A FIELD GUIDE TO FLORIDA

REPTILES AND AMPHIBIANS

D1603302

Gulf Publishing Company
Houston, Texas

FIELD GUIDE SERIES
Gulf Publishing
FIELD GUIDE SERIES

A FIELD GUIDE TO FLORIDA
REPTILES AND
AMPHIBIANS

RICHARD D. BARTLETT
PATRICIA P. BARTLETT

GULF PUBLISHING FIELD GUIDE SERIES:

A FIELD GUIDE TO FLORIDA
REPTILES AND AMPHIBIANS

Gulf Publishing Company
Book Division
P.O. Box 2608 □ Houston, Texas 77252-2608

10   9   8   7   6   5   4   3   2   1

Library of Congress Cataloging-in-Publication Data

    Bartlett, Richard D., 1938–
    A field guide to Florida reptiles and amphibians/R.D. Bartlett.
Patricia P. Bartlett.
       p. cm. — (Gulf's field guide series)
    Includes bibliographical references and index.
    ISBN 0-88415-277-4 (alk. paper)
      1. Reptiles—Florida.   2. Amphibians—Florida.   3. Reptiles—
Florida—Identification.   4. Amphibians—Florida—Identification.
I. Bartlett, Patricia Pope, 1949–.   II. Title.   III. Title: Florida reptiles
and amphibians.   IV. Series.
QL653.F6B37   1998
597.9'09759—DC21   98-34749
                                           CIP

Printed in the United States of America.
Cover photos by R.D. Bartlett.
Cover design by Senta Eva Rivera.

CONTENTS

AMPHIBIANS

SALAMANDERS, NEWTS, AND SIRENS (CAUDATA) 87

Mole Salamanders (Family Ambystomatidae)

Amphiumas (Family Amphiumidae)

Lungless Salamanders (Family Plethodontidae)

Waterdogs (Family Proteidae)

Newts (Family Salamandridae)

Sirens (Family Sirenidae)

Peripheral Amphibians

REPTILES

CROCODILIANS (CROCODYLIA) 131

Alligators and Caimans (Family Alligatoridae)

Crocodiles (Family Crocodylidae)

ORDER SQUAMATA

WORM LIZARDS (SUBORDER AMPHISBAENIA) (Family Amphisbaenidae) 137

LIZARDS (SUBORDER SAURIA) 139

Agamids (Family Agamidae)

Glass Lizards (Family Anguidae)

Geckos (Family Gekkonidae)

Anoles, Iguanas and Related Lizards (Family Iguanidae)

Skinks (Family Scincidae)

Racerunners and Whiptails (Family Teiidae)

TURTLES AND TORTOISES 211

Typical Sea Turtles (Family Cheloniidae)

Snapping Turtles (Family Chelydridae)

Leatherback Sea Turtle (Family Dermochelyidae)

Basking and Box Turtles (Family Emydidae)

Cooters, Red-Bellied and Box Turtles, and Sliders (Genera Pseudemys and Trachemys)

Color Plate

Mud and Musk Turtles (Family Kinosternidae)

Color Plate

African Mud (Primitive Side-Necked) Turtles (Family Pelomedusidae)

Color Plate

Tortoises (Family Testudinidae)

Softshelled Turtles (Family Trionychidae)

Peripheral Turtle Species

ACKNOWLEDGMENTS

The success of a publication such as this is due to the efforts and generosity of colleagues and friends. With this in mind, we gratefully acknowledge the comments and concerns of such biologists as Ray E. Ashton, Jr., David Auth, C. Kenneth Dodd, Jr., Kevin Enge, Richard Franz, James H. Harding, Paul E. Moler, Alan Tennant, Thomas Tyning, and R. Wayne VanDevender.

We are grateful to David Auth who allowed us access to the study collection of the Florida Museum of Natural History, where we were able to see the enigmatic Gulf hammock dwarf siren firsthand.

Johanna Boonstra, Karin Burns, Dennis Cathcart, Scott Cushnir, John Decker, Glen Fried, Billy Griswold, Roger Kilhefner, Steven Johnson, John Lewis, Michael Manfredi, Carl May, Brian Mealey, Flavio Morrissey, Brice Newnan, Lewis Ober, Regis Opferman, Greta Parks, Nicole Pinder, Joseph Wasilewski, Maria C. Wray, Kenny Wray, and Kevin Zipple, either provided photographic opportunities, or joined us in the field and made certain that we noticed specimens that would have otherwise gone unseen by us.

Bill Love, Rob MacInnes, Chris McQuade, and Eric Thiss all allowed us great latitude in photographing Florida reptiles and amphibians that they felt would be of interest to us.

Walter Meshaka shared with us his vast knowledge of the introduced reptiles and amphibians of Florida, and helped us find many alien species in the wild. Barry Mansell provided not only field companionship, but supplied images of some of Florida's more elusive amphibians and reptiles. David Godfrey of the Caribbean Conservation Corp. and L. Ehrhart provided us with photos of Atlantic hawksbill and leatherback turtles. Joan Alderson, Ray E. Ashton, Jr., Joseph Butler, C. Kenneth Dodd, Jr., Billy Griswold, James H. Harding, Brian Mealey, R. Wayne Van Devender, and Kenny Wray, also responded to requests for photographs. Thank you all.

Special thanks are due Dale Johnson for her painstaking preparation of the range maps and illustrations.

To Paul E. Moler we owe more than just a word of thanks. Paul unstintingly shared with us his knowledge of the herpetofauna of Florida, offered comments and criticisms on, and proofreading of, the text, and tried to steer us to habitats where we could photograph some of Florida's difficult-to-find native amphibians and reptiles. We are truly indebted.

To the late E. Gordon Johnston who, more than 40 years ago, introduced me (RDB) to Florida and its wonderfully diverse herpetofauna, I owe a never-ending debt of gratitude.

PREFACE

There is more interest today in the reptiles and amphibians with which we share our world than ever before. This doesn't necessarily mean that all are liked, or even that all are tolerated, but interest now exists, and it is growing daily. The most encouraging thing is that the interest spans all levels, from the most basic to the most advanced. Interpretive programs are presented regularly in many grade schools. Programs, assemblies, and studies continue through middle schools into high school and there is now a proliferation of undergraduate and post-graduate college courses.

Besides academic interests, reptiles and amphibians have become popular pet items, subjects of ecotours, and of interest to gardeners and backyard naturalists.

More than 230 species and subspecies of reptiles and amphibians occur in Florida. Of these, more than 40 (17%) are established alien species. A few additional alien species are known to occur in south Florida, but their populations are more tenuous. Most of these alien species are lizards (33+ species) which have either escaped from reptile importers and hobbyists or which have been deliberately released. But, because they are here—and some flourishing—these established aliens must be counted.

Today, the Florida herpetofauna consists of some 70 species and subspecies of snakes (see the *Field Guide to Snakes of Florida* by Alan Tennant, Gulf Publishing Company), 57 lizards, 40 turtles, 3 crocodilians, 36 frogs, and 32 salamanders. By any accounting, this is truly an impressive array. Because Florida continues to be a major hub for reptile importers, it seems likely that additional species will continue to escape (or be released), and, of these, some will become established.

In 1983, in *The Ecological Impact of Man on the South Florida Herpetofauna,* researchers Larry David Wilson and Louis Porras chronicled the presence and effects (as determined by those authors) of the 25 species of alien herpetofauna then established in the state. In the intervening 15 years the number of species of alien herpetofauna has increased by upwards of 60%! Wilson and Porras discussed the population statistics of many of the native south Florida herpetofauna—and a host of other things, including rampant human population increases. They used the term "ecocollapse" to describe what they felt were ever-worsening (and, 15 years later, still unreversed) environmental and ecological conditions in Florida, south of Lake Okeechobee. The result is a diminished native south-Florida herpetofauna and the establishing of more than 40 exotic species.

As seriously beleaguered as Florida is, myriad diverse (though often fragmented) habitats remain. These may be as specialized as the sand pine and rosemary scrub habitats of the Lake Wales (and other) ridges, or as general as flooded roadside ditches. In these two, and all between them, from salt marsh to hardwood hammock, reptiles and/or amphibians dwell. Some species, such as the Florida sand skink, *Neoseps reynoldsi,* and our gopher frog, *Rana capito* ssp., are highly specialized. Others such as the green anole, *Anolis carolinensis,* and the southern toad, *Bufo terrestris,* are habitat generalists.

We invite you to join us as we tour the habitats and look at each Floridian species and subspecies of amphibian, lizard, crocodilian, and turtle, both native and introduced, in detail.

Dick and Patti Bartlett
Gainesville, Florida

INTRODUCTION

In a mere nanosecond of geologic time (about 50 years, or two thirds of a human lifespan, by our reckoning), Florida has changed so dramatically in physical appearance and demographics that it is all but unrecognizable to many among us. The changes are nowhere more apparent than to naturalists. Florida's great lake, Okeechobee, has been diked and tamed, vast expanses of the Everglades have been drained and, where sawgrass once bowed before subtropical breezes, sugarcane and sodfields reign supreme. Miami—only 35 years ago a small, friendly town with open windows, doors and hearts—is now an impersonal, at times outwardly hostile megalopolis. Nor is Miami the only of Florida's cities to change. Ft. Lauderdale, Tampa, Ft. Myers, Orlando, Jacksonville, Tallahassee—all are now sprawling cities, bursting at their seams, with little room and few thoughts for things natural.

Changes have come to Florida's wildlife, too. In our very reduced natural areas some 50 species of introduced and established exotic creatures compete with Florida's native wildlife.

In some wetland areas one may encounter feral capybaras (an immense neotropical rodent). On the southern peninsula, native painted buntings now compete with introduced and established common mynahs, and flocks of parrots—including the occasional macaw—wheel screaming overhead or settle noisily to feed on the fruits of exotic fig and palm trees. In Dade County, boa constrictors breed regularly (but still in small numbers) and the accidental introduction of the spectacled caiman to our canals raises our complement of crocodilians to three species. Small native treefrog species are being outcompeted in some areas by the immense Cuban treefrog, and where once only one (some researchers say two) native species of anole lizard, the green anole, foraged and displayed, an observer may see up to *nine* additional species of exotic anoles. Among these exotic anoles is the world's largest species, the knight anole, an interloper from Cuba.

Escapees from the pet trade have created a night shift of lizards—the geckos. Florida has only one native species of gecko, a tiny, crepuscular species (the reef gecko) that is so secretive that it is seldom seen except by dedicated observers. But with the establishment of 11 less secretive species, most of which are nocturnal dwellers of urban and suburban areas, it is now difficult *not* to see geckos in many of Florida's more subtropical areas.

Biologists watching gecko populations on the Florida Keys and southern mainland have noted interesting successional changes. About 80 years ago a population of the small hemidactyline gecko, then known as the Turkish or warty gecko but now known as the Mediterranean gecko, was reported from Key West. Having no competition in its nocturnal niche, the Mediterranean gecko did well, working its way as far northward on the peninsula as Gainesville and Jacksonville. Then, 30 years ago, a congener, the Indopacific gecko, was reported from various locations in Dade County. It, too, began expanding its range, moving southward onto the Keys and northward up the peninsula. The Indopacific gecko, a parthenogenic (all female) species that is a prolific breeder, was an efficient competitor for existing habitat, and it slowly replaced the Mediterranean gecko where the ranges of the two overlapped. But then, about 20 years ago, the tropical house gecko, "bigger and badder" than either of its congeners, was found in Florida. As this voracious hemidactyline expanded its range, it seems to have driven before it, and replaced, the by-now seemingly firmly established Indopacific gecko and provided a new level of competition for the dwindling populations of the Mediterranean gecko.

End of story? Not yet! A few years ago, a fourth species of hemidactyline was found on the southern Keys. This is the small but feisty common house gecko. Will this species make inroads on the others? It's too soon to guess.

Although we certainly don't understand all of the dynamics, we see this succession of gecko species on the Keys rather as a "house that Jack built" progression, i.e., this is the gecko that displaced this gecko that displaced this gecko that . . .

It will be interesting to see what the ending of this biological tale of succession will be—if there ever is an ending.

So, as you will see in the species accounts herein, in about 50 years, Florida's herpetofauna has increased and diversified by 40 to 50 exotic species. These have either been deliberately released or escaped from captivity and have become established. There will assuredly be others.

Of those present today in Florida, some have become firmly established and, barring cataclysmic climatic changes, will be here for a long, long time—perhaps even longer than some of our beleaguered native species. Most of these exotics are so commonplace that folks who see them don't even realize that they are non-native species.

Other species are less adaptable and less temperature tolerant and it will take only one or two abnormally cold winters to extirpate the population. But now (1998), they are here and because you just might see them in the wild, we have included them in these pages. Among these tenuously established species are lizards such as the African red-headed agama, the Indochinese tree agama, and the Haitian green anole. The list includes frogs, such as the Australian great green treefrog and the Puerto Rican coqui. At present, the Florida populations of all of these are very localized. In fact, the coqui is restricted to only a half dozen bromeliad greenhouses in Homestead, Florida. Yet, after we bought some bromeliads in 1988 from a Dade County nursery, coquis sang in our garden for two years before succumbing to a freeze.

There are some reptiles and amphibians that have been collected or seen on one or two occasions, then not seen again. In most cases these have been geckos and they have appeared on urban warehouse complexes. The presence of most could be traced to one or two escapees from a reptile dealership. We have not included these.

In another category are those temperate species for which northern Florida is the southern most extreme of their range. These species are usually localized and may be rare—in Florida—but common north or west of Florida. Examples are the southern coal skink, the Gulf Coast smooth soft-shelled turtle, and the seal salamander.

A final category is of those species of herpetofauna that have been found in either Georgia or Alabama, within a very few miles of the Florida state line and may actually occur in Florida. These, the spotted salamander, three-toed amphiuma, and the southern painted turtle, are considered "peripheral species (see pages 127 and 263)."

Reptiles and amphibians vary not only in size and shape but in their activity patterns. Generally, they are categorized as diurnal, nocturnal, or crepuscular. While some lizards are actually restricted to daylight activity patterns, other lizards, as well as the turtles, crocodilians, and amphibians, may be active around the clock. This is especially true on overcast days and when the barometric pressure is low.

It is not always possible to generalize about the preferred activity patterns of our herpetofauna by *families*. For example, while most of the gecko species in Florida are crepuscular and nocturnal, the yellow-headed gecko is decidedly diurnal. Similarly, three of our four toads are crepuscular and nocturnal, but the tiny oak toad regularly indulges in diurnal activity.

Reptiles and amphibians live in a wide range of habitats. These habitats vary from the open ocean (sea turtles) and salt marshes (diamondbacked terrapins), to acidic hillside seeps (Pine Barrens treefrogs), woodland river edges (river frogs), shaded, sphagnaceous ravines (southern red salamander) the yielding sands of dry, interior ridges (sand skinks and gopher tortoises), to human habitations (various geckos). Reptiles and amphibians may be arboreal (anoles and some treefrogs), terrestrial (toads and curly-tailed lizards), aquatic (soft-shelled turtles and alligators) or sub-surface burrowers (worm lizards and mole skinks).

Although populations of many of our native reptiles and amphibians do not long persist in areas of urban and suburban sprawl, those of other species easily survive the changes wrought by man. Populations of most introduced exotic species actually thrive in the proximity of human-altered habitats.

How stable are populations of Florida's herpetofauna? Opinions vary widely. If for no other reason than the fact that commercial collecting of native reptiles and amphibians from the wild continues to be allowed, a conservationist could surmise that the stance of the state's Game and Fresh Water Fish Commission (GFC) is that most reptiles and amphibians continue to do well. This may not actually be the case. It just may be that the regulatory arm of GFC is moving a little more slowly than many of us would like in protecting our native reptiles and amphibians from exploitation. Currently the GFC offers some measure of protection to only 33 of our 198 species and subspecies (including snakes). No exotics are protected.

But biologists from other agencies (such as the Department of Environmental Protection [DEP], which administers the various state parks and appraises populations on a more local basis than GFC biologists) and myriad independent biologists and researchers feel that more protection should be offered to more species, and that the GFC should provide that protection *now*.

In the 40+ years that we have either visited or dwelt in Florida, we have seen innumerable individual populations of reptiles and amphibians dwindle or disappear. Discounting the American alligator, first driven nearly to extinction, then protected, we are unable to think of a single species of *native* amphibian, lizard, turtle, or crocodilian that has thrived in the wild *because* of man.

Despite an increasing tolerance of reptiles and amphibians, there remain many pressures on Florida's herpetofauna. Among them are:

• Continued habitat degradation
• Carnage on canalside, pondside, and other highways
• Collecting for the pet trade
• Collecting for scientific research

Assuring that *all* of the amphibians and reptiles of Florida are here for us and our descendants to view and appreciate in the wild will take a concerted effort on the parts of all persons. Whether we are researchers, herpetoculturists, or merely have an interest in the creatures with which we share our world, it is time for us to join forces and promote the conservation of these interesting, beneficial, and complex animals. We hope that our comments in this identification guide will help you to better understand and appreciate the intricate lifestyles of Florida's reptiles and amphibians.

As is so often said, "we're all in this together," so let's all work together.

HOW TO USE THIS BOOK

In these pages we discuss 175 species and subspecies of amphibians and reptiles. While many are of very dissimilar appearance, some are confusingly alike.

Many of these species have two or more color phases and many of the amphibians are capable of undergoing chameleon-like color or pattern changes. Because of this, it would be difficult to include all if we attempted to categorize them by color or pattern.

Therefore, we opted to list and discuss all in a traditional manner, divided by classes (amphibians or reptiles), families, genera, species, and subspecies.

We further believe that a guide of this sort is not the place to attempt to justify or decry "cutting-edge" taxonomy; we have opted, for the most part, to use the tried and true traditional names—both common and scientific. Future changes in *both* may occur.

We have fully listed and numbered all species and subspecies in the table of contents. The numbers assigned there will coincide with the numbers assigned in both text and photographs. If you know, or have a good idea what the species is you are researching, begin with the table of contents.

We have listed each major group, genus, species, and subspecies alphabetically by scientific names. Therefore, you may have to search some if you know only the common name of a species. Also, check the photo and range map provided for each species.

Scientific names are of Latin or Greek derivation. They can be binomial (two names) or trinomial (three names). Examples of each are:

- Broad-headed skink, *Eumeces* (you-me-sees) *laticeps* (lat-i-seps). This large skink has not subspeciated, thus it is identified by only a binomial.
- Bronze frog, *Rana* (ran-ah) *clamitans* (clam-i-tans) *clamitans*. The trinomial indicates that this small frog has subspeciated. The redundant specific and subspecific name of the bronze frogs tells

us that it was this subspecies that is the nominate race (the first subspecies identified). There is only one other race of *Rana clamitans*. This is the green frog, *Rana clamitans melanota*, which occurs north of Florida.

Amphibians are rather easily differentiated from reptiles. Amphibians lack scales and claws and usually have a moist skin (although the skin of toads and some newts is warty and rather dry). Florida examples include frogs, toads, treefrogs (all are typified by muscular hind legs used for jumping or hopping) and salamanders (which are elongate [some are superficially lizard-like] and have two or four tiny to moderate legs of about the same size).

Reptiles have dry skin, scales, and claws (if legs are present). Florida examples include crocodilians (immense, primarily aquatic, lizard-like reptiles), lizards (either legless or with four tiny to average-sized legs and movable eyelids), worm lizards (neither legs nor external eyes; dry, pinkish, annulated body) and turtles (shelled; some have flexible edges to the carapace).

Because they are readily recognized by most persons, let's use a familiar garden variety "hop-toad," found in the western panhandle, as an example.

Firstly, it has a dryish, warty skin, muscular hind legs, and no scales or claws. This combination of characteristics tells us it is both an amphibian and a toad. Additionally, its body is about 2 in. long. When we check the range maps, we find that it could be one of three species. If you compare the specimen at hand with the photos of the three possible species, you may be able to make an immediate identification. But if photo identification is not possible, move on to the species accounts. When we look at the accounts, we find that one of the possible species, the oak toad, is only about an inch in length when full grown. We can, therefore, discount it. The accounts then tell you that the southern toad has knobby protuberances on the back of its head, may be dark spotted and, if spots are present, they usually enclose only one, but sometimes enclose two or more warts.

Your specimen has no knobs on the head and has prominent light-edged dark spots, most of which contain three or more warts. So you discount the southern toad and are left, through elimination (a very non-scientific but often effective method of arriving at an answer), with the Fowler's toad. Check the photo again and you will probably now be able to see the resemblance.

An additional (but not infallible) clue in the identities of these two toads is in color. In the Florida panhandle southern toads are often quite red in color. Fowler's toads are almost always grayish.

FLORIDA'S HABITATS

To find a particular species or subspecies of amphibian or reptile in Florida, you must look first within its range and next in its proper habitat. The following pages contain a habitat chart that links each animal with where you are likely to find it. Be aware there is much habitat crossover. For example, you'll find a southeastern slimy salamander along the *shores* of streams and rivers, not in the water. Alternatively, you'll find a waterdog, which shares the same habitat description *only* in the water.

Despite the habitat destruction, Florida still contains many types of habitats. Each and every one hosts its complement of amphibians and/or reptiles.

Xeric (Dry) Uplands—Standing Water is Uncommon

Scrub—Sandy, rapidly drained soils typify this habitat as does a plant community of sand pine, opuntia cactus, rosemary, wiregrass, and lichens. *Typical inhabitants*: sand skinks, mole skinks, scrub lizards, gopher tortoises, and gopher frogs occur in this habitat.

Sandhills—Soils are sandy and fast draining. The typical plant community consists of turkey oak, longleaf pine, wiregrass, and saw palmetto. *Typical inhabitants:* gopher tortoises, mole skinks, scrub lizards, fence lizards, worm lizards, slender glass lizards, and gopher frogs.

Hammocks—Red, bluejack, live, and laurel oaks are typical trees that are replacing the pines in these successional areas, but poor soils restrict succession to true woodlands. Wire and other grasses are present. Shallow, ephemeral ponds may be present.

Mesic (Damp) Uplands—Ephemeral or Permanent Ponds or Streams May Be Present

Hardwoods—An overstory community of oaks, beeches, magnolias and other tall forest trees is present. Understory trees and shrubs, such as American holly and hophornbean, are also present. Catsclaw, grape, ferns, and other vines and forest floor plants are usually evident.

Pine—Longleaf pines are the dominant overstory tree in this community. A shrubby understory may or may not be present, but grasses and herbaceous growth grow thickly on the forest floor.

Mesic (Damp) Flatlands—Ephemeral or Permanent Ponds May Be Present

Pine Flatwoods—With stands of natural or cultured longleaf pine as the dominant overstory tree, pine flatwoods are typified by poorly drained soils, a sparse understory at best, but profuse ground cover. *Typical inhabitants:* coal skinks, ground skinks, green anoles, box turtles, flatwoods salamanders, slimy salamanders, oak toads, and pine woods treefrogs.

Prairie—A dense growth of herbaceous ground cover typifies this open, usually treeless, habitat. Such understory plants as saw palmetto and willows may be abundant, especially around waterholes and canals. *Typical inhabitants:* at waterholes, American alligators, pig frogs, leopard frogs, and spring peepers; also eastern glass lizards and southeastern five-lined skinks.

Hydric Flatlands—Flatlands Subject to Periodic Flooding

Wet Marl Prairies—These poorly drained prairies are most common on the southern peninsula. They are open treeless expanses that may support some stands of shrubs and a dense ground cover of wiregrass, rushes, spider lilies, and other flood tolerant plants are present. *Typical inhabitants:* alligators, box turtles, chicken turtles, southeastern five-lined skinks, and leopard frogs.

River Swamps—Sweet gum, bay, and maples are among the more commonly seen larger trees in this habitat. Both species of titi, wax myrtle, and other shrubs and myriad low-light, ground-dwelling herbs occur on the forest floor. *Typical inhabitants:* gray treefrogs, green treefrogs, spring peepers, mole salamanders, southern dusky salamanders, green anoles, and broad-headed skinks.

Cypress Swamps and Heads—This habitat is flooded for much, if not all, of each year. Besides cypress, trees such as sweet gum, and elder, grow. Where conditions permit, shrubs and emergent herbs occur. *Typical inhabitants:* American alligators, various turtles, three-lined salamanders, two-toed amphiumas, bullfrogs, pig frogs, and river frogs.

Everglades Hammocks/Swales—At one time this habitat, with its shallow, flowing waters, was found over much of Florida's southern peninsula. Today, it is restricted to outflows from Lake Okeechobee and the Big Cypress regions. Sawgrass and other plants that thrive with perpetually wet feet are typical of this habitat. *Typical inhabitants:* two-toed amphiumas, greater sirens, pig frogs, southern leopard frogs, chicken turtles, Peninsula cooters, red-bellied turtles, and American alligators.

Limestone Communities—Canals Have Been Dug Through Many of These Habitats

> **Pine Rocklands**—Restricted to the southern peninsula and the Keys, this habitat supports sparse to moderate stands of slash pines beneath which grows a ground cover of drought-tolerant ferns, terrestrial orchids, cat-briar, and harsh grasses. *Typical inhabitants:* greenhouse frogs, Cuban treefrogs, eastern glass lizards, southeastern five-lined skinks, and green anoles.
>
> **Limestone Hardwood Hammock**—Restricted to the southernmost areas of the state, these are elevated hammocks of densely growing tropical and temperate tree species such as live oaks, gumbo-limbo, poisonwood, tamarind, and Paurotis and sabal palms. *Typical inhabitants:* Cuban treefrogs, squirrel treefrogs, greenhouse frogs, giant toads, green anoles, and southeastern five-lined skinks.

Disturbed Habitats

> **Human Habitations**—Includes buildings, yards, urban parklands, roadside trashpiles, and recreational areas. *Typical inhabitants:* Puerto Rican coquis, greenhouse frogs, narrow-mouthed toads, great green iguanas, spiny-tailed iguanas, and most introduced anole species.
>
> **Modified Habitats**—Pastures, fields, farmlands, agricultural areas. *Typical inhabitants:* box turtles, gopher tortoises, broad-headed skinks, green anoles, brown anoles, oak toads, southern toads, and squirrel treefrogs.

Coastal Dunes and High Beaches

These are above the high-water mark in all but the most severe conditions: sea oats, beach morning glory, saw palmetto, and other shrubs are typical plants. *Typical inhabitants:* gopher tortoises, mole skinks, brown anoles, slender glass lizards, and six-lined racerunners.

Freshwater and Marine Habitats

> **Ephemeral Ponds and Flooded Ditches**—These are poorly drained, low-lying (often man-made) areas that fill regularly during the rainy seasons, but that dry regularly between heavy rains. Drought-tolerant aquatic vegetation and immersion-tolerant semi-terrestrial plants usually abound in these habitats. *Typical*

(text continued on page 24)

Habitat Types	Scrub	Sandhills	Oak hammocks	Damp upland hardwoods	Damp upland pinewoods	Pine flatwoods	Damp prairie	Wet marl prairie
FROGS, TOADS, TREEFROGS								
Toads								
1-Giant toad								
2-Oak toad			X		X			
3-Southern toad			X	X	X	X		
4-Fowler's toad			X	X				
Treefrogs and allies								
5-Northern cricket frog		X						
6-Florida cricket frog		X						
7-Southern cricket frog		X						
8-Pine Barrens treefrog								
9-Bird-voiced treefrog								
10-Cope's gray treefrog								
11-Green treefrog						X		
12-Pine woods treefrog		X			X	X		
13-Barking treefrog		X	X	X				
14-Squirrel treefrog		X				X		X
15-Cuban treefrog								
16-Australian green treefrog								
17-Southern spring peeper				X				
18-Northern spring peeper				X				
19-Southern chorus frog			X			X		
20-Florida chorus frog			X			X		
21-Little grass frog						X		
22-Ornate chorus frog								
23-Upland chorus frog								
Tropical Frogs								
24-Puerto Rican coqui								
25-Greenhouse frog	X	X	X	X				
Narrow-mouthed toads								
26-Eastern narrow-mouth toad	X	X	X			X		

River swamp	Cypress swamp	Everglades hammocks	South Florida pine rocklands	Limestone hardwoods	Human habitation	Pasture/field	Coastal dune	Ephemeral pond	Permanent pond	Stream/river	Freshwater marsh	Mangrove swamp	Saltmarsh	Ocean/bay
			X	X	X	X		X	X					
				X				X						
X	X			X	X	X		X	X	X	X			
					X	X			X					
X	X							X	X	X	X			
X	X							X	X	X	X			
X	X							X	X	X	X			
X									X					
X									X					
X	X							X	X	X				
X	X			X				X	X	X	X			
								X	X					
								X	X					
X					X			X	X					
				X	X	X		X	X			X		
					X			X	X					
X								X	X	X	X			
X								X	X	X	X			
							X	X	X		X			
							X	X	X		X			
X						X	X	X	X	X				
X	X						X	X						
X							X	X	X					
						X								
X			X	X	X	X								
			X	X	X	X								

(table continued on next page)

Habitat Types	Scrub	Sandhills	Oak hammocks	Damp upland hardwoods	Damp upland pinewoods	Pine flatwoods	Damp prairie	Wet marl prairie
Spadefoots 27-Eastern spadefoot		X	X	X	X			
True Frogs 28-Florida gopher frog	X	X	X					
29-Dusky gopher frog	X	X	X					
30-Bullfrog								
31-Bronze frog				X				
32-River frog								
33-Pig frog								
34-Florida bog frog						X		
35-Pickerel frog								
36-Southern leopard frog				X	X	X		
37-Florida leopard frog				X	X	X		
38-Carpenter frog								
SALAMANDERS & NEWTS								
Mole Salamanders 39-Flatwoods salamander						X		
40-Marbled salamander						X		
41-Mole salamander				X				
42-Eastern tiger salamander					X			
Amphiumas 43-Two-toed amphiuma								
44-One-toed amphiuma								
Lungless Salamanders 45-Apalachicola dusky salamander								
46-Southern dusky salamander				X			X	
47-Spotted dusky salamander				X				
48-Seal salamander				X				
49-Southern two-lined salamander								
50-Three-lined salamander								
51-Dwarf salamander								
52-Georgia blind salamander								

River swamp	Cypress swamp	Everglades hammocks	South Florida pine rocklands	Limestone hardwoods	Human habitation	Pasture/field	Coastal dune	Ephemeral pond	Permanent pond	Stream/river	Freshwater marsh	Mangrove swamp	Saltmarsh	Ocean/bay	Caves
					X				X	X					
	X							X	X						
	X							X	X						
X									X	X	X				
X									X	X					
X									X	X	X				
X									X	X	X				
								X	X	X					
										X					
		X	X	X					X	X	X	X			
		X	X	X					X	X	X	X			
X										X					
	X					X		X							
X								X							
X	X					X									
X						X		X	X						
X	X							X	X	X	X				
X	X									X					
X															
X															
X										X					
										X					
X	X									X					
X	X									X					
X	X								X	X	X				
															X

(*table continued on next page*)

Habitat Types	Scrub	Sandhills	Oak hammocks	Damp upland hardwoods	Damp upland pinewoods	Pine flatwoods	Damp prairie	Wet marl prairie
53-Four-toed salamander				X		X		
54-Southeastern slimy salamander				X	X	X		
55-Gulf Coast mud salamander				X				
56-Rusty mud salamander				X				
57-Southern red salamander				X				
58-Many-lined salamander								
Mudpuppies 59-Eastern Gulf Coast waterdog								
Newts 60-Striped newt			X		X			
61-Central newt								
62-Peninsula newt								
Sirens 63-Narrow-striped dwarf siren								
64-Everglades dwarf siren								
65-Slender dwarf siren								
66-Gulf Hammock dwarf siren								
67-Broad-striped dwarf siren								
68-Eastern lesser siren								
69-Greater siren								
Peripheral Amphibians 70-Spotted salamander (peripheral)						X		
71-Three-toed amphiuma								
CROCODILIANS								
Alligators and Caimans 72-American alligator								
73-Spectacled caiman								
Crocodiles 74-American crocodile								
AMPHISBAENIANS								
75-Florida worm lizard	X	X	X					

River swamp	Cypress swamp	Everglades hammocks	South Florida pine rocklands	Limestone hardwoods	Human habitation	Pasture/field	Coastal dune	Ephemeral pond	Permanent pond	Stream/river	Freshwater marsh	Mangrove swamp	Saltmarsh	Ocean/bay	Caves
X	X							X							
	X									X					
X	X														X
X	X														
										X					
								X	X	X					
											X				
	X							X							
X								X	X	X	X				
X	X	X						X	X	X					
X	X							X	X	X	X				
X	X	X						X	X	X	X				
X	X							X	X	X	X				
X	X							X	X	X	X				
X	X							X	X	X	X				
							X	X	X	X					
	X						X	X	X	X					
X								X							
								X	X	X					
X	X	X	X					X	X	X	X	X		X	
								X							
												X		X	
					X	X									

(table continued on next page)

Habitat Types	Scrub	Sandhills	Oak hammocks	Damp upland hardwoods	Damp upland pinewoods	Pine flatwoods	Damp prairie	Wet marl prairie
LIZARDS								
Agamas								
76-Red-headed agama								
77-Indochinese tree agama								
Glass Lizards								
78-Eastern slender glass lizard		X	X		X	X		
79-Island glass lizard	X	X	X			X		
80-Mimic glass lizard				X	X	X		
81-Eastern glass lizard						X	X	
Geckos								
82-Asian flat-tailed gecko								
83-Tokay gecko								
84-Yellow-headed gecko								
85-Common house gecko								
86-Indopacific house gecko								
87-Tropical house gecko								
88-Mediterranean house gecko								
89-Bibron's gecko								
90-Giant day gecko								
91-Ocellated gecko								
92-Ashy gecko								
93-Florida reef gecko								
94-White-spotted wall gecko								
95-Moorish wall gecko								
Anoles								
96-Green anole	X	X	X	X	X	X	X	X
97-Pale-throated green anole				X		X		X
98-Haitian green anole								
99-Puerto Rican crested anole								
100-Large-headed anole								

River swamp	Cypress swamp	Everglades hammocks	South Florida pine rocklands	Limestone hardwoods	Human habitation	Pasture/field	Coastal dune	Ephemeral pond	Permanent pond	Stream/river	Freshwater marsh	Mangrove swamp	Saltmarsh	Ocean/bay
					X									
					X									
					X	X	X							
						X	X							
X			X	X	X	X		X						
					X									
					X									
					X									
					X									
			X	X	X									
			X	X	X									
					X							X		
					X							X		
					X									
					X									
					X									
			X	X	X									
					X									
					X							X		
X	X	X		X										
X			X	X	X	X								
					X									
					X									
					X									

(table continued on next page)

Habitat Types	Scrub	Sandhills	Oak hammocks	Damp upland hardwoods	Damp upland pinewoods	Pine flatwoods	Damp prairie	Wet marl prairie
101-Green bark anole								
101-Florida bark anole								
102-Knight anole								
103-Barbados anole								
104-Marie Gallant sail-tailed anole								
105-Jamaican giant anole								
106-Cuban green anole								
107-Brown anole					X			
Basilisks 108-Northern brown basilisk								
Iguanas 109-Mexican spiny-tailed iguana								
110-Black spiny-tailed iguana								
111-Great green iguana								
Curly-Tailed Lizards 112-Northern curly-tailed lizard								
113-Green-legged curly-tailed lizard								
114-Red-sided curly-tailed lizard								
Horned Lizards and Swifts 115-Texas horned lizard								
116-Southern fence lizard	X	X	X		X	X		
117-Florida scrub lizard	X	X						
Skinks 118-Southern coal skink						X		
119-Florida Keys mole skink						X		
120-Cedar Key mole skink					X	X		
121-Blue-tailed mole skink	X							
122-Peninsula mole skink	X	X	X		X			
123-Northern mole skink		X	X			X		
124-Five-lined skink			X	X	X	X		
125-Southeastern five-lined skink		X	X	X	X		X	
126-Broad-headed skink				X	X	X		

River swamp	Cypress swamp	Everglades hammocks	South Florida pine rocklands	Limestone hardwoods	Human habitation	Pasture/field	Coastal dune	Ephemeral pond	Permanent pond	Stream/river	Freshwater marsh	Mangrove swamp	Saltmarsh	Ocean/bay
					X									
					X									
					X									
					X									
					X									
					X									
					X									
			X	X	X	X	X							
					X			X	X					
			X	X	X									
			X	X	X									
			X	X	X	X		X						
					X		X							
					X									
					X									
					X		X							
					X	X								
X							X		X					
							X							
							X							
					X		X							
X														
X	X		X	X	X	X								
X														

(table continued on next page)

Habitat Types	Scrub	Sandhills	Oak hammocks	Damp upland hardwoods	Damp upland pinewoods	Pine flatwoods	Damp prairie	Wet marl prairie	
127-Sand skink	X	X							
128-Ground skink	X	X	X	X	X	X			
Racerunners and Allies 129-Giant ameiva (green-rumped)									
130-Giant ameiva (dusky)									
131-Rainbow whiptail									
132-Giant whiptail									
133-Six-lined racerunner	X	X	X						
TURTLES									
Marine Turtles 134-Loggerhead turtle									
135-Green turtle									
136-Atlantic hawksbill turtle									
137-Atlantic ridley									
Snapping Turtles 138-Florida snapping turtle									
139-Eastern snapping turtle									
140-Alligator snapping turtle									
Leatherback 141-Leatherback turtle									
Basking Turtles 142-Spotted turtle									
143-Florida chicken turtle									
144-Eastern chicken turtle									
145-Barbour's map turtle									
146-Escambia map turtle									
147-Ornate diamondbacked terrapin									
148-Carolina diamondbacked terrapin									
149-Mississippi diamondbacked terrapin									
150-Mangrove diamondbacked terrapin									

River swamp	Cypress swamp	Everglades hammocks	South Florida pine rocklands	Limestone hardwoods	Human habitation	Pasture/field	Coastal dune	Ephemeral pond	Permanent pond	Stream/river	Freshwater marsh	Mangrove swamp	Saltmarsh	Ocean/bay
X					X	X		X						
					X									
					X									
					X									
					X									
						X	X							
														X
														X
														X
														X
									X	X				
									X	X				
									X	X				
														X
									X					
								X	X	X				
								X	X	X				
										X				
										X				
												X		X
												X		X
												X		X
												X		X

(table continued on next page)

Habitat Types	Scrub	Sandhills	Oak hammocks	Damp upland hardwoods	Damp upland pinewoods	Pine flatwoods	Damp prairie	Wet marl prairie		
151-Upper Keys diamondbacked terrapin										
152-Florida east coast terrapin										
153-Mobile cooter										
154-Suwannee cooter										
155-Florida cooter										
156-Peninsula cooter										
157-Florida red-bellied turtle										
158-Florida box turtle			X	X	X	X	X			
159-Eastern box turtle			X		X	X	X			
160-Gulf Coast box turtle						X	X			
161-Three-toed box turtle						X	X			
162-Yellow-bellied slider										
163-Red-eared slider										
Musk and Mud Turtles 164-Striped mud turtle										
165-Florida mud turtle										
166-Mississippi mud turtle										
167-Eastern mud turtle										
168-Loggerhead musk turtle										
169-Striped-necked musk turtle										
170-Common musk turtle										
Primitive Side-Necked Turtles 171-East Africa Black Mud Turtle										
Tortoises 172-Gopher tortoise	X	X	X							
Soft Shelled Turtles 173-Florida soft-shelled turtle										
174-Gulf Coast smooth soft-shelled turtle										
175-Gulf Coast spiny soft-shelled turtle										
Peripheral Turtles 176-Southern painted turtle										
177-Eastern painted turtle										

River swamp	Cypress swamp	Everglades hammocks	South Florida pine rocklands	Limestone hardwoods	Human habitation	Pasture/field	Coastal dune	Ephemeral pond	Permanent pond	Stream/river	Freshwater marsh	Mangrove swamp	Saltmarsh	Ocean/bay
												X		X
												X		X
									X	X		X		X
									X	X		X		X
									X	X	X	X		X
									X	X	X	X		X
									X	X		X		X
				X	X	X								
					X	X								
X					X	X								
X					X	X								
									X	X				
									X	X				
								X	X	X				
								X	X	X	X	X		
								X	X	X	X	X		
								X	X	X	X	X		
									X	X				
									X	X				
									X	X				
									X					
						X								
									X		X	X		
										X				
									X	X				
									X	X				
									X	X				

(text continued from page 9)

inhabitants: various treefrogs and toads, narrow-mouthed toads, and some turtles.

Permanent Ponds, Lakes, and Canals—Although water levels may fluctuate with rainfall, permanent ponds, lakes, and canals usually retain water year around. Shrubs often rim the perimeters and emergent vegetation may grow thickly in the shallows. Submerged vegetation of many kinds grow where the water becomes too deep for emergents. *Typical inhabitants:* frogs, toads, treefrogs, amphiumas, greater and lesser sirens, American alligators, and many turtles.

Streams, Creeks, and Rivers—These may fluctuate in depth, but are typified by flowing water throughout the year. Generally, rivers are larger than creeks and streams. Many originate from springheads in densely wooded areas but meander near their mouths through tidal marshlands or mangrove swamps. Dependent on water depth and soil conditions, both emergent and submerged vegetation may be abundant. *Typical inhabitants:* various terrestrial salamanders in protected areas on the banks; three-lined salamanders, two-toed amphiuma, greater and lesser sirens, river cooters, alligator snapping turtles, soft-shelled turtles, American alligators, and many other species in aquatic situations.

Freshwater Marshes—These are low-lying, poorly drained habitats that usually hold water. Cattail, pickerelweed, alligator flag, blue flag, and maidencane are commonly seen emergents, and shrubs such as wax myrtle and various willows often surround the area. *Typical inhabitants:* American alligators, various turtles, aquatic salamanders, and many true frogs.

Mangrove Swamps—These are low-lying, tidally influenced, zones of transition between fresh and saltwaters that are vegetated by red, black and white mangroves and buttonwood. *Typical inhabitants:* diamondbacked terrapins, Suwannee cooters, red-bellied turtles, striped mud turtles, and American crocodiles.

Saltmarsh—Heavily vegetated, open regions of tidally influenced shoreline. The salinity is very variable. Cord and salt grasses and rushes are usually the dominant plants. *Typical inhabitants:* various diamondbacked terrapins, cooters, and American crocodiles.

Open Ocean—Includes shorelines and estuaries. *Typical inhabitants:* marine turtles.

Panhandle Caves—Florida's only extensive cave system is in the western Panhandle. *Typical inhabitants:* it is in the full darkness of the deeper caves that the Georgia blind salamander occurs. Other salamanders may occur (not shown on chart).

REPTILES AND AMPHIBIANS PROTECTED IN FLORIDA

As of June 1, 1997, 5 taxa of amphibians and 28 taxa of reptiles including snakes are protected in some manner within the state of Florida. This list is subject to change at any time, hence it is offered only as a guide.

Current information is always available through the headquarters of the Game and Fish Commission. They may be contacted at:

> State of Florida Game and Freshwater Fish Commission
> 620 South Meridian Street
> Tallahassee, Florida 32399-1600

or through the United States Fish and Wildlife Service. Their contact address is:

> Office for Human Relations
> United States Fish and Wildlife Service
> Department of Interior
> Washington, DC 20240

The following applicable designations will precede the species name:

> G = protected by Florida's Game and Fish Commission
> F = protected by United States Fish and Wildlife Service
> B = protected in some manner by both of the above agencies
> E = endangered
> T = threatened
> S = species of special concern (a state designation only)
> ** regulated species not yet appearing on the official list

In some cases it is legal to keep a regulated species. However, regulated species cannot be sold or bartered. Check with the game commission for clarification.

Protected Amphibians

> GS *Haideotriton wallacei,* Georgia blind salamander
> GS *Hyla andersonii,* pine barrens treefrog
> GS *Rana capito aesopus,* Florida gopher frog
> GS *Rana capito sevosa,* dusky gopher frog
> GS *Rana okaloosae,* Florida bog frog

Protected Reptiles

BTS   *Alligator mississippiensis,* American alligator
BT   *Caretta caretta,* loggerhead turtle
BE   *Chelonia mydas,* green turtle
BE   *Crocodylus acutus,* American crocodile
BE   *Dermochelys coriacea,* leatherback turtle
GT   *Diadophis punctatus acricus,* Big Pine Key ring-necked snake
BT   *Drymarchon corais couperi,* eastern indigo snake
GS   *Elaphe guttata guttata,* corn snake (southern Keys populations only)
BE   *Eretmochelys imbricata imbricata,* Atlantic hawksbill turtle
GS   *Eumeces egregius egregius,* Florida Keys mole skink
BT   *Eumeces egregius lividus,* blue-tailed mole skink
GS   *Gopherus polyphemus,* gopher tortoise
GS   *Graptemys barbouri,* Barbour's map turtle
GE   *Kinosternon bauri,* striped mud turtle (southern Keys populations only)
BE   *Lepidochelys kempii,* Atlantic ridley turtle
GS   *Macrochelys temmincki,* alligator snapping turtle
BT   *Neoseps reynoldsi,* sand skink
BT   *Nerodia clarkii taeniata,* Atlantic salt marsh snake
GS   *Pituophis melanoleucus mugitus,* Florida pine snake
GS   *Pseudemys concinna suwanniensis,* Suwannee cooter
GT   *Stilosoma extenuatum,* short-tailed snake
GT   *Storeria dekayi victa,* Florida brown snake (lower Keys populations only)
GT   *Tantilla oolitica,* Rim Rock crowned snake
GT   *Thamnophis sauritus sackenii,* peninsula ribbon snake (southern Keys populations only)
**   *Terrapene carolina* (all subspecies), eastern box turtle
**   *Malaclemys terrapin* (all subspecies), diamondbacked terrapins
**   *Graptemys ernsti,* Escambia map turtle
**   *Sternotherus minor,* loggerhead musk turtle

Most of these amphibians or reptiles should not be collected or *molested* without permit. Bag limits of one or two without permitation are set for others. The term "molest" can be especially broadly interpreted by law enforcement personnel. Ostensibly, it can include even photographing in the wild if the progress of an animal is interrupted or if it is startled into motion. Because laws and regulations are subject to change, we suggest that you contact the appropriate regulatory agency for current listings and interpretations.

Amphibians and Reptiles as Captives

A word of caution: before collecting or molesting reptiles or amphibians in the wild, we urge you to check the list of protected or regulated species previously cited. In some instances, it is perfectly legal to collect a specimen (sometimes two) of state-regulated species of special concern, but check with the regulatory division of Florida's Game and Freshwater Fish Commission for particulars. Violating the laws protecting reptiles and amphibians is a serious offense. Don't become an arrest statistic.

Keeping reptiles and amphibians in captivity is a big-time hobby today. Millions of dollars are spent annually in the acquisition of herps and support equipment such as cages, cage furniture, food items, etc.

Many of Florida's reptiles and amphibians are major components of the pet trade. Although hobbyists are mostly interested in snakes, some of our frogs, salamanders, lizards and turtles also figure prominently.

There was a time when collecting amphibians and reptiles from the wild for the pet trade was an entirely valid occupation. This practice is less acceptable today than in bygone years. Yet, it is entirely legal in Florida to volume collect and commercialize on any non-protected or non-regulated herps. We decry this continuing practice of commercialization of *native* species for several reasons. There are fewer and fewer habitats remaining intact. Yet, from these, more and more amphibians and reptiles are collected to supply an ever-increasing number of hobbyists. Eventually something has to give, and we would much rather see a cessation of the collecting based on public opinion and cooperation between interested parties while species are still plentiful, rather than wait until the numbers of reptiles dwindle in the wild and and it becomes *necessary* to legislate against collecting just to preserve the presence of a species in the wild.

Please note that we have emphasized the term "native". Although we do get a degree of pleasure from seeing introduced species in the field in Florida, we acknowledge that none truly belong here.

Many species of Florida's reptiles and amphibians are now bred in captivity for commercial purposes. We advocate the purchase of domestically bred specimens whenever possible rather than continued collecting from the wild.

A Note on Toxicity and Other Potential Problems

Although it only makes sense to wash one's hands after handling an amphibian or reptile, we felt a word of caution about the possible toxicity and other potential dangers of a few species was needed. There are no lizards, crocodilians, or turtles with toxic potential. But, there *is* a chance of contamination by salmonella or other pathogens from these (and most other) sources. Additionally, all can, and many will, bite.

All amphibians are capable of exuding skin secretions that may retard desiccation or afford protection from predators. Giant toads, pickerel frogs, and Cuban treefrogs are noted for a particularly virulent exudate. This exudate is especially effective when it comes in contact with mucous membranes (nose, mouth, or eyes) or open wounds.

Again we offer this admonition; wash your hands after handling any amphibian or reptile!

A NOTE ON TAXONOMY

The science of classification is called taxonomy. As in any other discipline, there are diverging beliefs, techniques, and applications. Two such different applications are traditional systematics and cladistics. The proponents of either often vociferously decry the suggestions of the other.

Sadly, there is also a current school of thought that allopatrism (non-contiguous populations) equates, in all cases, to speciation. We feel that this is an incorrect assumption and every species/subspecies must be evaluated on its own merit.

Because traditional systematics has "worked well" over the years, and because we feel that a field guide is not the proper forum for arguing taxonomic principals, we have continued to take this comfortable and conservative approach in these pages. Is it good to be comfortable? Probably not, but . . .

Wherever we felt it possible, both the common and scientific names used in this book are those suggested in the publication entitled *Standard Common and Scientific Names for North American Amphibians and Reptiles (Fourth Edition)* by Joseph T. Collins.

However, we have diverged on some aspects. We do not advocate the use of "simplified" names when the simplification advocates bad grammar. Thus, instead of the proposed "diamondback terrapin" for example, we have used "diamondbacked terrapin."

In time, taxonomy may again become more standardized. We can at least hope so.

Amphibians and reptiles are classified as follows:

Amphibians

Kingdom: Animalia
  Phylum: Chordata
    Subphylum: Vertebrata
      Class: Amphibia
        Order: Gymnophiona (Caecilians)
              Caudata (Salamanders and Newts)
              Anura (Frogs, Toads, and Treefrogs)

Reptiles

Kingdom: Animalia
  Phylum: Chordata
    Subphylum: Vertebrata
      Class: Reptilia
        Order: Rhynchocephalia (Tuataras)
              Crocodilia (Crocodiles, Alligators, and Gavials)
              Chelonia (Turtles and Tortoises)
              Squamata
                Suborders: Amphisbaenia (Worm Lizards)
                          Sauria (Lizards)
                          Serpentes (Snakes, see the *Field Guide to Snakes of Florida* by A. Tennant, Gulf Publishing Co.)

Beyond this, each order is divided into families, sometimes subfamilies, genera, species, and subspecies.

AMPHIBIANS

Most believe the ancestors of today's amphibians evolved from the fishes some 350 million years ago, during the early Devonian period. Today, the class Amphibia contains three groups of rather divergent-appearing creatures. These are the frogs (including toads and treefrogs), the salamanders, and the caecilians. There are a total of about 4,000 species. Representatives of only the first two groups occur in Florida.

Though of diverse appearance, amphibians have many characteristics in common. They have moist skins that lack such cover as hair, feathers, or scales; they lack true claws, and by definition (but sometimes not in actuality) amphibians lead a "double life." Many breed and lay their eggs in the water. Those eggs hatch into aquatic larvae, which develop and eventually reach a point of metamorphosis. During metamorphosis, changes, such as the resorption of gills, the development of eyelids, skin cell changes, and others, occur and the aquatic larva leaves the water to begin life on land. However, at no point in its life is any amphibian truly divorced from an external source of moisture. Even in species adapted to aridland habitats, life-enabling moisture must be absorbed through the skin.

There are, of course, divergences, or seeming divergences, from the norm. Some amphibians are fully aquatic throughout their lives. Others are not dependent on the availability of free-standing water and live a fully terrestrial existence. But all amphibians—there are *no* exceptions—must, at sometime during nearly every day, be in contact with some source of external moisture.

A few amphibians give birth to living young. However, most, including all Florida species, reproduce by means of gelatinous covered eggs. The eggs are laid in the water or in moisture-retaining terrestrial situations, often very near water.

TOADS AND FROGS
Order Anura

Not all frogs are toads, nor are all frogs treefrogs, but all toads and treefrogs are frogs.

This is just another way of saying that the toads and the treefrogs are just frogs that have developed a certain set of characteristics that allows systematists to conveniently group them together.

Six families of anurans are found in Florida.

Family Bufonidae—Toads   (4 species)
Family Hylidae—Treefrogs and relatives   (16 species)
Family Leptodactylidae—Tropical Frogs   (2 species)
Family Microhylidae—Narrow-Mouthed Toads   (1 species)
Family Pelobatidae—Spadefoot Toads   (1 species)
Family Ranidae—True Frogs   (9 species)

No matter the family to which they belong, the frogs, toads, and treefrogs of Florida have lidded eyes, moist skins (sometimes difficult to determine on dusty toads), and muscular hind legs for hopping or leaping. The males (and sometimes the females) of all have one or more rather distinctive calls.

All except the two species of tropical frogs have an aquatic larval (tadpole) stage and all are terrestrial or semi-aquatic as adults. The two tropical frogs lay their eggs in moist pockets on land and full development occurs in the egg capsule.

How to Find Frogs, Toads, and Treefrogs in Florida

Found throughout the state, frogs, toads, and treefrogs are most easily spotted with a flashlight after nightfall when they are vocalizing at breeding ponds. They are most difficult to find at midday in mid-summer. They are most easily observed on fairly warm overcast or misty nights, especially when these nights occur in conjunction with lowered barometric pressure. Anurans can be very difficult to approach on brilliantly moonlit nights.

All species and subspecies, except the two species of tropical frogs, may be found at breeding ponds at some time of the year. They may be tracked, and are identifiable, by their voices. The two tropical frogs also call, but from moist gardens, greenhouses, and hammocks.

After they have left the breeding ponds, little information is available on most Florida frogs, toads, and treefrogs.

Treefrogs of many species voice "raincalls," often from some height in trees, at the advent of spring and summer storms.

For information on the species themselves refer to the sections designated "Abundance," "Habitat," and "Behavior" in the species accounts.

Terminology Defined

The following short list of selected terms may help you with the accounts on Florida's frogs, toads, and treefrogs. Additional terms may be found in the glossary.

Anuran—a tailless amphibian; a frog, toad, or treefrog.

Allopatric—not occurring together, but often adjacent.

Amplexus—the breeding grasp. This term is often prefixed by the word axillary (males grasp females just posterior to the forelimbs) and inguinal (the female is grasped around the waist).

Deposition site—the spot chosen for egg-laying.

Dimorphic/dimorphism—a (usually) sexually related difference in external morphology.

Dorsal/dorsum—pertaining to the upper surface.

Lateral—pertaining to the side.

Race—a subspecies.

Tubercles—warty protuberances.

SVL—snout-vent length

Tympanum—the external eardrum.

Ventral—pertaining to the belly.

A Note About Tadpoles

Tadpoles have gills, modified scraping mouthparts, and lack eyelids. They grow, develop hindlegs, then forelegs; their tails are resorbed, eyelids develop, mouthparts alter, and within a few weeks they metamorphose into tiny, essentially terrestrial, froglets. Newly metamorphosed frogs often are as difficult to identify as the tadpoles from which they transformed. However, within days identifying characteristics become more apparent.

Identifying tadpoles is a discipline in itself. Tadpole appearance is mentioned in the text only if some readily visible species-unique characteristic is present.

TOADS
Family Bufonidae

There are few persons who do not recognize a "hop-toad." Most have a rather dry-appearing warty skin and, except while breeding, are found in relatively dry habitats. There are four species in Florida, which range in size from the Brobdignagian, introduced giant toad to the Lilliputian oak toad.

The four Florida species all have exposed toxin-secreting parotoid (shoulder) glands. The secreted toxins may vary from distasteful (those produced by the three native species) to the potentially lethal secretions of the Latin American giant toad.

Except for the oak toad, which lays its eggs singly or in short strings, all Florida species lay their eggs in long paired strings.

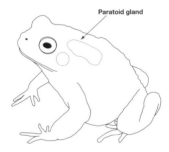

Paratoid gland

The 4 species of toads now found in Florida all have a venom-secreting shoulder (paratoid) gland and warty skin.

1 GIANT TOAD

Bufo marinus

Abundance The giant toad, primarily a native of tropical America, ranges naturally northward to the Lower Rio Grande Valley of Texas. The Florida population, resulting from both deliberate introductions and pet trade escapes, is probably of Colombian origin. It is abundant in Dade and some areas of Monroe counties, and also occurs, though in lesser numbers, in Broward, Glades, Lee, Okeechobee, and Pinellas counties.

Habitat In Florida this toad is associated with urban and agricultural areas. It breeds in canals, flooded ditches, shallow pools, and fishponds. It seeks shelter beneath ground debris in dry and cold weather but often congregates in some numbers to feed on insects drawn to street and porch lights.

Size Populations of this toad in Florida seem to now vary in the adult size attained. Specimens between 6 and 7 in. in length are still regularly found in the Miami, Homestead, and Florida City areas. Most of those seen in the Tarpon Springs area in recent years are in the 3- to 4-in. size range. We speculate that the size reduction of this northernmost population may be brought about by winter temperatures, which are normally cooler than optimum for this tropical species, as well as a winter reduction in available food items. Females are by far the larger sex.

Reproduction Giant toads begin chorusing at the onset of spring rains. A single large female is capable of producing more than 20,000 eggs. The egg strings may float freely but are more often secured to surface or submerged vegetation.

Coloration/pattern This immense toad may vary between brown and red in ground color. It may or may not have darker and lighter spots and marblings. Females are more heavily patterned than males. The body tubercles of breeding males are tipped with tiny spines. The parotoid glands are immense and extend far down onto the shoulders. The cranial crests are prominent, but the interorbital pair have no bulbous posterior projections.

Males have a comparatively small (but still very visible) subgular vocal sac and call while sitting on the shore or in shallow water.

Tadpoles are black above and light (often speckled with black) ventrally.

Voice A low-pitched, slowly pulsed, rattling trill is voiced by males. The largest males have the deepest voices.

Similar species The tremendous parotoid glands that angle downward onto the shoulders (all populations) and the tremendous adult size (south Florida populations) should identify this species.

Behavior Giant toads are interesting, but highly predacious, creatures. They eat all manner of native frogs and toads as well as dry dog food and the more usual fare of insects and other arthropods. When confronted by a potential predator, the giant toad lowers its head, elevates its rear, and butts the toxin-producing parotoid glands into the enemy. The toxins secreted are potent and have been implicated in the death of dogs and other predators. Unlike many other anurans, giant toads are able to recognize palatable inanimate products as food items. It is not uncommon to see one or more eating dog or cat food from a pet's food dish.

Comments Although the southernmost populations of this toad in Florida seem to retain their great size, those found in Pinellas County appear to be undergoing a reduction in the maximum size attained. As large as the southern specimens when first noted in the '60s, breeding specimens found in Pinellas County in the 1990s were hardly larger than the native southern toads.

Giant toads were initially released in Florida in the hopes of controlling crop insect pests. They are also a mainstay of the pet industry.

2 OAK TOAD

Bufo quercicus

Abundance Although seemingly less common now, the oak toad remains common-to-abundant in many areas of Florida. It does not seem to thrive in urban and suburban areas, but may remain common in agricultural areas.

Habitat The oak toad is associated with sandy pine scrublands. In such habitats, oak trees of various species may or may not exist. Because of rampant development, these well-drained uplands are among the most rapidly disappearing habitats in Florida. Oak toads use shallow semi-permanent ponds, temporary flatwood ponds, and roadside drainage ditches for breeding.

Size Although both sexes may attain slightly larger sizes, oak toads are adult at from .75 in. (males) to 1 in. (females).

Reproduction The 100 to 250 eggs are laid singly or in very short strings. They may float on the water surface or adhere to vegetation with which they come in contact.

Coloration/pattern This tiny toad may be very dark when cold, but rather brightly colored and well patterned with paired, light-edged dark dorsal spots when warm. The ground color is of some shade of brown to gray. At all times a *prominent* white, yellow, or orange vertebral stripe is visible. The warts are variable in color but may be russet, red, orange, or yellow.

The venter is light. Males have a dark throat that swells when the toad is calling into an enormous, anteriorly projecting, vocal sac.

The parotoid gland is prominent and elongate. The cranial crests, while present, are not well defined.

The tiny tadpoles are dark above and lighter below. The upper tailfin is spotted with dark pigment; the lower tailfin is not.

Voice The call of this toad is unlike that of any other Florida bufonid. Males produce a rapidly repeated, strident peeping, which can be almost overpowering when large choruses are heard.

Similar species The vocalizations of this toad are distinctive. Juvenile toads of other species usually do not have the prominent light vertebral line or well developed parotoid glands.

Behavior The oak toad may be encountered foraging in shady areas even on the hottest summer days. It may be inactive during the winter months. Although males may call sporadically during the daylight hours (especially on overcast or rainy days), the largest and most persistent breeding choruses are heard on humid or rainy summer nights.

Comments The shrill calls of this toad, often heard along Florida's more rural roadways, are frequently mistaken for bird calls. Oak toads blend remarkably with the grasses from which they often call and finding them can be a real chore.

3 SOUTHERN TOAD

Bufo terrestris

Abundance This is probably the most frequently seen toad in Florida. It can be found in every county. Possibly because it is eaten or otherwise outcompeted by the introduced giant toad, the southern toad is now uncommon in areas of Dade County where the giant toad has proliferated.

Habitat The southern toad is a habitat generalist. It may be encountered along lake and pond shores, wooded hammocks, highland scrub, and all habitats between.

Size Female southern toads are substantially larger than males. Males are adult at from 2–3 in., while females occasionally exceed 4.5 in. SVL (snout-vent-length).

Reproduction Southern toads lay dual strings of eggs at the edges of all manner of ponds, lakes, ditches, and canals. The eggs may number more than 4,000.

Coloration/pattern This is Florida's most variable toad. The ground color can be gray, brown, red, or nearly charcoal. Dark dorsal spots may or may not be present. If present, each spot often contains one or two (sometimes more) warts. A vestige of a lateral stripe is often visible. The venter is light but is usually variably pigmented with black spots or flecks. The parotoid glands are kidney shaped.

Males have a dark throat and a large, rounded vocal sac.

The small tadpoles are black above and dark below. The upper tailfin is more heavily pigmented than the lower.

Voice The voice of the southern toad is a penetrating, high pitched, rapidly pulsed, trill. Large choruses can be overpoweringly loud. Males call while sitting in exposed areas of the shoreline (occasionally in short grasses) or in very shallow water.

Similar species Although juveniles can be difficult to positively identify, no other Florida toad species has the very prominent cranial crests and interorbital knobs.

Behavior This is the common backyard hoptoad of Florida. Although active diurnally during overcast or rainy weather, the southern toad is primarily nocturnal in its activity patterns. It occurs in most areas but seems most common where sandy soils provide rapid drainage. From one to several toads often gather beneath porch lights to dine on falling insects.

Comments Despite massive habitat destruction in Florida, the southern toad remains a commonly seen species. When climatic conditions are suitable in the spring, immense breeding choruses may gather. These congregations may happen literally overnight. Following the breeding season, they disperse widely, and the few then seen give no indication of the true population in a given area.

4 FOWLER'S TOAD

Bufo woodhousii fowleri

Abundance This species, uncommon in Florida, is found only in the western panhandle.

Habitat Where found in Florida, the Fowler's toad is primarily restricted to bottomland habitats.

Size This is a fairly large, robust toad. Females may exceed 3.5 in. in SVL, but males are often somewhat smaller.

Reproduction Although Fowler's toads tend to breed where water retention is somewhat more stable than at sites chosen by the southern toad, temporarily flooded bottomland sites are also used. Wherever in Florida Fowler's toads are found breeding, they are usually vastly outnumbered by southern toads. They often breed a little later in the spring than the main concentrations of southern toad. Double gelatinous strings of eggs are laid by floating, amplexed females. Clutches of up to 8,000 eggs have been reported.

Coloration/pattern The Fowler's toad is usually of some shade of gray, more rarely a grayish-brown but, unlike the southern toad, never red. Fowler's toads have dark dorsal and lateral spots of irregular outline, but which are neatly edged in very light gray. The interorbital crests never bear large posterior knobs. The venter is light and usually has no, or little, dark pigmentation.

Males have dark throats and a single large subgular vocal sac.

The tadpoles are small, black dorsally, white ventrally, and have narrow unpigmented tailfins.

Voice Calling males produce a loud, unmusical, nasal, "waaaaaah" while sitting on open sandy banks, usually within a few inches of the waterline.

Similar species Most persons immediately recognize toads as such. Differentiating species can be more challenging, however. This is especially so of any toad that is not fully adult.

In the western Florida panhandle, three toad species occur sympatrically. They are easily differentiated by call. Fowler's toads voice a nasal "waaaah"; southern toads, *B. terrestris,* produce a high-pitched trill; and oak toads, *B. quercicus,* make a chick-like peep. Hybrids between Fowler's and southern toads produce an intermediate whirring trill.

Oak toads are adult at 1.25 in. SVL. If the specimen in question is larger, rule out the oak toad. Adult southern toads have greatly developed knobs at the posterior end of the interorbital crests. Southern toads may be red in color and, if dark spots are present, they often contain only one large wart. In general, most southern toads appear smoother-skinned than Fowler's toads.

See also the species accounts for the southern (3) and the oak toads (2).

The eastern spadefoot has vertically elliptical pupils.

Behavior Like most toads, the Fowler's toad moves in short hops. They are secretive, and usually hide by day beneath ground debris or in a burrow of their own making. They become active at dusk and are often found after dark beneath porchlights and streetlights where tired insects fall, crawl—and get eaten.

Comments It would appear that the Fowler's toad has never been very common in Florida. However, because so little is known with certainty about this species in the state, careful monitoring and life history studies would be of great benefit to biologists.

CRICKET FROGS, TREEFROGS, & CHORUS FROGS
Family Hylidae

The hylid frogs of Florida—the cricket, tree, and chorus frogs—are contained in 5 genera. Within these genera, there are 16 species (3 with 2 subspecies each) of which 14 are native. Of the two remaining species, one, the Cuban treefrog, is a firmly established alien species and the other, the Australian great green treefrog, seems tenuously established at the moment.

The **cricket frogs** (2 species, one of which has 2 subspecies) are of variable color, usually found near water and, lacking toepads, do not readily climb. Both are tiny species that attain a length of barely an inch. They have *fully webbed* hind feet, a dark interorbital triangle, and distinctive striping on the hidden surface of the thigh. To see the latter the frogs must be caught and their legs gently extended.

The **treefrogs** (9 species, none of which are subspeciated) all have toepads and are capable of climbing, although most species do not often climb to treetop height. These are more variably sized, ranging from the slender 1 in. length of the Pine Woods treefrog to the hefty 5 in. attained by female Cuban treefrogs. At a length of 2.25 in., the barking treefrog is the largest of Florida's *native* treefrog species. The amount of webbing on the hind feet varies, but is usually considerable. Except when hybridization occurs, all are easily identified in the field both by appearance and voice.

For the most part, the **chorus frogs** (5 species, 2 with 2 subspecies each) are also small frogs. The largest Florida species is the relatively robust ornate chorus frog that occasionally attains a 1.5 in. SVL. The chorus frogs have very small toepads and, although capable of climbing, except for the spring peeper, seldom do so. The toes bear only basal webbing. Of the chorus frogs, only the spring peeper is recognized by most folks. It is the most "treefrog-like" member of the genus.

All Florida hylids may be field identified by their distinctive breeding calls. The clicking calls of the two species of cricket frogs are the most confusingly similar. Although we have tried to describe the sounds made by each, anuran vocalizations do not lend themselves well to words. To learn these we recommend that you obtain *The Calls of Frogs and Toads of Eastern and Central North America* produced by Lang Elliott Nature Sound Studio. The croaking callnotes of the Australian great green treefrog are not on this recording.

All Florida hylids breed in "normal" fashion. The two sexes encounter each other in the breeding ponds, streams, or bogs. Females respond to the species-specific calls of the males, but hybridization does occasionally occur. Males grasp the females in an axillary (behind the forelimbs) embrace termed "amplexus." The eggs are fertilized as they are laid. Within a few days the eggs hatch and develop into the aquatic, free-swimming larvae known as tadpoles or polliwogs, most of which are confusingly similar. After a period of weeks, throughout which complex changes occur, the tadpole metamorphoses into a tiny froglet, which may still be difficult to positively identify for a few days or weeks.

CRICKET FROGS

Although not difficult to identify as cricket frogs, these frogs are often difficult to distinguish from each other. Cricket frogs lack toepads, have a dark triangular or V-shaped mark between the eyes, and striping on the hidden surface of the thighs. The southern and the northern chorus frogs have numerous tiny papillae on both sides of the vent. These papillae are absent in the Florida cricket frog.

Cricket frogs may be heard calling sporadically during cool weather, but they are actually hot weather breeders.

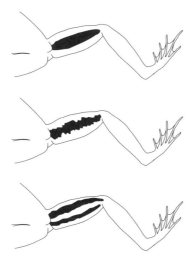

Differences in the thigh pattern of the southern cricket frog (top), northern cricket frog (center), and Florida cricket frog (bottom).

5 NORTHERN CRICKET FROG

Acris c. crepitans

Abundance This frog can be quite common in suitable boggy habitats. Although it ranges widely in the eastern United States, it occurs in Florida only in the western panhandle.

Habitat The northern cricket frog is associated with permanent water sources. They are particularly common in, but not restricted to, sunny shallows that are matted with sphagnum and emergent plants such as frogsbit and lizard's tail.

Size A minuscule frog, the northern cricket frog is fully adult at from 1–1.25 in. SVL. Females may be marginally the larger sex.

Reproduction The several small clusters of eggs are attached to submerged plants. A complete clutch numbers from 100 to 200 eggs. Tadpoles, in advanced stages of development, are dark dorsally and have a pinkish venter and a dark tailtip.

Coloration/pattern This tiny, warty, agile frog is variably colored and patterned. The ground color can be brown, tan, charcoal, some shade of green, or various combinations of these colors. The markings, usually oriented longitudinally, can be yellow, green, russet, or brown. The single broad thigh stripe is usually irregularly edged. The hind leg is comparatively short. If it is *gently* extended and drawn forward, the heel *usually* does not extend beyond the snout. A dark interorbital triangle is present. The webbing of the toes is extensive, reaching the tips of all except the longest toe. Males have a dark throat skin that distends into a single large subgular vocal sac.

Voice The initial notes in the lengthy sequence of clicking calls produced by the northern cricket frog are slower and more separated from the next note than those towards the end. The sound produced by a large chorus is harsh and shrilly discordant.

Similar species If the two species of cricket frogs are compared, the northern cricket frog is the shorter-nosed and shorter-legged of the two. It could be termed "chunky," while the southern cricket frog might be called streamlined and lithe. But we hasten to caution that the characteristics that separate the two species of chorus frogs are *all* variable and comparative. The extent of the webbing of the toes and shape of thigh stripe are the most constant differences. Also see the southern cricket frog (7). Chorus frogs have reduced webbing on the toes and treefrogs have discernible toepads.

Behavior Although they may sit atop floating or pondside mosses in patches of sunlight for long periods, northern cricket frogs are alert and agile when approached. While there may seem neither rhyme nor reason to their long, erratic hops, they are remarkably successful at avoiding capture.

Comments Although we always enjoy seeing these frogs, they are quick to flee if approached incautiously. If an observer sits quietly (often difficult to do amidst the clouds of mosquitos that also are found in these habitats), the cricket frogs will usually reassemble and may even start chorusing.

6 FLORIDA CRICKET FROG

Acris gryllus dorsalis

Abundance This subspecies is the most common of the cricket frogs in the state. It occurs in a wide range of aquatic habitats, often in dense populations.

Habitat Potholes, ponds, lakes, bogs, marshes, and open sphagnaceous swamp edges are among the habitats of this moisture-loving frog. They are often particularly common where extensive mats of sphagnum exist and blend remarkably with that medium.

Size This frog is fully adult at from .75–1 in. SVL.

Reproduction Several small clusters of eggs are deposited by amplexed females. They are attached to submerged vegetation. A total complement of 100–200 eggs is laid.

Coloration/pattern A great variability in both ground color and dorsal pattern typifies this warty, alert, and agile hylid. The ground color may run the gamut from a rather deep brown through tan and russet to green. The frog is darkest when cold. Dark diagonal bars are often present on the flanks and a broad, lengthwise, vertebral mark of a brighter and contrasting color is usually present. This often begins on the top of the snout, splits and outlines the large interorbital triangle, then converges and continues to the vent as a single stripe.

Males have dark throats and a single subgular vocal sac.

The legs are long (if carefully adpressed along the body, the heel extends beyond the tip of the snout). The toes are less fully webbed than those of the northern cricket frog. There are *two* dark stripes on the hidden surface of each thigh and no anal papillae.

Voice The clicking vocalizations are more metallic than those of the northern cricket frog and are produced in a series of 1 to 7 or 8 rapidly repeated notes.

Similar species See the northern cricket frog (5). Chorus frogs have very reduced webbing on the toes.

Behavior Alert, active, agile, normally unapproachable—all describe the Florida cricket frog well. This little frog explodes into a series of long, frenzied jumps when approached.

7 SOUTHERN CRICKET FROG

A. g. gryllus

The Florida cricket frog is replaced in the northwestern panhandle by the southern Cricket Frog, which is very similar in appearance, but has only a single rather even edged thigh stripe and has anal papillae.

TREEFROGS

All Florida species are easily identifiable in the field. They vary in size, color, webbing, habitat preference, breeding season, and much else. The same frog may undergo chameleon-like changes of color, being brown or heavily patterned one moment and green or unpatterned a short time later. Cold treefrogs are often the darkest in coloration. Most are easily approached on overcast, or especially on rainy nights, when they are at their breeding sites. In fact, except when they are vocalizing, their presence may be unsuspected.

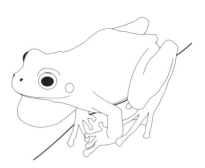

Treefrog. Note the expanded toetips. The circle behind the eye is the tympanum (exposed eardrum). The vocal sac beneath the chin is partially distended.

8 PINE BARRENS TREEFROG

Hyla andersonii

Abundance This is an uncommon, localized, and highly specialized treefrog. It is a protected species in Florida.

Habitat In Florida, the Pine Barrens treefrog is found only in hillside seepage bogs. These are uncommon habitats known to exist in only a few areas in the western Panhandle. Titi, red maple, mountain laurel, fetterbush, insectivorous plants, and sphagnum are among the plant species associated with these bogs.

Size In Florida, Pine Barrens treefrogs seem slightly smaller than those in the Carolinas and New Jersey. Adults in the Florida populations are from 1.25–1.50 in. in SVL.

Reproduction Small clusters of 150–250 eggs are deposited in shallow water. The egg clusters adhere to submerged vegetation.

Coloration/pattern If not the most beautiful treefrog in America, the Pine Barrens treefrog surely runs a close second to whichever species you may personally favor. Unless cold or stressed, when they may be an unattractive olive-green, *H. andersonii* varies from jade to leaf green dorsally. A broad purplish to brown stripe extends rearward from the nostri, through the eye and tympanum, to the groin. This is bordered dorsally with cream or yellow. The hands and feet are also purplish. Golden to orange spots and reticulation appear on the posterior side, beneath the legs, and in the groin. Except for where it is suffused with orange, the venter is white. Males have a dark throat that distends when the frog is vocalizing into a rounded subgular vocal sac.

The tadpoles are olive green with dark flecking on body and tail.

Voice The call of this species is often likened to the honking of a goose. However, the calls of the Florida populations are higher pitched than those of northern populations. The notes are an oft repeated, high-pitched "quank."

Similar species The green treefrog, *H. cinerea*, is occasionally found with or near the Pine Barrens treefrog. The green treefrog is more slender and has a metallic white to no lateral stripe.

Behavior This is a secretive, spring- and summer-breeding treefrog. Virtually nothing is known of its life history beyond the breeding bogs. Additional studies are needed of all populations, but none more than of those in Florida.

Comments Pine Barrens treefrogs from the Florida populations are known to have hybridized with pine woods and green treefrogs.

Neither the tadpoles nor adults of the Pine Barrens treefrog do well in captivity. Their captive husbandry remains as enigmatic as the details of their life away from the breeding ponds. This species is protected in Florida.

9 BIRD-VOICED TREEFROG

Hyla avivoca

Abundance This is a common-to-abundant treefrog, which is found from Leon County westward in the panhandle. Like many other treefrogs, once the breeding season is over, little is known of its life history.

Habitat The bird-voiced treefrog is a denizen of the great southern tupelo and sweet gum river swamps.

Size This is a small treefrog that is known to attain 1.75 in. SVL, but is usually smaller. Females are marginally larger than males.

Reproduction This small treefrog may lay upwards of several hundred eggs. The eggs are deposited in clusters of 10 to 30 and may adhere to surface or submerged vegetation.

Coloration/pattern The bird-voiced treefrog is a smaller and smoother-skinned version of the gray treefrog and has a very different voice. The dorsal coloration varies from pale- or pea-green through gray to charcoal. The same frog may be greenish at one moment and deep gray soon thereafter. Cold or stressed specimens are usually the darkest. A large, dark, central figure (outlined with charcoal or black) is usually visible on the back. Leg bars and a dark interorbital marking are present. The groin and concealed surfaces of the hind legs are greenish or a very pale yellow (but never orange). Males have a dark throat and a subgular vocal sac. A dark-edged, light (white to yellowish-green) spot, usually wider than high, is beneath each eye.

The tadpoles are pretty and quite similar in appearance to those of the gray treefrog. They are buff or light brown with a reddish or rose saddle and rose to pink(ish) fins.

Voice Of the Florida frog calls, that of the bird-voiced treefrog is our hands-down favorite. The calls are melodious flute-like whistles that have been likened to the ululations produced by some birds or of a person whistling for a dog.

Similar species The larger gray treefrog has orange in the groin and on the hind legs. The bird-voiced treefrog tends to have a lineate pattern on the rear of the thighs, while that of the gray treefrog is more reticulate.

Behavior Little is known about the life history of this treefrog once it has stopped chorusing for the year. We have found adults crossing roadways during late summer nighttime showers, and we have found new metamorphs emerging from the swamplands in September. This species typically choruses once the muggy nights of late spring and summer have set in, but we have heard choruses as early as late March, when periodic coolness could still be expected. Autumn showers may also induce sporadic vocalizations. Chorusing males typically call from perches 2–6 ft above the surface of the water. Calling densities are greatest in the interior of the swamp.

Comments Two subspecies of the bird-voiced treefrog are recognized by some authorities. These are *H. a. avivoca*, the western, and *H. a. ogechiensis*, the eastern. If you continue to recognize these subspecies, *H. a. avivoca* would be the race found in the Florida panhandle. The suborbital spot is usually white on this race.

10 COPE'S (OR SOUTHERN) GRAY TREEFROG

Hyla chrysoscelis

Abundance The southern gray treefrog is widely distributed across the northern one third of the Florida peninsula and is known from all of the panhandle counties. It is a common to abundant species.

Habitat *H. chrysoscelis* prefers wet woodland habitats where it breeds most frequently in pools and swamps. However, this species is more of a habitat generalist than many other treefrogs.

Size Large females may attain 2.25 in. SVL. Males are somewhat smaller. This is a heavy-bodied species.

Reproduction Females may lay more than 1,500 eggs, which are deposited in small clusters and may adhere to either surface or submerged vegetation or float free.

Coloration/pattern Gray treefrogs are capable of undergoing chameleon-like changes from pale- or pea-green through many shades of gray to charcoal. Cold or stressed frogs are often the darkest. A large and intricate darker dorsal figure is usually prominently visible. It is outlined in black. Leg bars and an interorbital bar are usually present. The interorbital bar may be broken midway. The groin and undersurface of the hind legs are orange-yellow to bright orange. The rear of the thighs is orange patterned with black reticulations. A dark-edged white spot, often taller than wide, is present beneath each eye. Males have dark throats and a large, round subgular vocal sac.

The attractive tadpole of this species is buff or gold with a rose tailfin.

Voice The call of this species consists of a loud, resonant, high-pitched, rapid trill that is not dissimilar to the call of a red-bellied woodpecker. The chosen calling station is often a foot to several feet above the water. It may call while sitting on a limb or it may choose to cling head up or head down to the trunk of a fairly large tree. Gray treefrogs may be heard in full chorus from late March or early April to June or July and more sporadically for several months thereafter.

Similar species In Florida, only the bird-voiced treefrog is apt to be mistaken for this species. The bird-voiced treefrog has a greenish or pale yellow rather than a golden or orange wash in its groin and on the underside of its hind limbs.

Behavior The gray treefrog is strongly arboreal and is quite apt to vocalize during summer storms from much higher in the trees than many other hylids. It is common near the periphery of woodland ponds and swamps but also calls from deep in swampy situations.

Comments Florida is one of the few states in which the taxonomy and identification of the gray treefrog doesn't seem problematic. To the best of our knowledge, of the two sibling species, *versicolor* (a genetic tetraploid) and *chrysoscelis* (a genetic diploid) only the latter occurs in Florida. The two are visually identical in the field, but because of the chromosomal differences, they do not usually inter-breed. Chorusing males can be field identified by comparing the trill rate of the calls of the two at *identical* temperatures. *H. versicolor* has a much slower trill rate, hence a much more melodious call.

11 GREEN TREEFROG

Hyla cinerea

Abundance Not only is this one of the most beautiful of Florida's treefrogs, it is one of the most abundant as well.

Habitat By day green treefrogs may occasionally be encountered resting, eyes tightly closed, on emergent or pondside vegetation. It is a common "backyard species" over much of Florida and is often drawn to porch lights by the profusion of insects. Green treefrogs are associated with more open areas than many other hylids, and are common around cattle tanks, pasture ponds, slowly flowing canals, lakes, and other such areas with a profusion of low herbaceous growth. At night they hunt and call while sitting on the leaves of cattails, arrowheads, and other such emergents.

Size The green treefrog is adult at a slender 1.75–2.25 in. Females are a little larger than the males.

Reproduction The complement of 400–600 eggs is laid in numerous clusters of 40 to 100 each. The eggs may float as a surface film but more often adhere to surface or subsurface vegetation.

Coloration/pattern Low temperature and/or stress produce a dorsal coloration of olive-brown to dark olive-green. Sleeping green treefrogs may be olive-tan. But when these little frogs are alert and relatively content, they are a beautiful bright- to forest-green and are among the prettiest of the hylids. The throat of a male green treefrog is green on the sides and yellowish-green to yellowish-white centrally. The distended subgular vocal sac is lighter in color than the throat. The sides are green and the venter is white. Green treefrogs often have an enamel white lateral stripe that extends from the tip of the snout to the groin. On some specimens the line may be foreshortened or entirely lacking. A white femoral and heel stripe is often present. Small, but well-defined, gold or orange dorsal spots may be present.

The tadpoles are rather nondescript, being olive to greenish with a yellowish stripe extending from nostril to eye.

Voice Some say the loud, frequently-repeated single notes of this treefrog sound like the peals of cowbells. We have never been able to discern this similarity. Instead, we hear a rather unmusical series of "quonks." The frogs often call from a foot or so above the water on the leaves of emergent arrowheads or similar vegetation. Occasionally, they call from water level while sitting on floating vegetation. They may be heard chorusing in Florida from early February (temperatures permitting) to late summer. They call most continually on warm overcast nights. On nights such as these they are also easily approached.

Similar species The squirrel treefrog, *H. squirella,* is smaller and lacks a distinct white lateral stripe. Pine Barrens treefrogs, *H. andersonii,* have a plum-colored stripe bordered dorsally with a narrow light line. Barking treefrogs, *H. gratiosa,* are larger and often patterned dorsally with light ovals or ocelli. See the individual species accounts for these three treefrogs.

Behavior This frog often strays from the breeding ponds into open woodlands during the day. There they are commonly seen hunkered down, legs drawn tightly to the body and eyes closed, on the foliage of broad-leafed plants. They are capable jumpers, but often walk unless frightened.

Comments Green treefrogs can be hardy pet treefrogs, living a decade or longer in captivity. They hybridize with barking treefrogs rather frequently. The appearance of such hybrids may be similar to a parent (apparently, most often the barking treefrog) or noticeably intermediate. The calls, however, usually differ from those of the parental species.

12 PINE WOODS TREEFROG

Hyla femoralis

Abundance This is another of Florida's common-to-abundant treefrog species.

Habitat The common name pretty well defines the habitat in which this frog is most commonly seen. However, it may also be encountered amidst cypress, near and on dwellings, and is a common breeder in roadside ditches.

Size This is one of the smaller of Florida's treefrogs. A slender frog, the pine woods treefrog is adult at from 1.25–1.5 in. Females are the larger sex and may occasionally attain 1.75 in.

Reproduction Clusters of from 20 to 100 eggs are laid by amplexed females until the total complement is deposited. The eggs may float freely but more often adhere loosely to surface and subsurface vegetation. Ephemeral ponds are often chosen as breeding sites.

Coloration/pattern Pine woods treefrogs are variable and can be difficult to identify. Although most often reddish in color, grays and greens are also assumed. A large dorsal figure of irregular shape is usually visible, as is a dark lateral line that begins at the nostril, passes through the eye, curves downward posterior to the tympanum, and continues to the groin. A dark interorbital blotch is also usually discernable. The most distinctive markings are the light (often yellowish, sometimes greenish) irregularly oval spots on the dark concealed surface of the thigh.

Males have a dark throat and a rounded subgular vocal sac.

Tadpoles are olive to olive-drab dorsally, purplish ventrolaterally, and yellowish ventrally.

Voice Pine woods treefrogs have a curious and characteristic dot-dash call that is often likened to the sounds produced by Morse Code transmissions. The call is rapidly paced at the breeding ponds, but slower when given as a "rain call." At some breeding ponds, calling males sit at night on open muddy shores; in other locations they may vocalize while sitting from 1 to 5 feet above the water on the leaves of shoreline shrubs. They are rather easily approached on overcast or rainy nights but are much more wary on brilliantly moonlit nights. The breeding calls may be heard as early as late February and as late in the year as early October.

Similar species The oval yellowish to greenish thigh spots are diagnostic but nearly impossible to see unless the treefrog is in hand. Also see species accounts for the gray, squirrel, Pine Barrens, and bird-voiced treefrogs.

Behavior Like many other treefrogs, the pine woods treefrog is strongly arboreal. It is seldom seen except when calling at the breeding ponds. Rain calls may be voiced from treetop positions.

Comments This species is known to hybridize with both the Pine Barrens and gray treefrogs. Visually, the hybrids may be difficult to differentiate from the parent species, but the calls are often intermediate.

13 BARKING TREEFROG

Hyla gratiosa

Abundance This largest native eastern treefrog remains common in some areas, but may be reduced in numbers where habitat alterations have occurred or where it is collected heavily for the pet trade. Some speculate that this species is naturally cyclic.

Habitat This frog is associated with open mixed woodlands, farmlands, and pasture ponds. It climbs high and well, apparently foraging both while high in trees and closer to the ground. One winter day I (RDB) found a dozen apparently dormant individuals in sandy soil at the base of a newly fallen pine in Hillsborough County. We have been told of a similar aggregation found beneath bark shards fallen from a long dead but still standing pine in Alachua County. Several others were found while people were digging near the base of a large oak at the edge of a clearing.

Size Although many are adult at 2 in. SVL, a record size of 2.75 in. has been confirmed. Females are the larger sex.

Reproduction These frogs call at night while floating in rather open, shallow waters, often in pasture or open woodland ponds. The 500–1000+ eggs may be deposited either singly or in sizable clusters and adhere to submerged or pond bottom vegetation. Choruses, drawn to ponds by warm, heavy rains, may be heard from early February to September.

Coloration/pattern Barkers are truly the chameleons of treefrogdom. The same frog may be yellowish-green, green, tan, or brown, and may be patternless at one time and profusely marked with solid rounded spots or open centered ocelli at another. Males have a greenish or yellow throat and a huge, rounded, subgular vocal sac. The upper lip is white and an irregular white lateral line may be present. The skin is strongly granular.

The tadpoles are rather pretty. They are often yellowish-green dorsally and pinkish ventrally with a very high tailfin. A light line may run from the tail musculature to the eye and a dark elongate marking may saddle the tail musculature somewhat anterior to midtail. Both the stripes and the dark saddle may be absent.

Voice The barking treefrog has two distinctly different calls. A loud, oft-repeated but hollow sounding "dooonk" is voiced by floating frogs, whereas the treetop raincall sounds more like a barking dog.

Barking treefrogs often call in conjunction with several other hylids but seem most often associated with choruses of green treefrogs. Hybridization with the green treefrog is well documented.

Although, in altered habitats, other observers have seen male green treefrogs intercept and amplex female green treefrogs, in unaltered habitats in central Florida, I (RDB) have seen the opposite. In these natural pothole environments, female green treefrogs are intercepted by male barkers floating near the edges of the ponds, as the female greens attempt to respond to the male green treefrogs calling from more central emergent vegetation.

Similar species When present, the dorsal ocelli are diagnostic.

Behavior Males often hold their calling position by grasping the stems of emergent vegetation or water surface plants with their fingers.

Comments Even on overcast or rainy nights, barking treefrogs are rather wary. Floating frogs will dive quickly if disturbed by ripples. They seldom resume calling at the site where they were frightened, surfacing, instead, several feet away.

14 Squirrel Treefrog

Hyla squirella

Abundance This treefrog remains one of the most common species in Florida.

Habitat This is a rather ubiquitous treefrog. It uses all manner of habitats, from open woodlands and cypress heads to pasturelands, gardens, and dwelling walls.

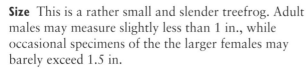

Size This is a rather small and slender treefrog. Adult males may measure slightly less than 1 in., while occasional specimens of the the larger females may barely exceed 1.5 in.

Reproduction This is a fecund species. Females may lay more than 800 eggs. The eggs may be deposited singly or in clusters. Breeding may occur in woodland or pasture ponds, flooded roadside ditches, or other suitable bodies of water. Males call while sitting on muddy shorelines or, more often, while hunkered down amidst low grasses in only 1–2 in. of water. Breeding activities begin at different times at different latitudes on the peninsula, but usually initially coincide with the onset of spring and summer rains. However, squirrely treefrogs are known to breed from late winter throughout the months of summer.

Coloration/pattern Squirrel treefrogs are both variable and rather nondescript. They change colors rapidly, varying between brown, a yellow green, and bright green. All shades between these colors are also assumed. Squirrel treefrogs often have a light upper lip and may have a vaguely defined light or dark lateral line. An interorbital blotch, spots, or triangle may be present. Darker orbital stripes, and/or dorsal and lateral blotches may be present.

Males have a rounded sub-gular vocal sac.

The tadpoles are olive-green dorsally and have a dark-centered yellow(ish) venter. The gills may show through the translucent skin with a reddish blush.

Voice The common name refers to the rapidly repeated raincall that is voiced from trees, shrubs, logs, and stumps during periods of unsettled weather. The breeding call is somewhat more slowly repeated and is more reminiscent of a duck's quack than a squirrel's churr.

Similar species The squirrel treefrog is best identified by considering what field marks it doesn't have.

The squirrel treefrog lacks a well defined white lateral stripe, while *most* green treefrogs have one.

The squirrel treefrog lacks orange or yellow in the groin, a color shared by several other Florida species.

The squirrel treefrog lacks light oval markings on the concealed surfaces of the thighs (pine woods treefrogs have these).

One positive characteristic is that squirrel treefrogs have well developed toepads. These are lacking in the cricket frogs and small in the chorus frogs.

Behavior Although squirrel treefrogs can be alert and agile, they often allow close approach without taking fright. This is especially true on cloudy or rainy nights at the breeding ponds and puddles. They are agile climbers but also seek refuge in moisture retaining natural and manmade ground debris.

Comments This is a frog you may need to catch to identify. Consider all of the negative field characters together and rule out the impossibilities.

15 CUBAN TREEFROG

Osteopilus septentrionalis

Abundance Common to abundant in urban and suburban settings from Charlotte County on the west coast and Indian River County on the east coast, southward through the Florida Keys. It occurs more sparingly in Hillsborough, Pinellas, and Sarasota counties (west coast) and Brevard County (east coast). Isolated specimens have been found elsewhere as well.

Habitat In Florida this West Indian frog is often associated with man, but also occurs in tropical hammocks of the southern mainland and throughout the Keys. It is common to abundant in garden settings, irrigated shrubs, along periodically flooded drainage ditches, and other such artificial habitats. By day and in dry weather this primarily nocturnal frog may secrete itself in open pipes, the axils of banana "trees," palms, and other such moisture retaining areas.

Size This is the largest *firmly established* treefrog in Florida. Males are adult at 1.5–2.75 in. Females regularly exceed 3 in. SVL and an occasional one may exceed a heavy-bodied 5 in.

Reproduction Clusters of 25 to 75 floating eggs are laid by amplexed females. A total complement of more than 200 may be laid.

Coloration/pattern The ground color of the Cuban treefrog may vary from an unpatterned to a heavily patterned tan or gray, through warm brown, to an olive (rarely bluish-) green. The dorsum is warty, the toepads are immense. Yellow is often present in the axil of each foreleg. The venter is white or off-white.

This frog may breed anytime from March throughout the months of summer in the Keys. On the mainland it is more apt to breed between mid-April and August, after warm weather has truly set in.

When inflated, the bilateral vocal sacs make the male Cuban treefrog appear to be wearing waterwings.

The tadpoles are nearly black dorsally with a lighter venter. The tail musculature may have a brownish tinge.

Voice Variable. Males snore and make sounds comparable to wet fingers being drawn over an inflated balloon.

Similar species At present, this frog occurs south of the range of the gray and bird-voiced treefrogs and lacks the white suborbital spot borne by both of those smaller species. No other treefrog in Florida has the proportionately immense toepads of the Cuban.

Behavior Cuban treefrogs usually allow close approach, but if startled are capable of making tremendous leaps. Although they are occasionally encountered on the ground or beneath debris, Cuban treefrogs are highly arboreal and the large toepads enable them to assume and retain precarious positions. Males may call from the tops of citrus or other such trees during rainstorms. The raincall is shorter and less varied than the breeding vocalizations.

Comments This frog seems to be expanding its range and increasing its numbers annually. They are still killed in immense numbers by the occasional freezes, but enough obviously survive to quickly repopulate an area. Males seem to live only one or two years (researcher Walter Meshaka considers males "annuals"), but females may survive more than a decade.

Despite the toxicity of the skin secretions, Cuban treefrogs are preyed upon by many Florida snakes. Alligators, raccoons, opossums, and birds of prey also eat these frogs.

Caution: The skin secretions of the Cuban treefrog are highly irritating to mucous membranes (eyes, nose, mouth). Wash your hands *thoroughly* after handling this species.

16 AUSTRALIAN GREAT GREEN TREEFROG

Litoria caerulea

Abundance If truly established in Florida, this magnificent frog remains rare and localized in distribution.

Habitat In Australia and Indonesia, this frog is a habitat generalist. It is often associated with manmade breeding facilities such as cattle tanks and cisterns and is often found in and on dwellings. It is capable of withstanding sustained droughts. The preferred habitat in Florida is unknown. A few specimens have been found along weed-choked canals in Lee, Collier, and Dade counties. The presence of this frog in Florida can be traced directly to pet trade escapees.

Size At an apparent maximum length of 2.5–3 in., males of this species are much smaller than females, which may slightly exceed 5 in. SVL.

Reproduction Clusters of floating eggs are laid by amplexed females, often while the frogs are floating amidst, or holding onto, surface vegetation. Females can produce from several hundred to more than 1,000 eggs. No congregations of metamorphs have yet been found in Florida.

The two small choruses of this species that we have heard have been in mid-May following heavy rains.

P. caerulea is now bred extensively for the pet trade by Florida herpetoculturists. The species can be induced to multiclutch in captivity through the use of luteinizing and releasing hormones (LHRH). It is doubtful whether multiclutching occurs in nature in Florida.

Coloration/pattern Cold and stressed or sleeping frogs may be an overall or blotchy brown, deep olive, or olive-drab. Improving conditions and wakefulness often bring about a considerable brightening of color. Jade to forest-green are the most normal colors. Occasional specimens may be a cobalt blue. Some specimens may have one or many enamel white spots. If present, these spots are often most numerous laterally. The venter is white. This is a stocky treefrog that may have from poorly developed to greatly developed supraorbital and supratympanal ridges.

Males have a proportionately small subgular vocal sac. Breeding males have well developed nuptial (grasping) pads on the thumbs.

The tadpoles are of a rather uniform olive-drab to olive-green color.

Voice A series of hoarse croaks is given. The calls are given more slowly at low temperatures.

Similar species There are no other giant green treefrogs, either native or introduced, now known to occur in Florida. The typical jade green coloration should distinguish juveniles of this species from the bright green native species.

Behavior While this species is associated with disturbed habitats, often near human habitations, in its native countries, virtually nothing is known of its natural history in Florida. Because of its tolerance for drought conditions and cool temperatures (Australian specimens), *P. caerulea* may be well adapted to the climatic vagaries of subtropical Florida.

Comments Both Indonesian and Australian *P. caerulea* are now bred for the pet trade. It seems probable that Indonesian specimens would be less tolerant of Florida's occasional freezes than the Australian frogs. Unlike *P. caerulea* of Australian origin, those from Indonesia seem not to develop the fleshy ridges over the eyes and tympanum. Indonesian specimens also seem of a more olive hue than those from Australia.

CHORUS FROGS

This group of hylid frogs contains Florida's smallest species, the little grass frog. Even the largest Florida chorus frog, the ornate, attains an average length of only 1.25 in.

The toepads of chorus frogs are relatively tiny. Most often the frogs are encountered in terrestrial situations. However, the spring peeper climbs readily. During the breeding season, chorus frogs enter shallow water situations to vocalize and breed. They may be heard by day (especially on overcast days) or night. These are well-camouflaged, secretive frogs that can be difficult to locate.

17 SOUTHERN SPRING PEEPER

Pseudacris crucifer bartramiana

Abundance This is one of the most ubiquitous and abundant frogs of the northern two fifths of the Florida peninsula and the eastern half of the panhandle.

Habitat Peepers are frogs of open woodland and woodland ponds, of marshes, and of bogs. Although their breeding biology is rather well understood, little is known about their life away from the breeding ponds. Peepers have been occasionally found in the summer months sitting on the leaves of low-to-the-ground herbs (such as trilliums and jacks-in-the-pulpits). Although rather closely allied to the chorus frogs, and currently in the genus *Pseudacris*, unlike other chorus frogs which are secretive ground-dwellers, peepers sometimes chorus while sitting in shrubs 2 to 6 feet above the water.

Size This small but attractive treefrog is adult at .75–1.25 in. The females are noticeably larger than the males.

Reproduction In Florida the spring peeper—a harbinger of impending northern spring weather—would be better referred to as a winter peeper. These little frogs begin vocalizing at the onset of cool weather (usually during the rains of late October or early November) and may be heard at the ponds throughout the winter until shortly after the warm days of spring have set in. Males may choose to seclude themselves in a clump of grass when calling or be completely exposed on a patch of mud or a low branch. The eggs, which may near or slightly exceed 200 in number, are laid singly or in small clusters. They adhere to submerged vegetation.

Coloration/pattern Variable, but to a lesser degree than many hylids. The dorsal ground color may be tan, russet, or of some shade of brown to brownish-gray. Some peepers seem vaguely suffused with olive. Cold or stressed frogs are darkest. A dark X is usually at least vaguely discernible on the dorsum. The sides of the snout are often darker than the top and a dark lateral stripe is often present on each side. The venter is variably pigmented with black spots and stipplings on a light ground color. Males have a yellowish to grayish chin and a single subgular vocal sac.

The tadpole is quite nondescript. The body, which is darkest dorsally, is greenish with vague stipplings or reticulations. The tail musculature and finnage is of the same color as the body but may be more strongly patterned.

Voice The vocalizations of this small hylid are probably recognized by more persons than those of any other North American frog. The calls, whistled peeps with a rising inflection, are produced in series. The calls are most slowly given on cold nights. Peepers may produce occasional short trills. Once choruses are in full swing, peepers may call even on nights when temperatures dip into the low-40s. However, at such cold temperatures the little frogs take fright easily and may not resume calling once disturbed.

Similar species The pine woods treefrog, *Hyla femoralis,* has orange to greenish oval spots on the rear surface of each thigh. Brown-toned squirrel treefrogs, *H. squirella,* can be very similar to peepers in appearance. However, *H. squirella* lack the dark dorsal X. Other chorus frogs tend to have dorsal markings in the form of stripes and a white(ish) upper lip.

Behavior Much about the life of the spring peeper remains a mystery. Its natural history is badly in need of study.

Comments The spring peeper was long considered a member of the genus *Hyla,* the "true" treefrogs. Although it has been relegated to the current genus, it does not fit well here. Some suggest that the peeper differs sufficiently from the treefrogs and the chorus frogs to warrant the erection of a new genus.

18 NORTHERN SPRING PEEPER

Pseudacris c. crucifer

In Florida's western panhandle (and throughout much of the eastern USA) the southern spring peeper is replaced by the northern spring peeper, which *may* be slightly smaller, is often somewhat duller in dorsal coloration and has little, if any, black pigmentation on the belly.

19 FLORIDA CHORUS FROG

Pseudacris nigrita verrucosa

Abundance Because of its secretive nature, population statistics of this once (and possibly still) common frog are difficult to ascertain. In recent years we have found this species rare or absent in many Florida locations where it was once common, but still abundant in others. Whether populations undergo normal cyclic fluctuations or whether other causes exist for the seeming number reductions is unknown. This race occurs over the southern four fifths of the peninsula.

Habitat These tiny, agile, and seldom seen frogs call from flooded fields, rain-swollen marshes, drainage ditches, pine woodland ponds, and other such open habitats. They are also associated with ponds and flooded shallows in woodlands with thick herbaceous understories.

Size This hylid frog is adult at a slender 1 in. in length. Occasional females may attain 1.25 in. SVL.

Reproduction Although these frogs are often spoken of as winter breeders, in Florida the breeding time is dictated by the occurrence of rains. Winter rains occur in the northern parts of Florida and allow winter and early spring breeding to occur. In more southerly areas of the state, winter rains may occur, but the rainy season is usually in the late spring to autumn. Thus, the Florida chorus frog may breed at any time of year in that area. The up-to-several-hundred eggs are laid in loose clusters and attached to submerged twigs and vegetation.

Coloration/pattern As do most other hylid frogs, the Florida chorus frog can vary tremendously in color and intensity of pattern. Cold frogs can be so dark a gray that the charcoal markings are barely discernible. When warm, the same frog can display a ground color of the lightest of gray with boldly contrasting elongate spots of deep charcoal. Even the lateral markings are in the form of spots. Rarely, the spots may join to form stripes. Striping seems more common at the northern end of the range than in the south. The upper lip may be mostly white or mostly black but always has alternating patches of those colors. It is never solid white.

The venter is light. Males have a dark throat, which distends into a large subgular vocal sac.

The small tadpoles are dark with yellowish or golden flecks.

Voice Although the trill rate varies with temperature (being slower when cold), the voice of this frog is best described as the noise made when a fingernail is drawn over the teeth of a pocket comb.

Similar species Cricket frogs have very extensive webbing on their hind feet and distinct stripes on the rear of the thigh. The dorsal markings of the brownish-tan upland chorus frog are usually a deeper brown, not black, and the white lip stripe may not be as precisely delineated dorsally.

Behavior When calling, Florida chorus frogs are usually backed into and under emergent grasses. Often only their head or head and anterior body are above the water surface.

20 SOUTHERN CHORUS FROG

Pseudacris n. nigrita

The nominate subspecies occurs in the northern one fifth of the peninsula and throughout the panhandle. Although not invariable, the dorsal spotting of this subspecies often coalesces into ragged stripes. The dark lateral markings are usually heavy and in the form of stripes rather than spots. The upper lip of the southern chorus frog is an unbroken white and is usually precisely delineated dorsally.

Both races of this frog are often difficult to observe at the breeding sites and nearly impossible to find once breeding has ceased for the year.

21 LITTLE GRASS FROG

Pseudacris ocularis

Abundance This is an abundant but difficult to observe species.

Habitat This little hylid is a denizen of grassy pond and cypress bay margins, swamp and marsh edges, flooded meadows, grassy pasture ponds, and roadside drainage ditches. It is found throughout all of Florida save the westernmost panhandle.

Size Males of this diminutive frog—the smallest anuran of the United States—are slender and attain an SVL of only .5 in. Occasional large females may attain a .625 in. SVL.

Reproduction Despite their small size, females of the little grass frog may lay more than 200 eggs. These are laid in several clusters of 25 or more and are attached to underwater twigs and grasses.

Coloration/pattern The ground color of this species is variable, but almost always ranges somewhere between light tan, rusty red, and dark brown. More rarely, the frog may be suffused with olive. It is often brighter dorsally than laterally. A darker vertebral stripe and/or two dorsolateral stripes may be visible. A prominent dark lateral stripe begins at the tip of the snout and continues along each side, often to the groin. A dark interorbital triangle is usually visible. Little grass frogs are often most brightly colored during periods of daytime activity, lightest and less contrasting on warm nights, and darkest when the weather (and the frog) is cold. The belly is light, often with a yellowish tint anteriorly. Males have a dark throat and proportionately huge subgular vocal sac.

The tadpole is olive dorsally and pinkish ventrally. The pinkish color, or a yellowish suffusion, extends onto the tail musculature. A dark line is usually present centrally on the tail musculature and dark spots are present on the edges of the fins.

Voice The tinkling calls of this tiny hylid may be heard throughout most of the year.

Similar species Cricket frogs (*Acris* sp.) have more extensively webbed hind feet and stripes on the rear of the thighs. Other chorus frogs (*Pseudacris* sp.) are larger, and most have a pattern of dorsal and dorsolateral spots that are either discrete or coalesced into stripes.

Behavior This frog may hop from grasses when startled, but is usually not seen unless a concerted effort is made to find it. Even then, it is easily overlooked. It is most easily found as it calls at night in roadside ditches. Look for it just above surface level to 2 ft above the water on emergent grasses.

Comments When calling, this hylid often aligns itself with the stem on which it is sitting. The striped pattern allows it to blend almost indiscernibly into its background. At other times the little grass frog may position itself crossways to the stem and become slightly more visible.

Many taxonomists feel that the little grass frog is more closely related to the treefrogs than to the chorus frogs. It is often referred to the genus *Limnaoedus*.

22 ORNATE CHORUS FROG

Pseudacris ornata

Abundance Locally common, but invariably secretive, the ornate chorus frog is found on the northern half of the peninsula and all of the panhandle of Florida.

Habitat Pine and mixed woodland ponds, seasonally flooded meadows, and roadside ditches are among the many habitats used.

Size This is the largest and most robust of Florida's chorus frogs. Males, the smaller sex, are adult at from 1–1.25 in. SVL. Occasional females may near 1.5 in.

Reproduction The more than 100 (probably to several hundred) eggs are laid in small clusters and attached to submerged twigs and vegetation.

Coloration/pattern This is the most variably colored of the chorus frogs. The ground color may vary from dull to bright green, or be gray, brown, or russet. A dark interorbital triangle *may* be present. Broad dorsolateral stripes may be prominent or barely visible. If present, the vertebral stripe is usually the weakest. Prominent light-edged black markings are present laterally. These exist as a stripe that begins on the tip of the snout and continues rearward to the tympanum or beyond, a side stripe or spot (this may coalesce with the eyestripe), and (usually) two elongated diagonal spots in and above the groin.

The venter usually has a yellowish blush, strongest posteriorly. Males have a dark throat and a rounded subgular vocal sac.

The nondescript tadpoles are brownish dorsally and somewhat lighter ventrally.

Voice The metallic, abruptly ended, peeps are voiced in series and are unlike the calls of any other Florida chorus frog.

Similar species Peepers, *Pseudacris crucifer,* have an X on the back. Squirrel treefrogs lack the black lateral markings.

Behavior A persistent burrower, the ornate chorus frog is usually seen above ground only when at the breeding ponds or when foraging during rainy weather. Males call while sitting either exposed or concealed in grasses on the shore or in very shallow water, or hold onto grasses or twigs with their fingers and vocalize while floating.

Comments This is the most distinctively marked of the eastern chorus frogs. The prominent black lateral markings make identification easy, no matter the dorsal color or pattern.

23 UPLAND CHORUS FROG

Pseudacris triseriata feriarum

Abundance This little frog occurs in Florida in only a few of the western panhandle counties where it follows river floodplains southward. It seems uncommon, or at least of local distribution.

Habitat In Florida, the upland chorus frog is a floodplain and low woodland species. It breeds in marshes, swamps, and temporarily flooded areas.

Size The record size for a female (the larger sex) of this frog is 1.5 in. This is a slender species.

Reproduction The several hundred eggs are laid in small clusters, which adhere to subsurface vegetation and twigs.

Coloration/pattern Although the ground color of the upland chorus frog may occasionally border on gray, more often it is of some shade of brown. Like most frogs, the colors are the lightest during periods of activity and darkest when the frogs are cold.

Light to dark brown is the most commonly seen ground color. The dark vertebral and dorsolateral stripes are relatively narrow and often broken into elongate spots. The dorsolateral stripes are often more prominent than the vertebral stripe. The lateral stripes are the most prominent and are usually not broken. A dark interorbital triangle is often visible. The venter is light but may bear dark pepper spots anteriorly. Males have a dark throat and rounded subgular vocal sac.

The tadpoles are very dark dorsally, gold ventrally, and the tail is dark tipped.

Voice This is another of the chorus frogs with a "combtooth" voice. The pulse rate of the trills is usually more rapid and of a higher pitch than the vocalizations of the southern chorus frog, but the two calls can be difficult to distinguish.

Males are usually well concealed in emergent grasses while calling.

Similar species Spring peepers have a dark X on the back. Cricket frogs have fully webbed rear feet and stripes on the rear surface of the thighs. Southern and Florida chorus frogs are gray with black markings.

Behavior Very little is known about the behavior of this frog in Florida. Field studies of its natural history are badly needed.

Comments North of Florida this species is associated with highland habitats, while the southern chorus frog is a coastal plain species. In Florida the range is restricted to two disjunct river drainages on the western panhandle.

LEPTODACTYLID FROGS
Family Leptodactylidae

The two representatives of this family now found in Florida are both alien species. The coqui is a very temperature-sensitive species that is tenuously established at best. The greenhouse frog is firmly established.

These two species are the only frogs of Florida to undergo direct development in the egg. Because there is no free-swimming tadpole stage, neither the coqui nor the greenhouse frog are dependent on standing water for breeding.

These frogs lack webbing between the toes.

24 PUERTO RICAN COQUI

Eleutherodactylus coqui

Abundance This is a rare and local species in
Florida. It is known to exist only in and around a few
greenhouses in southern Dade County. Although it has
been seen and heard in Florida for well over a decade,
the fact that it remains very localized and seems unable to
expand its range causes us to continue to consider its
presence here tenuous. Even where present in some numbers,
this frog is seldom seen except at night.

Habitat In Puerto Rico, this is an arboreal frog that is known to
climb to canopy positions. Those we have watched in Florida have,
for the most part, remained fairly close to the ground (.5 to 7 ft). We
have seen males calling from the trunks of citrus and ornamental
shade trees, as well as on the leaves of both epiphytic and terrestrial
bromeliads.

Size Although coquis are known to attain 2.25 in. SVL in Puerto
Rico, those in Florida seem considerably smaller. Of the several that
we have seen, all have been between 1.25 and 1.75 in.

Reproduction In Puerto Rico, the coqui breeds year-round. Little is
known about the reproductive biology of this frog in Florida, but
breeding activities here may be more heavily skewed towards our
very hot, humid, and often unstable late spring, summer, and early
autumn weather. The one to two dozen eggs are laid in moisture-
retaining pockets amid ground debris or, occasionally, in protected,
elevated sites. Males tend the clutches from deposition until shortly
after hatching. There is no free-swimming tadpole stage. Hatchling
coquis have a tail nub.

Coloration/pattern In ground color, the coqui varies from grayish-
brown through tan to rich brown, either with or without a pattern. If
a pattern is present, it may be obscure or prominent. Many specimens have a dark W-shaped marking discernible above the forelimbs.
A light dorsolateral stripe may be present. A broad, light interorbital
bar is often present. This species has large digital discs.

   The venter is primarily light, but often with at least some dark pigmentation. Males have a large, rounded subgular vocal sac.

Voice This species has derived its common name from its two-syllabled call of "co-qui," the accent being on the last syllable.

Similar species The greenhouse frog, *Eleutherodactylys p. planirostris*, is smaller, more slender, and, although variable, usually with rusty overtones. See also the species account and the photograph of the squirrel treefrog, *Hyla squirella* [14].

Behavior Except on strongly overcast or rainy days when it may be active, the coqui retires to the seclusion of rockpiles, the axils of bromeliad leaves, or beneath ground debris during the day. Both sexes are very active, and males are *very* vocal after dark.

Comments Whether or not this little frog was actually entitled to a page in these species accounts was, and is, problematic. Although it could once be found in some numbers amid the tropical plantings at Fairchild Tropical Gardens in south Miami, the coqui seems to no longer occur there. If our current information is accurate, the coqui is now restricted to about a half dozen bromeliad nursery/greenhouses in south Dade County. Whether the populations are self-sustaining, even in the artificiality of these habitats, is unknown. It may be that new coquis, arriving in bromeliad shipments from Puerto Rico, continually replenish the populations.

25 GREENHOUSE FROG

Eleutherodactylus p. planirostris

Abundance Although a decidedly tropical species that is adversely impacted by cold temperatures, the introduced greenhouse frog is a firmly established species that has slowly extended its range northward. It is now found as far north as Duval and Columbia counties, as well as in many isolated populations in the panhandle.

Habitat This is a ubiquitous species. It may be found in yards, woodlands, scrub, and other diverse habitats. Greenhouse frogs are particularly common in gardens, greenhouses, nurseries, or wherever else occasional sprinkling prevents a complete drying of the substrate. They seek seclusion beneath boards, mulch, fallen leaves, or stepping stones, and are adept at gaining quick access to the smallest of crevices and cracks.

Size Male greenhouse frogs are adult at about .75 in. SVL, but occasionally grow slightly larger. Females, which may exceed an inch in length, are more robust than the males.

Reproduction In Florida the greenhouse frog breeds during the hot days of late spring, summer, and early autumn. The one to two dozen eggs are laid in moisture-retaining debris or damp pockets of earth. Full metamorphosis occurs in the egg capsules. The tiny froglets emerge with a tail nub but are otherwise minuscule replicas of the adults.

Coloration/pattern Greenhouse frogs occur in both a mottled and a lineate phase. One or the other usually predominates in a given population. No matter which phase is at hand, mixtures of rust to orange and brown make up the dorsal and lateral colors. The venter is usually an off-white but may be gray. The skin is warty.

Males call on rainy days or at night from the seclusion of garden plants or woodland herbs. They may call while on the ground amid leaf litter or while sitting several inches above the ground on the leaves of plants.

Despite the presence of a subgular vocal sac, the calls have little carrying power.

Voice Greenhouse frogs produce a varied series of insect-like chirps and trills. The calls of this species are very apt to be mistaken for the stridulations of a cricket or other garden insect.

Similar species Spring peepers, *Pseudacris crucifer,* may be pinkish but usually have a dark X on the back. Other chorus frogs (*Pseudacris* sp.) are associated with marshes and pond edges and have a lineate pattern of dark spots or stripes. Cricket frogs (*Acris* sp.) have extensive webbing on the feet and stripes on the rear of the thigh. Squirrel treefrogs, *Hyla squirella,* may be brown but lack the rusty highlights that are characteristic of the greenhouse frog.

Behavior This little frog thrives in settings as diverse as urban gardens and pristine woodlands. It is one of the most secretive of frogs. After having dwelt with greenhouse frogs in our yard for more than 25 years, we have not yet seen a male vocalizing. These frogs are active on warm, heavily overcast or rainy days, but are essentially nocturnal. In southern Florida terrestrial bromeliads provide favored hiding places.

Comments This tiny frog was introduced to Florida from the West Indies. It is very successful and is a firmly established alien species.

NARROW-MOUTHED TOADS
Family Microhylidae

The eastern narrow-mouthed toad is the only representative of this family in Florida. It is so rounded that its appearance has been likened to a marble with legs and a nose. Termites and ants seem the major food items of this frog. Narrow-mouths are so secretive that they may be present in large numbers, but their presence not suspected.

Narrow-mouths run or make short erratic hops rather than graceful leaps.

26 EASTERN NARROW-MOUTHED TOAD

Gastrophryne carolinensis

Abundance Even in many urban and suburban habitats, this is a common but secretive and seldom seen frog. It is found in every county in the state.

Habitat Eastern narrow-mouthed toads are found in a wide variety of habitats from urban lots to woodlands and sandy pinelands. Where drainage is sharp, these toads are most common near the environs of ponds, lakes, swamps, and marshes. They persist in suburban lawns and may be especially abundant in sandy soils where lawn and garden sprinkling is carried out daily. Narrow-mouths are accomplished burrowers and are seldom seen on the surface of the ground. They may be found beneath boards, rocks, leaf-litter (including mats of pine needles), and other moisture-retaining debris.

Size Males are adult at an inch or less in length. Occasional females may slightly exceed 1.25 in.

Reproduction These little toads may breed in situations as ephemeral as shallow drainage ditches or where water is somewhat more permanent. The shallows of grassy, semipermanent ponds and irrigated agricultural areas are especially favored. Narrow-mouths often call while hunkered down amid grasses and, when so positioned, are difficult to see even when calling. Occasionally, they may call while floating or while sitting exposed on a bank. The floating eggs are deposited in small clusters. A total of more than 800 eggs has been recorded from a single female. Amplexus is axillary (behind the forelimbs).

Coloration/pattern Narrow-mouthed toads are darker dorsally than laterally. The back varies from charcoal to olive-brown to bluish-gray. A broad, (often dark-edged) brown, russet to terra cotta dorso-lateral stripe is present on each side. The lower sides and venter are heavily pigmented gray, and males have a darker throat. A fold of skin crosses the back of the head just posterior of the eyes. This little toad is ovoid when viewed from above, and has short, heavy legs.

The single subgular vocal sac is round.

The black tadpoles are flecked with slate blue and may have a tan lateral line. When viewed in profile, the anterior venter slopes sharply upwards into a pointed head. The tailfins are dark-flecked and dark-tipped.

Voice The call of the male is a penetrating, sheep-like bleat.

Similar species No other toad in Florida has a pointed head with a skin-fold behind the eyes.

Behavior This little burrower is primarily nocturnal. It is drawn to the breeding ponds by heavy spring and early summer rains. Sticky skin secretions assist amplexing males in retaining their position.

Comments Males have been observed calling on rainy nights while buried in damp sand with only their head and vocal sac exposed.

SPADEFOOTS
Family Pelobatidae

This frog family is represented in the United States by only six species, and in Florida by only one. These are burrowing anurans that are often referred to as spadefoot toads. Indeed, these creatures look much like toads, but such external features as the parotoid glands are lacking or indistinct, and the pupil is vertically elliptical rather than horizontal. A single dark-edged spade is present on the heel of each foot. There are internal differences as well.

The breeding embrace of these toads is inguinal, that is, amplexing males grasp the females around the waist instead of just posterior to the forelimbs. Spadefoots breed in ephemeral pools. Breeding activity is stimulated by heavy (read that torrential) rains. Tadpole development is rapid and metamorphosis, and if hastened by drying pools, can occur in a matter of only two to three weeks. If the pools are more stable, metamorphosis may take six weeks or more.

Scaphiopus h. holbrookii

Abundance Eastern spadefoots occur in most peninsular counties and in all panhandle counties. Where present, they can be abundant.

Habitat In Florida the eastern spadefoot colonizes open woodlands and woodland edges with sandy or yielding soils. Spadefoots sometimes persist in suburban areas where the use of insecticides is not rampant. This anuran burrows deeply. It is capable of undergoing rather extended fasts and emerges from its burrow to feed at irregular intervals.

Size Large females occasionally attain a 2.75 in. SVL. However, males seldom exceed 2 in., and most are smaller.

Reproduction Spadefoots are explosive breeders in temporarily flooded depressions. Breeding, which is induced by torrential rains, may occur annually or only every several years. Breeding congregations may occur during nearly any month of the year. The 150 or more eggs are laid in strings or in many irregular elongated clusters. The eggs may hatch in less than two days and tadpole development and metamorphosis are rapid. If hastened by receding water levels and deteriorating water quality, the complete process from deposition to metamorphosis can take less than two weeks.

Coloration/pattern This is a brownish or olive-brown toad with cream to yellow markings and sparse reddish tubercles. The dorsum usually bears a light (often cream, yellow, or greenish) lyre-shaped marking. The sides are lighter than the dorsum and may bear dark spots. The venter is white. The round parotoid glands are quite indistinct. Pupils are vertically elliptical and a single, sharp, digging spade is present on each heel.

The white subgular vocal sac is large but somewhat flattened.

Tadpoles are usually brownish dorsally and laterally. The translucent belly skin is yellowish.

Voice Although researchers have reported occasional muffled, moaning grunts being produced by spadefoots still in their burrows, most often they call only while floating. Each loud, moaning croak seems the result of a prodigious effort. As a male calls, the center of his back is bowed downward and his head and throat are lifted almost clear of the water.

Similar species Toads have horizontal pupils, prominent parotoid glands, and two tubercles rather than a single spade on each heel.

Behavior These nocturnal anurans are among the most secretive of Florida's tailless amphibia. Eastern spadefoots stay well under the soil surface at most times. Lowering barometric pressure, especially when associated with a wet front, heavy thundershower, or tropical storm, may induce spadefoots to emerge from their burrows.

Comments A toad in appearance, but not a toad in actuality accurately describes the eastern spadefoot. These intriguing little anurans are present in numbers in some sandy areas but may be entirely absent from what appear to be other similar habitats. Skin secretions, which smell vaguely like garlic, are distasteful and may cause allergic reactions.

TRUE FROGS
Family Ranidae

The ranids are the typical, long-legged, far-jumping frogs that are, with one exception in Florida (the gopher frog), associated with damp meadows or lakes, ponds, rivers, ditches, and other moist or wet habitats. Most Florida species have extensive webbing between the toes and web-free fingers. None in Florida have toepads.

Breeding is often initiated by rains, but may occur spontaneously in dry weather if all other conditions are suitable.

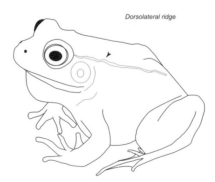

Dorsolateral ridge

Some true frogs have a ridge of skin (the dorsolateral ridge) on each side of their back.

Although many species are warm-weather breeders, others may breed during the short days and long nights of winter, while water temperatures are still cold. The tympani (exposed eardrums) of adult males of the bull, bronze, pig, river, and carpenter frogs are conspicuously larger than the eye. The tympani of adult females of these five species are about the size of the eye. Despite the Florida bog frog being closely allied to the bronze frog, the tympani of adult males of the bog frog are only marginally proportionately larger than those of the adult females.

The tympani of both sexes of the pickerel, southern leopard, and the subspecies of the gopher frog are similarly sized.

Adult males of some species (bull and bronze frogs) have yellow throats.

The arms and thumb-bases of all reproductively active male ranids are enlarged.

Vocal sac morphology varies in Florida ranids. It is bilateral and internal (causing the vocalizing male to look like it has mumps) on some species, and bilateral and external (like waterwings) on others.

The skin is usually relatively smooth, but may bear tubercles or glandular ridges. The presence or lack of dorsolateral ridges must be considered in species identifications.

28 FLORIDA GOPHER FROG

Rana capito aesopus

Abundance Usually uncommon, the Florida gopher frog can be fairly common locally but is a secretive habitat specialist. Once found over most of peninsular Florida, it has become less common in recent years. Thorough population studies are needed to determine the actual remaining numbers of this frog.

Habitat Unlike most frogs, which are associated with wet areas, the Florida gopher frog is a denizen of sandy scrub areas, which also support the most viable colonies of gopher tortoises. When not in the ephemeral ponds, which it prefers for breeding activities, the gopher frog often seeks refuge in the burrows of the gopher tortoise. More rarely, the gopher frog may be associated with stumpholes, rodent burrows, and ground debris.

Size Although usually smaller, Florida gopher frogs occasionally attain a length of slightly more than 4 in.

Reproduction Breeding activities by this frog are usually associated with heavy rains. In many cases, these same rains refill a breeding pond that has been dry, or nearly dry, through seasonal non-rainy months. Gopher frogs are among the frogs to breed earliest in the year. Sizeable choruses assemble at suitable ponds during heavy rains of February, March, and April. Males call while floating, often in water several feet in depth. The egg masses are attached to vegetation and may contain several thousand eggs.

Coloration/pattern The Florida gopher frog has a ground color of grayish-white to a rather dark gray, rarely with purplish overtones. Cold frogs are often the darkest. Dark, rather well defined oval to round spots are present dorsally. The dorsal spots may be vaguely outlined with a lighter pigment. The lateral spots are often of more irregular shape and may be more poorly defined. A prominent orange or yellow (males) or yellow to dark (females) dorsolateral ridge is present. Some yellow *may* be present in the axillae and groin. A second, similarly colored, but often less prominently delineated, ridge runs along the lip, above the forelimb to the groin. The light venter has little dark pigmentation.

The Florida gopher frog is comparatively short-bodied and stubby and has a proportionately large head.

Males have huge bilateral vocal sacs.

The tadpoles are greenish, lighter cranially with dark supraorbital spots. The upper tail fin is profusely spotted. The tailtip may be dark.

Voice Males produce a loud, roaring snore.

Similar species Leopard frogs are proportionately slender and have a ground color of green, tan, or brown (or combinations of all). The slenderness alone should differentiate leopard frogs from the stocky gopher frog. Pickerel frogs have bright yellow in the groin and *squared* dorsal spots.

Behavior Following their breeding activities, Florida gopher frogs may disperse for long distances. Unlike most other frogs (except the highly predacious bullfrog), gopher frogs readily consume smaller frogs (including their own species) and toads. The more standard frog fare of insects is also eaten.

29 Dusky Gopher Frog

R. c. sevosa

In Florida's western panhandle the Florida gopher frog is supposedly replaced by the slightly smaller (but no less stocky) dusky gopher frog, *R. c. sevosa*. This may not be a valid subspecies in Florida. While some researchers feel that the Apalachicola River is the dividing point between the two races, others believe the range of the dusky gopher frog begins much farther west, either in the floodplain of the Escambia River or, perhaps, west and north of Mobile Bay, Alabama. This darker race has not been as extensively studied as the Florida gopher frog. The dusky gopher frog is also restricted to sandy habitats. The ground color is darker, often with a brownish blush; the venter is quite heavily pigmented. It should be kept in mind that, when they are cold, Florida gopher frogs darken considerably in color, then closely fitting the description of *R. c. sevosa*.

30 Bullfrog

Rana catesbeiana

Abundance This highly aquatic frog may be found over the northern two thirds of the state but is most common in the northern half of Florida. Metamorphs and juveniles are seen more frequently than the adults.

Habitat Ponds, lakes, large ditches, canals, slow rivers, and their oxbows are all suitable habitats for this frog. Immature bullfrogs often sit on the shore or in shallow water near the shore, but adults are often seen in deep water, well away from shore. Adults may sit on or float among lily pads or other surface vegetation.

Size Although sexes are of nearly equal size, females are slightly larger. The record size of this, North America's largest frog, is 8 in. A SVL of 4–6.5 in. is more common.

Reproduction Huge rafts of several thousand to about 20,000 floating eggs are produced. These hatch in several days and the tadpoles may attain a length of more than 3 in. prior to metamorphosis.

The tip of the bullfrog's longest toe extends well beyond the webbing.

Although in the north, metamorphosis may take two years or longer, in the comparatively warm waters of Florida, bullfrog tadpoles may metamorphose in a year or less. Males may call from pondside positions or while sitting on floating debris or mats of vegetation. We have also found them calling while floating on the water surface, usually while amidst floating plants.

Coloration/pattern Although bullfrogs are of some shade of green, some specimens may be so dark that they look black. The sides of the face and lips are usually the brightest green. The forelimbs may have dark spots, the hind legs may be prominently banded with darker pigment. Males often have yellow throats. Females have white throats. The light venter may or may not be heavily pigmented. A prominent skin ridge extends back from the rear of the eye around the back of the tympanum and terminates above the foreleg. The last joint of the longest toe is devoid of webbing.

The vocal sac is internal, precluding a great swelling of the throat.

The tadpoles are olive (lighter ventrally), appear stippled and have well-developed lateral lines.

Voice The easily recognized voice of this species is a far-carrying, two- or three-syllabled "brrr-ummmmm" or "jug-o-rum." The larger the male, the deeper his voice.

Similar species For a ranid, bullfrogs have a rather broadly rounded snout (when viewed from above). Pig frogs, *Rana grylio*, have a more sharply pointed snout, are heavily pigmented under the hind legs, and have *fully* webbed hind feet. River frogs, *R. heckscheri*, have dark spots on the upper lip, white spots on the lower lip, and a heavily pigmented, dark throat. Bronze frogs, *R. c. clamitans*, have dorsolateral ridges.

Behavior Large, predacious, solitary (even intraspecifically confrontational during the breeding season when males avidly battle other males) describe the bullfrog. Bullfrogs are usually wary by day but rather easily approached at night. However, those floating are easily "spooked" by water ripples. Approach them carefully.

Comments This huge frog, once the staple for frogs' legs, is still hunted for food, the pet trade, and for biological studies throughout much of its range. Bullfrogs, probably intended as a food source, have been introduced to our western and Pacific states as well as elsewhere in the world.

31 BRONZE FROG

Rana clamitans clamitans

Abundance Bronze frogs can be common (but usually not abundant) in the northern two fifths of peninsular Florida and occur throughout the panhandle. They are uncommon at the southern extreme of their range.

Habitat Streams and associated pools, river edges and vegetated oxbows, ponds and lakesides are all acceptable habitats to this adaptable frog. It often sits concealed in water-edge vegetation, emitting a startling high-pitched cry as it jumps to safety when approached.

Size Occasional adults may attain, or slightly exceed, 3 in. SVL.

Reproduction The surface film of one to several thousand eggs often adheres to emergent vegetation.

Coloration/pattern More often than not, this small frog is an unrelieved bronzy-brown dorsally and laterally. The snout and upper lips vary from a brown lighter than the body to a lime-green. There are light spots on the lower lip. A light stripe is often present beneath the eye. The belly is light (almost white) with profuse dark vermiculations. Metamorphs have a more strongly patterned venter than adults. Prominent "three-quarter length" dorsolateral ridges are present. The center of the tympanum (external eardrum) of the male is elevated.

The bilateral vocal pouches are internal. Both body and throat swell noticeably when the frog choruses. Males may have a yellowish throat.

Tadpoles are dark brownish-green dorsally, light ventrally. The upper tailfin is prominently dark-spotted, the lower is less so.

Voice This is the "banjo-frog" of woodland streams and ponds. The call notes, usually given while the frog sits in shallow water or concealed in water-edge vegetation, is a single strong "plunk." Several plunks of diminishing volume may follow. Both sexes produce a shrill scream when captured by a predator (including man) and a high-pitched cry of shorter duration is often given when a startled frog jumps into the water.

Similar species Adults of the pig, river, and bull frogs are much larger and all lack dorsolateral ridges. The bronze frog-sized carpenter frog (found in Florida only in Baker and Columbia counties) also lacks dorsolateral ridges. Southern leopard frogs have a sharper nose and are spotted. The Florida bog frog is smaller, may have prominent spots posteriolaterally, has reduced webbing on the hind feet and is restricted to the panhandle counties of Okaloosa, Santa Rosa, and Walton.

Behavior Bronze frogs are active by both day and night, and they often sit in the patchy sunshine of water-edge grasses. When on the shore, these frogs leap quickly into the water when approached by day, but are less easily startled at night. Males call while floating or while lying atop floating vegetation.

Comments These pretty little frogs are not extensively exploited commercially in Florida. The banjo-twang calls are enjoyable additions to quiet summer days at many favored fishing holes.

32 PIG FROG

Rana grylio

Abundance The pig frog occurs in every county in the state. It does not seem as common now as in past days, but may still be found on nearly any warm night.

Habitat Pig frogs are generally distributed in most waterways, including rivers, streams, lakes, ponds, swamps, and marshes. They are highly aquatic, and may either float in open water or choose a station on or amid floating or emergent vegetation. They are among our most aquatic frogs.

Size Smaller and somewhat slimmer than the bullfrog, this frog, once referred to as the southern bullfrog, can attain nearly a 6.5 in. SVL.

The webbing on the hind foot of the pig frog extends to the tip of the longest toe.

Most, though, are 3.5–5.5 in. Males are usually notably smaller than females.

Reproduction The more than 10,000 eggs are laid as a surface film. They may adhere to surface or emergent vegetation. Although tadpoles at the northern edge of the range reportedly take more than a year to metamorphose, those in the southern part of the range probably develop in considerably less time.

Coloration/pattern Adult pig frogs may vary in coloration from gray-brown through olive-brown to a pleasing rather bright green. Green specimens often have scattered large dark marks dorsally and laterally. The belly is light anteriorly but heavily vermiculated with dark pigment posteriorly. Juvenile pig frogs have light stripes on a dark body and look superficially like carpenter frogs. However, the toes of the pig frog are webbed to the tips. Pig frogs lack dorsolateral ridges and have a sharply pointed snout.

Voice The common name says it all; the vocalizations are one or a series of pig-like grunts. Pig frogs have a single, broadly expanded internal vocal sac.

Similar species The bullfrog has a blunter snout, can attain a greater size, has slightly less extensive webbing on the hind feet and usually has a less pigmented belly. Adult carpenter frogs (which are quite similar in both dorsal and ventral color to juvenile pig frogs) have less extensive webbing on the hind feet than the pig frog does. Bronze frogs have dorsolateral ridges. Florida bog frogs (found only in the western panhandle) are very small and have reduced webbing on the hind feet. River frogs have dark and light spots on the lips.

Behavior Pig frogs are easily startled. They are very difficult to approach by day, but at night, using a flashlight, you'll be more successful.

Comments Long a staple of the frog-leg industry, pig frogs are hunted and gigged at night from air and John boats. Many commercial hunters have indicated that pig frog populations currently seem diminished. However, it is known that populations of this frog are cyclic, declining in drought and erupting in wet years.

33 RIVER FROG

Rana heckscheri

Abundance River frogs can be quite common in proper habitat. They occur from Hillsborough County on the Gulf Coast and Volusia County on the Atlantic coast northward through the peninsula and panhandle.

Habitat Despite the implications of its common name, the river frog may be found in and along lakes, ponds, swamps, and marshes as well as rivers. It often sits on the shore or on a floating log or other such vantage point.

Size With an occasional adult reaching a 6.25-in. SVL, this is one of the three largest frogs in Florida. Most adults are fully grown at 4–5.5 in.

Reproduction The several thousand eggs are laid as a surface film, often among emergent vegetation to which they adhere. Tadpoles overwinter and take about a year to metamorphose.

Coloration/pattern The river frog has a grayer and more rugose dorsum than the other large ranids with which it shares its habitat. The dorsal color varies between gray, grayish-green, and brownish-green. Poorly defined darker smudges are often present both dorsally and laterally. Light and dark spots may be present on the lips and variably defined dark bars are on the hind legs. The belly is gray with light markings. The throat may be darker than the belly. Males often have a yellow(ish) suffusion on the throat. There are no dorsolateral ridges. Webbing extends to the last phalanx of the longest toe.

The vocal sac is single and internal.

Tadpoles undergo ontogenetic color changes. Small tadpoles are very dark (often black) with a narrow but well-defined light ring around the body, posterior to the eyes. With growth the ring obscures, the color lightens (at least somewhat), and the tailfin becomes edged with dark pigment.

Voice Reproductively active males of this large frog have a deep, rolling, roaring snore. Shorter grunting calls are also emitted. The vocalizations of smaller river frogs are of a higher pitch than the sounds produced by large examples. Males call while sitting in shallow water or on the shore.

Similar species Bronze and Florida bog frogs are much smaller than adult river frogs, have dorsolateral ridges, and do not have heavily mottled gray bellies. Carpenter frogs are smaller and have four bronzy stripes. Pig and bullfrogs have no light spots on their lips.

Behavior This is a highly aquatic but often rather easily approached frog. This is especially so after dark, with the help of a flashlight. River frogs often choose to sit and call from rather conspicuous stations along clear(ed) banks or on floating logs or other such solid debris.

Comments Rather than struggling to escape when captured, the river frog goes entirely limp. The noxious skin secretions are odorous.

The tadpoles of this frog school, at times in vast numbers, and seem to show fidelity to certain areas in a body of water. Prior to metamorphosis they attain a length of more than 4 in. When moving slowly, the schools of tadpoles move in a rather synchronized manner; when disturbed they mill about. It is probable that the schooling is an antipredator mechanism and in addition to the protection afforded by the noxious secretions present in the skin of the large tadpoles, there is safety in numbers.

34 Florida Bog Frog

Rana okaloosae

Abundance This uncommon frog is found only in a few acidic streams in Walton, Santa Rosa, and Okaloosa counties in Florida's western panhandle.

Habitat This is a frog of slowly flowing acidic seeps and stream backwaters. Black titi, Atlantic white cedar, and sphagnum moss are among the plants commonly associated with these habitats.

Size At an adult size of slightly less than 2 in., the bog frog is the smallest of Florida's ranid frogs.

Reproduction The several hundred eggs are laid in a surface film.

Coloration/pattern In appearance the Florida bog frog is very similar to the bronze frog. The dorsum varies from yellowish-green to greenish-brown or brown. The three-quarter length dorsolateral ridges are often light in color. The light venter bears dark vermiculations. There may be light spots on the green jaw. The tympanum is brown and has no raised center. The webbing of the hind feet is very reduced. At least two phalanges of each of the four shortest toes and three phalanges of the longest toe extend beyond the webbing.

The vocal sac is single and internal.

The tadpole of the bog frog is slender and has an elongate tail. It is brown dorsally and darker with white spots ventrally. The sides and tail have many light spots.

Voice The series of low-pitched single clucking calls has little carrying power. The calls slow noticeably toward the end of the series. Males call while resting in shallow water, or while sprawled atop floating vegetation.

Similar species The bronze frog has more extensive webbing on the hind feet and the center of the male's tympanum is elevated. Neither the bull nor the pig frog has dorsolateral ridges.

Behavior Because of its limited distribution, precise habitat requirements and, apparently, low numbers, the bog frog is badly in need of extensive research.

Comments Little is known with absolute certainty about the natural history of this tiny, Florida endemic. It seems uncommon in some of its very specialized habitats and potentially susceptible to population reduction in others. This species is fully protected in Florida.

35 PICKEREL FROG

Rana palustris

Abundance If the pickerel frog exists (or existed) in Florida, it was and is the state's rarest frog. Although records are questioned by some biologists, Florida museum specimens have reportedly come from the Pensacola area.

Habitat North of Florida, pickerel frogs are associated with both cool woodland ponds and streams and the warmer more silted waters of the coastal plain. It is suspected that if pickerel frogs do occur in Florida, they will be found in the streams associated with the cooler ravines of the extreme western panhandle.

Size Although occasional females may attain 3.5-in. SVL, males and most females are an inch or more shorter.

Reproduction In Florida, unknown. Elsewhere, the eggs, which may number several thousand, are laid in one or more clumps. Each clump is attached to subsurface (often bottom) vegetation such as sticks or grasses. Males call while submerged, while floating, while sprawling atop or clinging to floating vegetation, or while sitting in wateredge grasses.

Coloration/pattern Pickerel frogs usually have paired brown spots between the light dorsolateral ridges and another row of large spots beneath the ridges. In some cases there may be three rows of spots, especially posteriodorsally, and smaller spots beneath the large lateral ones. The spots are usually squared or rectangular and may coalesce into bars or stripes. The ground color is tan or light brown. The venter is white (sometimes smudged with dark pigment) but suffused with bright yellow or orange in the groin and on the concealed surfaces of the hind legs. Juveniles are less colorful ventrally than adults.

Proportionately, the bilateral external vocal sacs of this ranid are rather small.

The tadpoles are greenish to greenish-brown dorsally, lighter (off white to cream-yellow) ventrally, and have grayish fins that are smudged with patches of darker pigment.

Voice The low-pitched rolling snore of male pickerel frogs may be produced either above or beneath the water surface. North of Florida, pickerel frogs call on cool spring evenings, often in conjunction with peepers and American toads.

Similar species Other than in Escambia County, any spotted frog encountered in Florida will be a southern leopard frog. Southern leopards have rounded or oval spots, those of the pickerel frog are squared or rectangular.

Behavior Although it occasionally wanders afield in damp weather, we have found the pickerel frog to be quite closely associated with water at all times of the year. It is agile, alert, and when startled may make several leaps before stopping.

Comments Pickerel frogs have fairly toxic skin secretions. Other frog species housed with pickerel frogs usually rapidly succumb. Although you should wash your hands after handling any amphibian or reptile, it is a particularly good idea to do so after handling pickerel frogs, river frogs, giant toads, or Cuban treefrogs.

36 FLORIDA LEOPARD FROG

Rana sphenocephala sphenocephala

37 SOUTHERN LEOPARD FROG

Rana sphenocephala utricularia

Note: Combined, these two subspecies, which are impossible to distinguish in the field, are the most abundant ranids of Florida (also see **Comments**).

Abundance These are the most abundant frogs in Florida.

Habitat Both of these leopard frogs may wander far from the water into damp pastures, fields, and sodlands but are more often found in the environs of ponds, lakes, flooded ditches, irrigation and drainage canals, stream and river edges, backyard goldfish pools, and virtually any other body of water. This is one of the few frogs able to colonize brackish coastal waters.

Size Although the record size is 5 in., most are adult at 2.25–3.5 in.

Reproduction The egg-clump is often found adhering to surface or subsurface vegetation. More than 1,000 eggs have been recorded either in a mass or in several clumps. Males call while floating in quite shallow water, usually while amid emergent grasses.

Coloration/pattern These are the most variably colored of Florida's frogs. The ground color may be brown, green, or a combination of both. The rounded to oval dark spots may be profuse or sparse, but are often more sparing on the sides than on the back. Usually each tympanum has a light center. The rear limbs are usually prominently marked with light-edged, elongate, dark spots. The snout is rather sharply pointed. The prominent dorsolateral ridges are light in color.

When inflated during vocalizations, the paired, bilateral vocal sacs of the male look like waterwings. When deflated, the sacs of some males remain visible as skin folds at the angle of the gape. Those of other males (especially those from peninsular Florida) are not outwardly visible when deflated.

The tadpoles are dark olive-green dorsally and lighter ventrally. Both upper and lower tailfins are spotted.

Voice Variable; chuckles or chicken-like clucks are interspersed with sounds best described as those made when rubbing your finger over an inflated, wet balloon. Southern leopard frogs may be heard most frequently during the winter and spring months, but may call occasionally during even the hottest weather.

Similar species Of Florida frogs, only the two leopard frogs and the pickerel frog are prominently spotted. The pickerel frog is known only from Escambia County in the westernmost panhandle. Pickerel frogs have squared or rectangular spots; those of the leopard frogs are more rounded or oval.

Behavior Leopard frogs are active and alert. If approached when ashore, they as often make several leaps away from the water as towards it. Each leap is often in a different direction.

Comments Taxonomically, largely due to a similarity of appearance, and disagreement on affinities, there is no more muddled group of frogs in North America than various leopard frogs.

You may see southern leopard frogs referred to as either subspecies of *R. utricularia* or of *R. sphenocephala,* or you may see the southern leopard frogs referred to by either of those names but treated as an unsubspeciated form.

Males of *R. s. utricularia* bear vestigial oviducts; those of *R. s. sphenocephala* do not. The former is said to be largely restricted to the panhandle in Florida while the latter ranges southward to and including the Keys.

Wright and Wright observed that southern leopard frogs become browner in coloration when away from the water for an extended period.

They are also darker in color when cold.

38 CARPENTER FROG

Rana virgatipes

Abundance Because in Florida the carpenter frog is found largely in the remote southern drainages of Georgia's Okefenokee Swamp, it is not a frequently seen species. Look for it only near the Florida-Georgia state line in Baker and Columbia counties.

Habitat In Florida, this persistently aquatic frog is associated with acidic cypress and tupelo swamps. It seems most common where extensive mats of sphagnum moss grow. It often sits amid emergent grasses.

Size This is one of the smaller of Florida's true frogs. An adult size of 2.5 in. may be attained, but most examples are smaller.

Reproduction From 300 to more than 700 eggs are laid in a floating mass that usually adheres to, or wraps partially around, emergent vegetation. Tadpoles overwinter before metamorphosing.

Coloration/pattern Although this is a four-striped frog, its dorsum is often so dark that the two dorsolateral stripes are hard to see. The ground color is a greenish-brown. The two dorsolateral stripes are tan to light brown. The two lateral stripes seem invariably better defined. They are light tan to off-white and separate the dark dorsum from the strongly vermiculated black on white venter. The throat is only weakly pigmented. Carpenter frogs lack dorsolateral ridges. The webbing does not extend to the tip of the longest toe.

Males have large, external, bilateral vocal sacs. When deflated these remain visible as dark folds at the angle of the jaws.

Tadpoles are dark olive-black overall. The tailfin is not strongly spotted, but the spots on the upper fin may coalesce into a vague stripe halfway between the top of the fin and the musculature.

Voice The series of half dozen (or so) two-syllabled, clacking calls diminish in volume towards the end. The calls are usually likened to hammerings, hence the common name of this frog. The carpenter frog is a spring and summer breeder.

Similar species Bronze frogs have dorsolateral ridges. Florida bog frogs are found only in Florida's western panhandle. Bullfrogs lack dorsolateral striping. Immature pig frogs often have dorsolateral striping, but the webbing of the hind foot extends to the tip of the longest toe.

Behavior Carpenter frogs may haul out onto sphagnum mats or floating debris. They often sit among emergent grasses where they blend, almost imperceptably, into their background. They call while floating (often while grasping grass or a twig with their fingers) and while sitting atop floating sphagnum and other surface or subsurface vegetation.

Comments This has proven to be an uncommon and secretive frog in Florida. It is much more easily found north of the state line where it occurs as far north as the Pine Barrens of New Jersey.

SALAMANDERS, NEWTS, AND SIRENS
Order Caudata

Salamanders and newts are attenuate, secretive creatures. Some found in Florida are so attenuate that they appear eel-like.

Florida salamanders fall naturally into six families.

Family Ambystomatidae—Mole Salamanders	(4 species)
Family Amphiumidae—Amphiumas	(3 species)
Family Plethodontidae—Lungless Salamanders	(13 species)
Family Proteidae—Waterdogs	(1 species)
Family Salamandridae—Newts	(2 species)
Family Sirenidae—Sirens	(4 species)

When the members of all families are considered, it will be found that they are of more divergent appearance than the frogs, toads, and treefrogs.

Externally, adults of the mole, all but one of the lungless salamanders, and the newts, look rather like smooth, scaleless, moist-skinned, clawless, lizards. They are slender bodied, have short but fully functional legs, and apparent tails. The single divergent lungless salamander is a permanent larva that retains external gills throughout its life, has no functional eyes, and lives in the perpetual blackness of caves. In general form, this creature looks much like a waterdog, but the waterdog has functional, though lidless, eyes.

The salamanders in the two remaining families are eel-like and aquatic. The amphiuma have no external gills and four *tiny* legs that are virtually useless from the viewpoint of aiding in mobility. The sirens, on the other hand, have bushy external gills and two fully usable, but small forelimbs. They lack hindlimbs.

Most of Florida's salamanders have the normal two (or more) staged life, but some are neotenic (permanently aquatic larvae) or deposit terrestrial eggs in which direct development occurs.

Unlike the frogs, toads, and treefrogs of Florida, all of which have loud advertisement calls, salamanders are virtually voiceless. It is reported that some of the aquatic forms produce clicking sounds while under water and yelping noises when they are restrained above water. But other than these seemingly rather inconsequential vocalizations, caudatans make no sounds. It is probable that they find each other by following scent trails (pheromones) with the tenaciousness of a prize bloodhound.

An explanation of the following selected terms may help you better understand the discussion of salamanders. Additional pertinent terms are contained in the glossary on pages 266–269.

Adpress—extend a foreleg directly rearward and a rear leg directly forward to count the number of body (costal) grooves between them.

Caudata—the taxonomic order containing all salamanders. The word Caudata is occasionally replaced with "Urodela."

Cirri—fleshy downward projection from the nostrils of some plethodontid salamanders.

Costal grooves—vertical grooves on the sides of some salamanders.

Direct development—complete development occurs in the egg capsule. The baby emerges as a diminutive of the adult in appearance.

Naso-labial groove—a groove between the nostril and upper lip of some lungless salamanders.

Neotenic—a salamander that is a permanent larvae.

How to Find Salamanders and Newts

Salamanders might be said to be very much where you find them. And to find them, you must look carefully in the places they are.

Collectively, salamanders are among the most secretive of vertebrates.

Few, except cave-dwelling varieties to which day and night make little difference, are active during the hours of daylight. Rather, some do not emerge from their lairs until well after darkness. Even after nightfall, those, which are wait-and-ambush predators, sit with only their head and shoulders protruding from their burrow while they quietly await the arrival of a bug or worm.

To find the amphiumas, sirens, and newts, look in the shallows of streams, reservoirs, ponds or lakes. Unless you intend to search through clumps of vegetation (a sometimes productive method of finding juveniles), look along the edges of these waters with a flashlight after dark. Search waterlogged leaf mats in streams for the larvae of brook salamanders and waterdogs.

Dusky and related salamanders forage at night along the edges of brooks and streams or sit on protruding rocks in the streams.

Some salamanders can be found by carefully turning streamside or ravine-side rocks or by rolling decomposing logs in the woodlands. Be sure to replace all ground cover that you move.

Other salamanders can be found in the twilight zones of caves or other darkened areas; one species is restricted to ground-water situations in the dark interiors of deep caves.

Remember that salamanders are delicate beasts. If you pick one up, do so carefully and with clean hands. Topical insecticides will quickly kill amphibians. Do not allow them to become warm or to dry out.

When you have finished looking at or photographing it, put the salamander right back where you found it. Only in this way will one again be there when you wish to see it.

MOLE SALAMANDERS
Family Ambystomatidae

There are four species of this family known to occur in Florida, and a fifth, the spotted salamander, may eventually be found. The four species known to occur in Florida are the flatwoods, marbled, mole, and tiger salamanders. While the first three are rather small, the tiger salamander is the largest terrestrial salamander of not only Florida, but the eastern United States as well.

The common family name comes from the propensity of all members of this family to burrow. In Florida two of the four species are considered winter breeders. They are induced to breeding ponds by heavy winter rains, usually not until after a few weeks of cold weather has occurred. The marbled and flatwoods salamanders lay their eggs on land, in soon-to-be-flooded situations, in the autumn months. Their breeding strategies, therefore, differ from those of the other two Florida ambystomatids as well as the peripheral spotted salamander.

Once the ambystomatids leave the breeding ponds, their lives are cloaked in mystery. All species are badly in need of study.

Ambystomatid salamanders are difficult to sex. During the breeding season, reproductively active males develop a conspicuously swollen vent. Only at that time is the external appearance of the adults sufficiently different to make a determination. Immatures and non-breeding adults are unsexable externally.

The flatwoods and tiger salamanders are considered uncommon and seem to be diminishing in numbers in Florida. The mole and the marbled salamanders remain relatively common.

39 FLATWOODS SALAMANDER

Ambystoma cingulatum

Abundance Flatwoods salamanders are known to have once occurred from Marion County northward to Duval and Baker counties, but seem to now be absent from many historic sites. It is also found from the panhandle's Wakulla County westward to the Alabama line. Thought to be rare in general, it may have also been rather recently extirpated from many areas in the panhandle.

Habitat This species burrows in the soils of seasonally flooded natural pine and wiregrass flatwoods, and breeds in associated shallow ponds and cypress heads. Flatwoods salamanders are known to use crayfish burrows as retreats.

Size The flatwoods salamander is one of the smaller of the ambystomatids. It is adult at about 3 in. in total length and seldom reaches 4 in.

Reproduction Egg-laying by this species occurs during the passage of late autumn or early winter storm systems. The nudging and bumping courtship activities occur at night on land or in grassy shallows. The courtship induces the female to pick up a previously deposited sperm packet with her cloacal labia. After so doing, a female flatwoods salamander usually selects damp-to-wet shoreline areas or a soon-to-be-flooded depression to distribute her 75 to 150 eggs singly or in small clusters. Instinct leads the female to areas that are normally flooded by autumn or early winter rains. Once covered by water, the eggs hatch in two to three days. If not covered within two to three weeks after deposition, the eggs desiccate and succumb.

Coloration/pattern Adults of this small-headed, robust species are so variably patterned that they were once divided into "reticulated" and "frosted" subspecies. The dorsal ground color is dark, varying from blackish-brown to black. The pattern, be it a precise reticulum or a busier frosted pattern, is silvery-white to white. The lower sides and venter are dark, peppered with white(ish) flecks or spots. The slender, attenuate, dark larvae, rather nondescript at first, develop prominent light vertebral and lateral lines. The cheek is light. At this stage, they are very pretty and easily identifiable, but become less diagnosable as the pattern fragments at metamorphosis.

Similar species Adult marbled salamanders have a proportionately larger head, and better defined and broader dorsal crossbars than the flatwoods. Larval marbled salamanders have dorsolateral spots and less prominent stripes than flatwoods salamander larvae.

Behavior This is a typical, autumn-breeding mole salamander in every sense of the word. During damp weather, it is occasionally possible to find adults beneath fallen trunks and other woodland debris. However, at most times they are burrowed more deeply below the ground.

Comments As agricultural entities and normal vegetational succession alter more and more of the natural pine and wiregrass flatwoods, the flatwoods salamander is becoming increasingly uncommon. It cannot exist in drained areas or deepened ponds. Larvae of the flatwoods salamander may still be found in some numbers in a few isolated ponds and cypress heads, but extensive searches have shown other historic sites to be devoid of these beautiful salamanders. The adults are always more difficult to find.

40 MARBLED SALAMANDER

Ambystoma opacum

Abundance This was once the most widely distributed of Florida's mole salamanders. It still may be the most commonly seen of them. Perhaps this is because the marbled salamander seems not to be as persistently fossorial as other mole salamanders, or at least it doesn't dig as deeply as some. Although this species now seems to be confined to the panhandle and the Suwannee River Valley, it was once found at least 125 miles south of this. In the mid-1960s I (RDB) found two examples beneath debris under an isolated railroad bridge near Lithia Springs (Hillsborough County).

Habitat Marbled salamanders occur in Florida in damp hardwood hammocks, usually in river floodplains. We have frequently found them beneath moisture-retaining trash as well as under, and occasionally in, mouldering logs. They require ephemeral ponds for breeding.

Size Marbled salamanders are adult at from 3–4 in.

Reproduction This pretty salamander is an autumn breeder. Courtship, which consists of nudging, butting, and chin-rubs, occurs in damp terrestrial situations. Males deposit spermatophores at the bases of grass clumps or beneath leaves. These are picked up by females with their cloacal labia. The female then seeks a damp, protected place in a soon-to-be-flooded woodland depression and deposits her clutch of 30 to more than 100 clustered, but single, eggs in a nest (often of her construction). Until autumn rains flood the depression and immerse the eggs, the female remains in attendance of the clutch. The eggs hatch in from one to several days following immersion and from that point on, development is normal. Larvae overwinter in the ponds.

Coloration/pattern This beautiful little salamander is sexually dimorphic. While the dorsal ground color of both sexes is black, the bands of the female are gray or silver and those of the male white. Sides and venter are unrelieved black. Marbled salamanders are short-tailed, stocky, and broad-headed.

The larvae are buff to green(ish) and have a somewhat darker dorsal stripe that usually contains some evidence of banding or spotting.

Similar species The flatwoods salamander is less precisely marked, has *much* narrower dorsal banding, a narrow head, and a proportionately longer tail.

Behavior Although it is a burrower in damp woodlands, the marbled salamander seems to surface and wander more often during rains than other members of the genus. We have occasionally encountered it crossing paved roads after dark, during or after storms.

Comments This small and pretty salamander is the most strongly dimorphic of any of Florida's ambystomatid species. Although fully capable of burrowing, marbled salamanders often remain rather close to the surface of ground except during extended droughts.

41 MOLE SALAMANDER

Ambystoma talpoideum

Abundance This remains a rather common but locally distributed ambystomatid. The range of the mole salamander in Florida includes the the northern one third of the peninsula (from Marion County northward) and the entire panhandle.

Habitat This persistent burrower is a denizen of damp pine, mixed, or hardwood woodlands. It breeds in temporary woodland ponds.

Size This is another of the smaller ambystomatids. Mole salamanders are adult at from 3–4 in. in total length.

Reproduction In Florida the mole salamander is a pond breeder during the long nights of winter. It usually enters the ponds during heavy rains or only after cool weather has chilled the ground somewhat. Males attach stalked spermatophores to pond-bottom leaves, twigs, rocks, or similar litter. Following a nudging, bumping, chin-rubbing courtship, the female picks the sperm packet from the top of the spermatophore with her ventral labia. She then deposits eggs in several small clusters until the total clutch of 100 or more is laid. The egg clusters are attached to stems or twigs.

Coloration/pattern Mole salamanders are short-bodied, short-tailed, and have a proportionately immense head. They are dark brown, dark gray, or nearly black with bluish or silvery flecks dorsally and laterally. The light-flecked belly and lower sides are lighter than the dorsum. The rather nondescript larva is buff to gray, blotched or mottled with darker pigment dorsally or laterally, but has a distinctive, unpigmented, midventral stripe.

Similar species None in Florida. The immense head of the mole salamander should be diagnostic.

Behavior Both the common and specific names bring attention to the burrowing habits of this small but robust salamander. Despite this propensity, mole salamanders are seen on the surface of the ground with some degree of regularity.

Comments Although it is the most nondescriptly colored of Florida's mole salamanders, the proportionately large head and short, stubby body of *A. talpoideum* are of interest. Currently, this species seems quite abundant in the northern third of the state.

42 TIGER SALAMANDER

Ambystoma t. tigrinum

Abundance In Florida this is a rare, and rarely seen, salamander. It occurs locally in suitable habitat in the northwestern one third of peninsular Florida as well as throughout the panhandle. It apparently has been extirpated in several areas where it once occurred.

Habitat Although they are known to occur in many variable woodland habitats, the alteration (both draining and deepening qualify here) of a single breeding pond may extirpate an entire population. These salamanders prefer moderately to heavily vegetated ponds that contain no predacious fish. Adult tiger salamanders burrow deeply into yielding loamy soils, but may be most common in sandy pinelands.

Size At up to a foot in total length, the eastern tiger salamander is the largest terrestrial salamander of the east. Florida specimens seem to attain a length of 7–9 in. Larvae often attain a length of 6 in. or more prior to metamorphosing.

Reproduction In north Florida, tiger salamanders are activated and induced to make breeding migrations by only the heaviest of winter rains. Usually these are during the passage of a frontal system that markedly lowers barometric pressure and that has been preceded by a week or two of rather cold weather. As with many ambystomatids, male tiger salamanders usually enter the breeding ponds before the females and may remain in the ponds for many days longer than the females, which again depart the water for the woodlands soon after laying. The eggs are large and the clump may contain as few as 25 to more than 100 eggs. The larvae often attain a length of 4–6 in. before metamorphosing.

Coloration/pattern Eastern tiger salamanders are of variable color and pattern. Florida examples tend to be sparsely spotted. However, north of Florida, some tiger salamanders may be so profusely marked that they appear to be light salamanders with dark reticulations. Such specimens may eventually be found in Florida. The dorsal ground color varies from brown to nearly black. The light dorsal and lateral spots are of irregular shape and arrangement, but seem to never be in the rather precise rows seen on the smaller spotted salamander. The light spots can vary from an off-white or cream to a rather intense butter-yellow or olive-green. The belly is light (light-olive to yellow) with dark markings.

Larvae are often an unrelieved olive-brown dorsally and laterally and somewhat lighter ventrally.

Similar species The spotted salamander, not yet known from Florida, has rounded, more regularly arranged spots.

Behavior Like adults of most mole salamanders, those of the tiger salamander are extensively fossorial and rarely seen. On the infrequent occasions that they do emerge from their burrows, they do so at night. Occasionally, they may wander into swimming pools or other such difficult-to-escape "traps." The larvae are occasionally netted from ponds.

Comments Because populations seem to be declining, the tiger salamanders of Florida are in need of nearly continuous monitoring. It is particularly important that their breeding ponds are preserved.

AMPHIUMAS
Family Amphiumidae

Although they may be common, the aquatic amphiumas are so persistently nocturnal and secretive that their presence in any body of water is easily overlooked.

Of the three described species, two are well known in Florida and the third nears our borders.

These are slender, attenuate salamanders that have four *tiny* legs. Their common names combine the number of toes on each foot with the generic name of *Amphiuma,* but when used in common parlance the amphiuma is not capitalized. The one-toed and two-toed amphiumas occur in Florida, and the three-toed amphiuma nears the Florida state line in central southern Alabama.

While little is known with certainty about the natural history of the one-toed amphiuma, the lives of the two- and three-toed amphiumas are at least somewhat less enigmatic.

43 TWO-TOED AMPHIUMA

Amphiuma means

Abundance When coupled with their secretive behavior and aquatic lifestyle, the nocturnal activity patterns of the two-toed amphiuma easily explain why these salamanders are not more often seen and readily recognized by Floridians. While populations may not be dense, two-toed amphiumas dwell in most aquatic habitats throughout the state.

Habitat The shallows of lakes, ponds, streams, ditches, rivers—even some not-so-shallow areas of straight-sided drainage canals—all harbor sizable populations of two-toed amphiumas. These salamanders seem most at home in silted or heavily vegetated waters, amid detritus, or in areas with easily burrowed muddy bottoms.

Size Most two-toed amphiumas seen are 8–20 in. long. Exceptional adults may exceed 3.5 ft.

Reproduction The water-edge or shallow-water nesting site is usually beneath a log, board, or matted vegetation or is similarly concealed. If water levels recede, the nests may be left some distance from the water. The bead-like string of 150 or so jelly-covered eggs is often folded into a flattened ball. The female amphiuma remains with the eggs during their several-month incubation. For a short time after hatching, hatchling amphiuma have barely discernable external gills. Hatchlings are about 1.5 in long. Females in south Florida lay their eggs during the winter or early spring months. Those in north Florida lay in late spring or early summer.

Coloration/pattern Two-toed amphiuma are dark mud-gray dorsally, lighter ventrally, and have no well defined line of demarcation between the two colors. Hatchlings are black (or nearly so) dorsally.

As suspected, the tiny legs are *usually* tipped with two toes each. Examples with one and/or three toes have been found.

The nose is rounded when viewed from above, but flattened in profile. The eyes are small, non-protuberant, and lidless. Prior to shedding, the eyes (the entire salamander, in fact) appear bluish and opaque. An oval or elliptical gill opening is present on each side of the head.

Similar species To date, the three-toed amphiuma is not known to occur in Florida. The one-toed amphiuma is much smaller, has a more rounded head profile, only one toe on each of the four *very tiny* legs, and is adapted to a habitat of oozy black mud rather than open water. Sirens of all species have external gills throughout their lives and lack rear legs. American eels (true fish) have fins and typical gills and gill covers.

Behavior A salamander that bites? Indeed! Two-toed amphiumas will bite, and bite strongly, in feeding response or if carelessly handled. The strong jaws, powerful enough to overpower crayfish, frogs, and small snakes, require respect. If a relatively stationary object such as a finger is grasped, the salamander will rotate on its long axis, peeling the skin away. Stitches may be necessary to repair a bitten area.

Amphiuma may occur in ponds that occasionally dry. Should this happen, the salamanders, in a manner similar to that of sirens and lungfishes, burrow deeply into the bottom mud, and form a (nearly) moisture-impervious cocoon in which to await the return of the rains. These interesting salamanders may be found foraging by night in the shallows or in thick mats of vegetation. Besides the mentioned items, amphiuma eat all manner of aquatic insects, worms, fish and their eggs, and other aquatic organisms.

Comments Amphiuma are occasionally caught by fishermen. As much because it is believed poisonous as for its writhing and biting, hooked specimens are either cut free with hook and line still in place, or are killed. One large, long-term captive in Dr. R. W. Van Devender's lab ravenously consumes adult mice.

44 ONE-TOED AMPHIUMA

Amphiuma pholeter

Abundance The true population statistics of this salamander remain unknown. It is so secretive that details of its natural history will continue to unfold for decades. It occurs in suitable habitats across the panhandle, southward to the Gulf Hammock area on Florida's northwestern peninsula.

Habitat The one-toed amphiuma dwells in deep beds of soupy, organic muck—a particularly difficult habitat to sample. Because of this anaerobic habitat, it has been nearly impossible to learn any details of the life history of this salamander.

Size The smallest of the three species in this genus, *A. pholeter*, appears to be adult at 9–10 in. and seems to top out in size at just about a foot.

Reproduction Much about the breeding biology of this species remains conjecture. It is thought that *A. pholeter* lays its eggs in the early summer and that, like the other members of the genus, a female remains in attendance of the eggs until hatching. Clutch size is unknown or unpublished. It is unknown whether this salamander has an aquatic larval stage, or whether complete development occurs in the egg-capsule.

Coloration/pattern This salamander is nearly uniformly dark brown or blackish-brown both dorsally and laterally, and only slightly (if at all) lighter ventrally. The legs of *A. pholeter* are proportionately the tiniest of any member of the genus and each is tipped with one toe. Two oval gill openings, one on each side, are located posterior of the head. The snout is rather rounded in profile. The eyes are lidless and non-protuberant.

Similar species Sirens have external gills and no hind legs. The two-toed amphiuma is larger, and has a lighter belly, a flattened snout, and usually two toes on each foot. The three-toed amphiuma has not yet been found in Florida (see page 128).

Behavior This streamside, muckland salamander is so secretive that it is seldom seen unless raked from its anaerobic habitat. Many invertebrates also occur in such habitat, and it is probable that the smaller worms, molluscs, and insects are the foods of the one-toed amphiuma. It is unknown where these salamanders go when water levels rise and cover their habitats. It is known that at such times habitats that usually harbor a fair number yield few or none to researchers. Certainly the decreased visibility during times of high water figures prominently in the inability of researchers to find specimens. Researcher Paul Moler refers to the habitat of this salamander during periods of high water as "liquid slurry," and at other times as having the consistency of "chocolate pudding."

Comments Dr. D. Bruce Means has studied this enigmatic salamander for more than 20 years. When published, the results of his study should offer more insight into the biology and life history of this species than has been collectively gathered to date.

LUNGLESS SALAMANDERS
Family Plethodontidae

This family contains a hodgepodge of salamanders and is represented in Florida by 14 diverse species. These fall into 2 rather natural groups (subfamilies), the dusky salamanders, subfamily Desmognathinae, with 4 Floridian species, and the Plethodontinae, with the remaining 10 species.

Attempting the identification of the dusky salamanders will prove to be, at the very least, an exercise in true dedication. At its worst it will seem an exercise in futility. It is most often necessary to note the negative, rather than the positive, characteristics. They are easily separated from the other plethodontids, but less easily from each other. Knowing the geographic origin of a specimen will be nearly mandatory. Tail shape, taken in cross-section, is an important consideration. All members of the dusky salamander group have hind legs that are much heavier than the forelegs, a characteristic not shared with the members of the subfamily Plethodontinae. Dusky salamanders have a light line running diagonally rearward from the eye to the angle of the jaws. Additionally, although it is less often observable, the jaw structure of the two groups differs. Dusky salamanders open their mouths by lifting the top of the head rather than by dropping their lower jaw.

In all, the lungs are lacking. Respiration is accomplished through the skin and mucous membranes that must always be moist. The salamanders in this family have a nasolabial groove, an indentation that extends downward from the nostril to the lip. In males of some species the grooves end below the lip on downward projections called nasal cirri. The cirri are visible during the breeding season on such Florida species as the southern two-lined salamander [49].

All of the plethodontids usually hide by day (some may be active during overcast or rainy weather, especially when barometric pressure is dropping during the passage of a frontal system), but emerge to forage on damp or dewy nights. Some species are largely restricted to the environs of springs or brooks, others wander rather far afield but are *always* in damp areas and microhabitats.

The most divergent of the Florida plethodontid species in external appearance is the Georgia blind salamander [52], a troglodytic paedomorph that seems far more common in the caverns of Florida than in its namesake state.

Florida plethodontids vary in size from the slender 2.75-in. overall length of the dwarf salamander to the more robust 6-in. length of the southern red salamander [57].

The reproductive strategies of the salamanders in this group are variable. One constant, both of aquatic and terrestrial plethodontids, is the "tail-straddling walk." In this, following stimulation, a female closely follows, and straddles with her forelegs, the tail of a walking male about to deposit a spermatophore. The male may stimulate the female by nudging, and/or by secretions from the mental gland. These secretions are transferred by the male rubbing or slapping the snout of the female, or by dragging his mental gland and teeth along her nape and shoulder area. At the culmination of the tail-straddling walk, the male deposits the spermatophore and the female walks

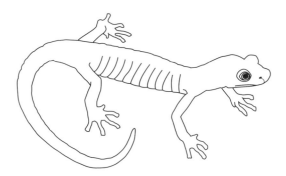

Plethodontid salamander. The nasolabial groove (the groove from nostril to lip) is characteristic of many lungless salamanders. Salamanders of many families have vertical grooves along the side (costal grooves).

over it and picks the spermcap off with her cloacal labia. Egg-laying follows.

Details of the life histories of most plethodontids are sparse. All species are badly in need of extended field studies.

45 Apalachicola Dusky Salamander

Desmognathus apalachicolae

Abundance In its very limited range, this is not an uncommon salamander. In Florida the Apalachicola dusky salamander will be encountered only near the Georgia state line in the drainages of the Ochlockonee and Apalachicola rivers.

Habitat Deep and relatively cool ravines, with extensive growths of sphagnum moss and permanent clear streams, are home to the Apalachicola Dusky Salamander.

Size Although occasional specimens near 4 in. in total length, most found are 2.5–3.5 in.

Reproduction Little is known about the reproductive strategy of the Apalachicola dusky salamander. I (RDB) have found two clutches of salamander eggs containing about 10 ova each beneath a sphagnum covered limb at the edge of a stream in a deep ravine in Liberty County. An Apalachicola dusky salamander was near, but not actually in attendance of each. Because this is the reproductive strategy of the rather similar but more northerly mountain dusky salamander, I suspect these eggs to have been *D. apalachicolae*.

Coloration/pattern The term nondescript best covers this, and most other dusky salamanders. *Desmohnathus apalachicolae* may be unicolored (older examples) or rather prominently spotted or blotched (younger examples). If patterned, the spots are often outlined, at least on their outer edges, with some black pigment. The spots may be discrete or coalesce into bands or even stripes. The dorsal ground color is brown(ish). The venter is usually white, but may show traces of dark pigment. Except at its tip where it is attenuate and compressed, the long tail is nearly round in cross-section.

Dusky salamander larvae, netted from among leaves barely submerged in the shallows of the stream, were brownish dorsally, had vague dorsal spotting, and a very low tailfin. Because the Apalachicola dusky seemed to be the only "desmog" in the ravine, we speculate that these were its larvae.

Similar species There are two confusingly similar species found within the range of the Apalachicola dusky salamander. These are the southern dusky salamander and the spotted dusky salamander. Both have teardrop-shaped tails (in cross-section). The southern dusky salamander has a dark venter, while the belly of the spotted dusky salamander is light with prominent black flecking.

Behavior Secretive by day, the Apalachicola dusky salamander is found foraging on the top of sphagnum mats and even a foot or more up in low herbs at night.

Comments This is a rather newly described dusky salamander. Range and microhabitat are at least as important in identifying this species as appearance.

46 SOUTHERN DUSKY SALAMANDER

Desmognathus auriculatus

Abundance Once common to actually abundant in suitable habitats on the northern one half of the peninsula and the entire panhandle, the southern dusky salamander seems far less common today. In some areas unknown causes seem to have decimated or actually extirpated populations.

Habitat Southern dusky salamanders were once commonly seen residents of seepages, streamside, and riverside situations, sphagnum bogs, and other such areas. They dwell by day beneath fallen limbs, rocks, and leaf mats, and forage, sometimes widely, by night. They are most active on rainy or foggy evenings and especially so during the passage of barometric-pressure-dropping frontal systems.

Size Most southern dusky salamanders seen are 3.5–5 in. long. Occasional specimens have been found that slightly exceed 6 in.

Reproduction As do the females of most dusky salamanders, those of the southern dusky attend the clutch of 12–36 eggs throughout the 30± day incubation period. The egg cluster (actually a folded string) is laid in the late summer or autumn beneath wet to saturated leaf mats or in the mud beneath a log or rock.

Coloration/pattern This is most usually a dark salamander. It may be dark brown to nearly black dorsally and laterally, with a white-spotted dark belly. Although some specimens (particularly older ones) may be largely devoid of lateral markings, most have one or two irregular rows of small whitish, cream, or orangish spots ("portholes") on each side. The tails of some specimens have an orangish or buff upper edge. The tail is teardrop-shaped (in cross-section) near the body, but is more strongly compressed with a sharp upper edge posteriorly.

The larvae are very dark dorsally, have a translucent belly skin, and may have indications of the light portholes on their sides.

Similar species The Apalachicola dusky salamander has a tail that is round in cross section anteriorly. The spotted dusky salamander lacks small, light round spots (termed portholes by some) on its sides and tends to be more colorful dorsally.

Behavior Southern dusky salamanders were once easily found by rolling wet waterside logs or turning similarly placed rocks. They were also plentiful in or beneath vegetable debris on muddy banks. In many areas where they were once common, southern dusky salamanders are now rare.

Comments Immediate studies are needed to determine the cause of population reductions. The agent(s) affecting the populations of this salamander may also be affecting those of other species.

47 SPOTTED DUSKY SALAMANDER

Desmognathus fuscus conanti

Abundance The spotted dusky salamander is a locally common species in suitable habitat. It ranges from Florida's Leon and Wakulla counties westward to and beyond the Alabama line.

Habitat Although outside of Florida the spotted dusky salamander may be found in a wide variety of habitats, in Florida it is most commonly encountered near springs and the edges of clear streams in the ravines of the western panhandle. Its exact range in Florida is imprecisely known. Many of the specimens formerly thought to be spotted dusky salamanders (based on pattern) are now known (based on DNA samples) to actually be Apalachicola dusky salamanders. The reassignment of these populations has left large gaps, and a greater lack of understanding, of the range of the spotted dusky salamander.

Size Although not large, the spotted dusky salamander is of rather robust build. While most adults are smaller, southern duskies occasionally attain an overall length of somewhat more than 4.5 in.

Reproduction The clusters of 8 to 30 eggs are often laid beneath a rock, log, or mat of vegetation sitting at streamedge on very wet ground. The bottom eggs of the clutch may actually be *in* the water. The females usually remain in attendance of the eggs through the 30–40-day incubation period. The gilled larvae may develop in shallow water, but as often as not are found in mats of very wet, but not submerged, leaves or sphagnum.

Coloration/pattern Although no dusky salamander could be considered brightly colored, some specimens of this race are more brightly colored than most. The sides are tan and the dorsum may be brown or buff with or without dark-edged irregularly paired brighter buff to dull golden or orangish spots. The belly is white(ish) but variably patterned with light and/or dark pepperings. The tail is teardrop-shaped in cross-section.

The larvae are dark and not too dissimilar in appearance from the adults they will become.

Similar species This can be a difficult salamander to identify. Its tail is less compressed than the southern dusky, but more so than that of the Apalachicola dusky. It is also often more brightly colored than either. See the comments contained in the species accounts for the Apalachicola dusky salamander [45] and the southern dusky salamander [46].

Behavior Like most small salamanders, the spotted dusky hides by day and forages by night.

Comments As a group, dusky salamanders are difficult to identify. Some examples of the Apalachicola dusky salamander closely approach the spotted dusky in appearance. Tail shape (in cross-section), habitat, and range are important tools in the identification of these salamanders.

SALAMANDERS, NEWTS, AND SIRENS

Desmognathus monticola

Abundance The seal salamander is restricted in Florida to a few ravine streams in northwestern Escambia County.

Habitat In Florida seal salamanders are known only from streams with rocky bottoms in cool ravines. The aquatic larvae are found in gravelly areas of streams.

Size The Florida specimens of this salamander are smaller than those in the Appalachians. Florida specimens can be up to about 4.5 in. long.

Reproduction The two dozen or more eggs of this rather aquatic salamander are attached to the bottoms of flat rocks in seepages and other such areas. The female remains in attendance of her clutch throughout the lengthy incubation period.

Coloration/pattern The dorsum of young adults is often mottled buff and olive-brown. The sides are abruptly lighter. The venter is also light. A row of light flecks or dots extends along each side from front to hind legs. There is a tendency for seal salamanders to become darker and more unicolored, both dorsally and ventrally, with advancing age.

The larvae and newly transformed juveniles often have four or five pairs of light dorsolateral dots on the trunk and additional light dots on the tail.

Similar species The range of the Apalachicola dusky salamander is well to the east of that of the seal salamander. The ranges of the southern and spotted dusky salamanders overlap with the range of the seal salamander. See the individual accounts.

Behavior Seal salamanders may be found beneath litter or in burrows by day, but often leave their areas of seclusion to forage by night.

Comments This is an uncommon salamander in Florida. It is most easily found at night on the edges of the streams near and in which it lives.

49 SOUTHERN TWO-LINED SALAMANDER

Eurycea cirrigera

Abundance This is a tiny, pretty, and common salamander that may be seen from Dixie and Columbia counties westward throughout the panhandle to the Alabama state line.

Habitat *E. cirrigera* is found beneath natural and man-made litter along brooks, streams, and seepages (both in and out of the water) and may also be found well out into damp woodlands. The larvae are common in leafbeds in shallow to moderately deep flowing water.

Size Although this species may attain a length of 4 in., its extreme slenderness makes it look much smaller.

Reproduction The 12–48 stalked single eggs are attached to the underside of stable submerged debris such as stones (which are not common in Florida habitats), submerged logs, and roots. The female remains in attendance of her clutch throughout the two months of incubation.

Coloration/pattern This is a pretty, variable, but rather easily recognized salamander species. The dorsal color may vary from grayish-tan or buff to a very bright orange. The lateral color may be the same as that of the dorsum on the paler specimens, but somewhat paler than the dorsum on the orange ones. A black dorsolateral stripe is present on each side. This is usually complete (but may be broken) from the eye to the tailtip. *Vestiges* of a dark vertebral stripe may be present. There are 5 toes on each hind foot. Males have well-developed nasal cirri.

The aquatic larvae are quite nondescript when young, but develop the characteristic stripes as they age.

Similar species The dwarf salamander is of quite similar appearance but has 4 toes on each hind foot. The three-lined salamander has a well-developed middorsal stripe.

Behavior Two-lined salamanders follow the norm by being inactive and secretive by day but foraging rather widely at night. They may ascend well above the ground into herbaceous vegetation on damp nights.

Comments The larvae of the southern two-lined salamander may be found in panhandle streams in the same submerged leafbeds as waterdogs. Adults wander well out into moist woodlands.

50 THREE-LINED SALAMANDER

Eurycea guttolineata

Abundance In suitable habitat the three-lined salamander can be quite common. It occurs from Jefferson County in the eastern panhandle westward and northward to (and beyond) the Alabama and Georgia state lines.

Habitat This pretty salamander can be particularly common near seepages, grottoes, and caves, and is the salamander regularly encountered during cave tours in Florida Caverns State Park. It is also found in damp areas of many hardwood woodlands and along stream and riveredges.

Size This is a long-tailed, slender salamander. Adults vary from about 4.5 to 7 in.

Reproduction Egg-deposition occurs from late autumn through the months of winter. The several dozen eggs are laid and attached singly to the underside of submerged or wateredge shelters such as rocks or logs, or in subsurface tunnels and passageways. The larvae are aquatic. The female provides nest protection for the month and a half or two months of incubation.

Coloration/pattern The yellowish to buff dorsum is divided by a dark middorsal stripe and bordered at each side by a broad, dark lateral stripe. Infiltration by light pigment may appear in the lateral stripes, which may break into broad vertical bars on the sides of the tail. The vertebral stripe (which may be broken or incomplete) may be variably divided by a thread-thin line of light pigment. The venter is light with a profusion of dark spots. The legs are prominently spotted and there are 5 toes on each hind foot.

Except for the fact that the vertebral stripe may be weak or, rarely, lacking, the gilled, aquatic larvae are very similar to the adults in appearance.

Similar species The two-lined and dwarf salamanders lack a well developed vertebral stripe. Dwarf salamanders have only 4 toes on each hind foot.

Behavior Outside of caves the three-lined salamander hides by day beneath rocks and logs. It emerges to forage by night. This salamander is active around the clock in the twilight areas and interior of caves and grottoes.

Comments This is one of the prettiest of Florida's salamanders. It has only recently been afforded full species status. Older texts refer to this salamander as *E. longicauda guttolineata*.

51 DWARF SALAMANDER

Eurycea quadridigitata

Abundance This small, attenuate salamander occurs farther southward on Florida's peninsula than any other plethodontid. It has been found from Dade County northward to (and beyond) the Georgia state line, as well as throughout (and west of) the panhandle.

Habitat Although the dwarf salamander may wander away from permanent water in the damper woodlands of north Florida, in the seasonally dry south it seems more restricted to the immediate environs of water. This is a common species in the sphagnum beds of north Florida and remains so in the tangles of frogsbit and hydrocotyl roots in the central part of the state. In the south it is associated with dense patches of water lettuce and water hyacinths. It may shelter beneath matted shoreline vegetation or damp logs. On rainy nights, adults are often seen crossing roadways that closely parallel canals, drainage ditches, or vegetation-choked rivers.

Size This is a very long-tailed salamander that is adult at less than 3.5 in. total length.

Reproduction Egg deposition occurs from late autumn through the winter months. The one to nearly four dozen eggs are laid singly, but often close to each other in aquatic or wateredge vegetation. We have seen eggs just beneath the waterline on the bladders of hyacinths and on the undersides of the lowest leaves of water lettuce.

Coloration/pattern This attenuate salamander has a brown dorsum (often with an apparent herringbone pattern) and lighter sides that are separated from each other by a broad, dark dorsolateral stripe. There may be some indication of a darker middorsal stripe. Reproductively active males develop nasal cirri. There are only four toes on each hind foot. The gilled larvae are darkest dorsally and, when nearing metamorphosis, develop a dark dorsolateral line on each side.

Similar species Except for the uncommon four-toed salamander (known in Florida only from portions of the panhandle) which has an enamel-white belly prominently spotted with black, the dwarf salamander is the only currently described, non-gilled (terrestrial) Florida salamander with four toes on the hindfeet.

Behavior These salamanders may be seen foraging at night amid floating hyacinths and water lettuce. They may also be encountered at night, at times in numbers, crossing rainswept roadways. Dwarf salamanders may be extensively subterranean, using the burrows of other small creatures during dry weather.

Comments It has been rather recently found that there are considerable biochemical differences in some populations of the salamanders currently considered *E. quadridigitata*. It is probable that this is actually a species complex.

52 Georgia Blind Salamander

Haideotriton wallacei

Abundance Unknown. Because of restricted access to its Stygian habitat, population statistics for this species can only be guessed at. Few adults have been seen but many juvenile specimens are known from a series of caves in Jackson County and another couple of caves in adjacent Georgia.

Habitat *Haideotriton* occurs in ground-water (*not* runoff) pools in the darkness of caves, and in deep wells and underground solution chambers.

Size Most specimens seen in caves are juveniles 1–2 in. long. Occasionally, 3-in. adults have been seen.

Reproduction Unknown, but almost certainly this salamander is an egg-layer. Gravid females have been found both in the spring and early winter.

Coloration/pattern Juveniles of this species are an overall translucent (sometimes pinkish) white with a vague overwash of dark pigment. Adults are pure white. The gills of Georgia blind slamanders of all ages are pink or red. Immature specimens have dark eyespots. These become more obscure with advancing age.

Similar species None. This is the only eyeless salamander of Florida.

Behavior *Haideotriton* is a permanently gilled aquatic species. It is found in deep and shallow cave pools in Jackson County, Florida. It readily and rapidly responds to disturbances of the water, perhaps as much to procure food as to avoid danger. Eyeless crayfish and amphipods occur in the same pools as this salamander.

Comments The first known Georgia blind salamander came from a deep well in Albany, Georgia. Since its discovery, however, far more specimens of this troglobitic paedomorph have come from caves in Florida than from its namesake state. Therefore, the alternate name of Southeastern blind cave salamander has been proposed.

53 FOUR-TOED SALAMANDER

Hemidactylium scutatum

Abundance This salamander is rare in Florida. It is currently known only from the Florida panhandle counties of Gadsden, Leon, and Walton.

Habitat Extensive, acidic, sphagnaceous areas and nearby woodlands seem to be the favored habitat of the four-toed salamander. In such habitats four-toed salamanders seek refuge beneath logs, limbs, and debris, but seem invariably most common beneath sphagnum mats.

Size This is a small salamander species. Most adults are 2.25–3 in. long. Occasional specimens near 4 in. in length.

Reproduction Up to three dozen (often fewer) eggs are laid above the water level in sphagnum mats or other such suitable areas. Communal nestings are not uncommon. Females remain in attendance of the clutch(es) throughout the 1½–2-month incubation period. The short-tailed larvae are aquatic.

Coloration/pattern The four-toed salamander is clad in earthen tones dorsally with a fine, but variable, peppering of black spots. The belly is enamel-white with discrete black spots. There is a basal tail constriction. The top of the tail is often brighter in color than the dorsum. The short nose is bluntly rounded. Larvae are short tailed and of a rather nondescript brown dorsally. The ventral spotting can be seen on nearly mature and mature larvae. The tailfin of the larva comes far forward onto its back.

Similar species The only other terrestrial Florida salamander with four toes on the hind feet is the dwarf salamander. The dwarf salamander lacks the prominently black-spotted white belly and the basal tail constriction.

Behavior As with many of our salamanders, little is known about the life history of the four-toed salamander in Florida. In many areas north of Florida, the four-toed salamander is known to make autumn breeding migrations. Whether it does so in Florida is unknown.

Comments This species is badly in need of life history studies in Florida (and elsewhere). It is hoped that additional field studies will divulge that this salamander is actually more common in Florida than now thought.

54 SOUTHEASTERN SLIMY SALAMANDER

Plethodon grobmani

Abundance Locally common in the woodlands of northern Florida (including the entire panhandle), the southeastern slimy salamander has been recorded as far south on the peninsula as the Tampa Bay area.

Habitat This is a member of the "woodland salamander" group. Wherever there is even a modicum of moisture, the slimy salamander is capable of surviving. It burrows into and beneath rotting logs and mats of leaf-litter, beneath rocks, and in other such areas. This species has no aquatic larval stage.

Size Adults range from 5–6.5 in. in length. Rarely, they may exceed 7 in.

Reproduction The 8–24+ eggs are laid in the protection of the interior of, or beneath, a rotting log, in an underground nest, or beneath a rock. The nesting site must be moist but not wet. Direct development occurs, with the larvae remaining in the egg capsule until metamorphosis is completed. Nesting has been observed in the spring, incubation takes about 12–15 weeks, and the female usually remains with the clutch throughout the incubation period.

Coloration/pattern This is a slender black salamander with a variable amount of white flecking on the back and sides. The sides are usually more heavily flecked than the back. The belly is dark, but lighter than the back.

Similar species The mole salamander is the closest in color to the slimy salamander. However, the mole salamander [41] is short, stocky, has a proportionately large head, and lacks the naso-labial groove.

Behavior As do all woodland salamanders, *P. grobmani* hides persistently by day, but emerges from its burrows and lairs to forage at night. They often sit with only the head and shoulders out of the burrow, awaiting the approach of an insect, spider, or worm.

Comments The slimy salamander complex consists of at least 16 species of biochemically distinct, largely look-alike salamanders. Of these, only *P. grobmani* occurs in Florida.

The slimy salamanders take their name from the copiously exuded skin secretions. In this case, though, the specific name of *glutinosus* better describes the cloying stickiness of the anything-but-slimy secretions.

55 RUSTY MUD SALAMANDER

Pseudotriton montanus floridanus

Abundance This species is secretive and of local distribution but probably not particularly uncommon.

Habitat This race of the mud salamander has been found northward from Orange County to (and beyond) the Georgia-Florida state line, including the eastern panhandle. They inhabit muddy seeps, spring edges, brook overflows, swamps, and wet lowland hammocks. Mud salamanders are persistent burrowers.

Size Although they may occasionally near 4.5 in. in total length, most adult rusty mud salamanders are 3–4 in. long.

Reproduction Little is known with certainty about the reproductive biology of either subspecies of the mud salamander in Florida. It is probable that the 50 to 200 eggs are laid beneath submerged logs during the late autumn or early winter months. The female may remain in attendance until hatching. The eggs probably take more than a month and a half to incubate. The larvae are aquatic. The mud salamanders in some populations breed biennially. It is unknown whether this is the case with Florida specimens.

Coloration/pattern A blotchy patina of dark pigment dulls most of the orange-red on the back and much of it on the sides. The venter is lighter with orange-red flecking. The eyes are (usually) relatively dark. The larvae are reddish-brown dorsally and variably pinkish ventrally. The venter has dark spots. Both the adults and larvae of this southeasternmost race of mud salamander are comparatively dull in color.

Similar species The southern red salamander [57] is stockier and liberally flecked with *light* spots dorsally and laterally.

Behavior Mud salamanders are aptly named. They actively burrow through the soupy mud of seepage areas and wet lowland hammocks. As you might surmise, this choice of habitat makes mud salamanders difficult to observe. Those that are seen are usually deliberately sought by researchers. Adults may sometimes be found crossing roadways on rainy nights.

56 GULF COAST MUD SALAMANDER

Pseudotriton m. flavissimus

A second, larger, stockier, and much more brilliantly colored race, the Gulf Coast mud salamander occurs in the western Florida panhandle. Adults of this subspecies near 5 in. in length. Young adults are a rather brilliant black-flecked orange-red to salmon dorsally and laterally, and an unmarked pink ventrally. The tail is yellowish dorsally.

All mud salamanders dull in color with advancing age. Some turn a solid brown with an orangish patina.

57 SOUTHERN RED SALAMANDER

Pseudotriton ruber vioscai

Abundance Like the mud salamander, the congeneric southern red salamander is locally distributed and, although common in certain habitats, seldom seen in Florida. Its main distribution is in the Florida panhandle from Leon County westward, but an apparently disjunct population occurs in Hamilton County.

Habitat In Florida the southern red salamander is associated with acidic, sphagnaceous, hardwood ravines through which small streams flow. The salamanders live in burrows beneath well-settled

Scrub

andhills

Oak Hammocks

Damp Upland Hardwoods

Damp Upland Pinelands

Pine Flatwoods

Damp Prairie

Wet Marl Prairie

River Swamp

Cypress Swamp

Everglades Hammocks

South Florida Pine Rocklands

Limestone Hardwoods

Human Habitation

Pasture/Field

Coastal Dune

Ephemeral Pond, Woodlands

Ephemeral Pond, Openlands

Permanent Pond

Stream/River

Freshwater Marsh

Mangrove Swamp

Saltmarsh

Ocean/Bay

1 **Giant Toad,** *Bufo marinus*

2 **Oak Toad,** *Bufo quercicus,*
chorusing

3 **Southern Toad,** *Bufo terrestris*
chorusing

4 **Fowler's Toad,**
Bufo woodhousii fowleri

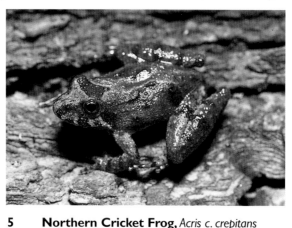

5 **Northern Cricket Frog,** *Acris c. crepitans*

6   **Florida Cricket Frog,** *Acris gryllus dorsalis*

7   **Southern Cricket Frog,** *Acris gryllus gryllus,*
chorusing

8   **Pine Barrens Treefrog,** *Hyla andersonii*

9   Bird-voiced Treefrog,
Hyla avivoca

10   Cope's Gray Treefrog,
Hyla chrysoscelis, chorusing

11a   Green Treefrog, *Hyla cinerea*
chorusing

11b   Green Treefrog,
H. cinerea, newly metamorphed

12   Pine Woods Treefrog, *Hyla femoralis*

13   **Barking Treefrog,** *Hyla gratiosa,* chorusing

14a   **Squirrel Treefrog,** *Hyla squirella,* brown phase, chorusing

14b   **Squirrel Treefrog,** *H. squirella,* green phase

15   **Cuban Treefrog,** *Osteopilus septentrionalis*

16   **Australian Great Green Treefrog,** *Pelodryas (Litoria) caerulea*

17   **Southern Spring Peeper,** *Pseudacris crucifer bartramiana,* chorusing

18   **Northern Spring Peeper,** *Pseudacris crucifer crucifer*

19   **Florida Chorus Frog,** *Pseudacris nigrita verrucosa*

20   Southern Chorus Frog, *Pseudacris nigrita nigrita*

21   Little Grass Frog,
Pseudacris ocularis, chorusing

22a   Ornate Chorus Frog,
Pseudacris ornata, brown phase,
chorusing

22b   Ornate Chorus Frog,
Pseudacris ornata, green and red phase

23   Upland Chorus Frog,
Pseudacris triseriata feriarum

24   Puerto Rican Coqui,
Eleutherodactylus coqui

25   Greenhouse Frog,
Eleutherodactylus p. planirostris

26   Eastern Narrow-mouthed Toad,
Gastrophryne carolinensis

27a   Eastern Spadefoot,
Scaphiopus holbrookii

27b   Eastern Spadefoot, *Scaphiopus holbrookii,*
chorusing

28a Florida Gopher Frog,
Rana capito aesopus

28b Florida Gopher Frog,
Rana capito aesopus, vocal sacs distend

29 Dusky Gopher Frog,
Rana capito sevosa

30 Bullfrog, *Rana catesbeiana*

31 Bronze Frog, *Rana clamitans clamitans*

32   **Pig Frog,** *Rana grylio*

33a   **River Frog,** *Rana heckscheri*

33b   **River Frog,** *Rana heckscheri,* tadpole

34   **Florida Bog Frog,** *Rana okaloosae*

35   **Pickerel Frog,** *Rana palustris*

36a **Florida Leopard Frog,**
Rana sphenocephala sphenocephala, green phase

36b **Florida Leopard Frog,**
Rana sphenocephala sphenocephala, black phase

37 **Southern Leopard Frog,**
Rana s. utricularia, amplexing pair, brown phase

38 **Carpenter Frog,** *Rana virgatipes*

39 **Flatwoods Salamander,** *Ambystoma cingulatum*

40 **Marbled Salamander,** *Ambystoma opacum*

41   **Mole Salamander,** *Ambystoma talpoideum*

42   **Eastern Tiger Salamander,**
Ambystoma tigrinum tigrinum

43   **Two-toed Amphiuma,** *Amphiuma means*   **44**   **One-toed Amphiuma,**
Amphiuma pholeter

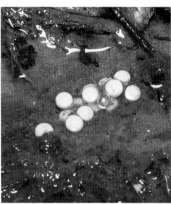

45a Apalachicola Dusky Salamander,
Desmognathus apalachicolae

45b Apalachicola Dusky Salamander,
Desmognathus apalachicolae, eggs

46 Southern Dusky Salamander,
Desmognathus auriculatus

47 Spotted Dusky Salamander,
Desmognathus fuscus conanti

48   Seal Salamander, *Desmognathus monticola*

49   Southern Two-lined Salamander,
Eurycea cirrigera

50   Three-lined Salamander,
Eurycea guttolineata

51   Dwarf Salamander, *Eurycea quadridigitata*

52   Georgia Blind Salamander,
Haideotriton wallacei

53   Four-toed Salamander, *hemidactyluim sctatum*

54   Southeastern Slimy Salamander,
Plethodon grobmani

55a   Rusty Mud Salamander,
Pseudotriton montanus floridanus

56b Rusty Mud Salamander,
Pseudotriton m. floridanus, larvae

56 Gulf Coast Mud Salamander,
Pseudotriton montanus flavissimus

57 Southern Red Salamander,
Pseudotriton ruber vioscai

58 Many-lined Salamander,
Stereochilus marginatus

59 Eastern Gulf Coast Waterdog,
Necturus species cf *beyeri*

60a   Striped Newt, *Notophthalmus perstriatus*

60b   Striped Newt, larvae

61   Central Newt, eft stage
Notophthalmus viridescens louisianensis

62   Peninsula Newt,
Notophthalmus viridescens piaropicola

63   Narrow-striped Dwarf Siren,
Pseudobranchus axanthus axanthus

64   Everglades Dwarf Siren,
Pseudobranchus axanthus belli

65   Slender Dwarf Siren,
Pseudobranchus striatus spheniscus

67 **Broad-striped Dwarf Siren,**
Pseudobranchus striatus striatus

66 **Gulf Hammock Dwarf Siren,**
Pseudobranchus striatus lustricolus

68 **Eastern Lesser Siren,**
Siren intermedia intermedia

69a **Greater Siren,**
Siren lacertina

69b **Greater Siren,** *Siren lacertina*,
immature

70   Spotted Salamander,
Ambystoma maculatum

71   Three-toed Amphiuma,
Amphiuma tridactylum

72a   American Alligator, *Alligator mississippiensis*

72b   American Alligator, *Alligator mississippiensis,*
hatchling

73   Spectacled Caiman, *Caiman crocodilus crocodilus*

74   American Crocodile, *Crocodylus acutus*

75a   Florida Worm Lizard, *Rhineura floridana*

75b   Florida Worm Lizard,
Rhineura floridana,
closeup of head

76a African Red-headed Agama,
Agama agama, warm, dominant male
clinging to vertical wall

76b African Red-headed Agama,
male when cool

77   Indochinese Tree Agama,
Calotes mystaceus

78   Eastern Slender Glass Lizard,
Ophisaurus attenuatus longicaudus

79   Island Glass Lizard, *Ophisaurus compressus*

80   Mimic Glass Lizard, *Ophisaurus mimicus*

81a Eastern Glass Lizard,
Ophisaurus ventralis

81b Eastern Glass Lizard, *Ophisaurus ventralis,*
old male

82 Asian Flat-tailed House Gecko,
Cosymbotus platyurus

83 Tokay Gecko, *Gekko gecko*

84a Yellow-headed Gecko,
Gonatodes albogularis fuscus, male

84b Yellow-headed Gecko,
Gonatodes albogularis fuscus, female

85 Common House Gecko, *Hemidactylus frenatus*

86   Indopacific House Gecko, *Hemidactylus garnotii*

87   Tropical House Gecko,
        Hemidactylus mabouia

88   Mediterranean Gecko,
        Hemidactylus turcicus

89   Bibron's Gecko, *Pachydactylus bibroni*

90b **Giant Day Gecko,** hatchling

91 **Ocellated Gecko,**
Sphaerodactylus argus argus

90a **Giant Day Gecko,**
Phelsuma madagascariensis grandis

92a   Ashy Gecko, *Sphaerodactylus elegans elegans*

92b   Ashy Gecko, *Sphaerodactylus elegans elegans,* juvenile

93   Reef Gecko, *Sphaerodactylus notatus notatus,* female

94   White-spotted Wall Gecko,
Tarentola annularis

95   Moorish Wall Gecko,
Tarentola mauretanica

96   Green Anole,
Anolis carolinensis carolinensis

97   Pale-throated Green Anole,
Anolis carolinensis seminolus

98   Haitian Green Anole,
Anolis chlorocyanus

99 **Puerto Rican Crested Anole,**
Anolis cristatellus cristatellus

100 **Large-headed Anole,**
Anolis cybotes cybotes

101a Bark Anole, *Anolis distichus* ssp.

B. Griswold

101b Bark Anole, *Anolis distichus* ssp.

102a Knight Anole,
Anolis equestris equestris

102b Knight Anole,
Anolis equestris equestris, juvenile

103 Barbados Anole, *Anolis extremus*

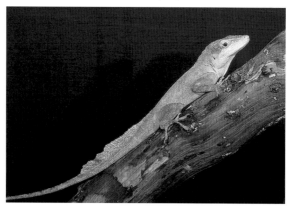

104 Marie Gallant Sail-tailed Anole,
Anolis ferreus

105 Jamaican Giant Anole,
Anolis garmani

106 Cuban Green Anole,
Anolis porcatus

07 Brown Anole, *Anolis sagrei*

"Green-headed" Variations

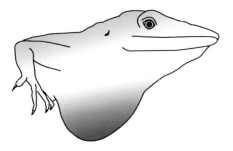

96 *Anolis carolinensis carolinensis*

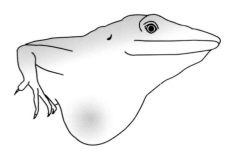

97 *Anolis carolinensis seminolus*

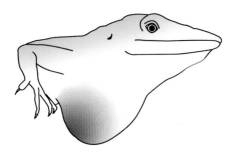

98 *Anolis chlorocyanus*

102 *Anolis equestris*

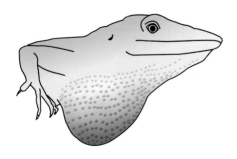

105 *Anolis garmani*

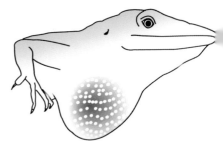

106 *Anolis porcatus*

"Brown-headed" Variations

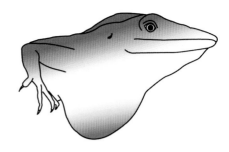

99   *Anolis cristatellus*

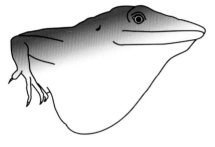

100   *Anolis cybotes*

101   *Anolis distichus distichus*

101   *Anolis distichus dominicensis*

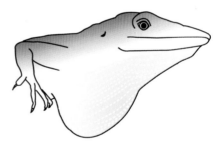

103   *Anolis extremus*

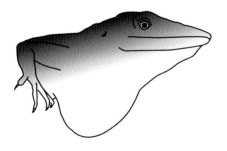

104   *Anolis ferreus*

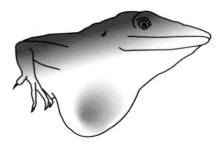

107   *Anolis sagrei*

108a Northern Brown Basilisk,
Basiliscus vittatus, male

108b Northern Brown Basilisk,
Basiliscus vittatus, juvenile

B. Griswold

109   Mexican Spiny-tailed Iguana,
Ctenosaura pectinata

110a Black Spiny-tailed
    Iguana, *Ctenosaura similis*

110b Black Spiny-tailed Iguana,
    Ctenosaura similis, hatchling

◀ 11   Great Green Iguana,
Iguana iguana, young male

**13   Green-legged
Curly-tailed Lizard,**
Leiocephalus personatus scalaris

112a   Northern Curly-tailed Lizard,
Leiocephalus carinatus armouri, subadult

112b   Northern Curly-tailed Lizard,
Leiocephalus carinatus armouri

114   Red-sided Curly-tailed Lizard,
Leiocephalus schreibersi schreibersi

115   Texas Horned Lizard, *Phrynosoma cornutum*

116a Southern Fence Lizard,
Sceloporus undulatus undulatus, male, bottom

**116b Southern Fence
Lizard,** *Sceloporus u.
undulatus,* male belly

117a Florida Scrub Lizard, *Sceloporus woodi,* male

**117b Florida Scrub
Lizard,** *Sceloporus
woodi,* male belly

118a Southern Coal Skink,
Eumeces anthracinus pluvialis

B. Mansell

118b Southern Coal Skink,
Eumeces anthracinus pluvialis, juvenile

119a Florida Keys Mole Skink,
Eumeces egregius egregius

J. Alderson

119b Florida Keys Mole Skink,
newly hatched clutch

120 Cedar Key Mole Skink,
Eumeces egregius insularis

121 Blue-tailed Mole Skink,
Eumeces egregius lividus

122   Peninsula Mole Skink, *Eumeces egregius onocrepis*

123   Northern Mole Skink, *Eumeces egregius similis*

24a Five-lined Skink, *Eumeces fasciatus,*
male, breeding colors

124b Five-lined Skink, juvenile

125 Southeastern Five-lined Skink,
Eumeces inexpectatus

26a Broad-headed Skink,
Eumeces laticeps, male,
breeding colors

126b Broad-headed Skink,
Eumeces laticeps, hatching

127 Sand Skink, *Neoseps reynoldsi*

128 Ground Skink, *Scincella lateralis*

129 Giant Ameiva,
Ameiva ameiva, dusky phase,
pair, male bottom

130 Giant Ameiva, green-rumped phase

131a Rainbow Whiptail, *Cnemidophorus lemniscatus*

131b Rainbow Whiptail,
Cnemidophorus lemniscatus, female

132 Giant Whiptail, *Cnemidophorus motaguae*

133 Six-lined Racerunner,
Cnemidophorus sexlineatus sexlineatus

134a Loggerhead Turtle, *Caretta caretta*

134b Loggerhead Turtle,
Caretta caretta, hatchling

135 Green Turtle, *Chelonia mydas*

136 Atlantic Hawksbill Turtle,
Eretmochelys imbricata imbricata

137 Atlantic Ridley, *Lepidochelys kempii*

138 Florida Snapping Turtle,
Chelydra serpentina osceola

139 Common Snapping Turtle,
Chelydra serpentina serpentina

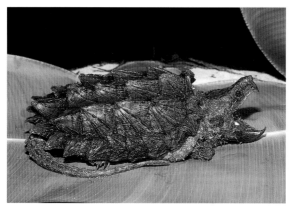

140 Alligator Snapping Turtle,
Macrochelys temminckii

141a Leatherback, *Dermochelys coriacea*

141b Leatherback, *Dermochelys coriacea,* hatchling

142   Spotted Turtle, *Clemmys guttata*

143 Florida Chicken Turtle,
Deirochelys reticularia chrysea

144 Eastern Chicken Turtle,
Deirochelys reticularia reticularia

145 Barbour's Map Turtle, *Graptemys barbouri*

146 Escambia Map Turtle, *Graptemys ernsti,* female

147a Ornate Diamondbacked Terrapin, **147b Ornate Diamondbacked Terrapi**
Malaclemys terrapin macrospilota *Malaclemys t. macrospilota,* hatchling

148 Carolina Diamondbacked **149 Mississippi Diamondbacked**
Terrapin, *Malaclemys terrapin centrata* **Terrapin,** *Malaclemys terrapin pileat*

150 Lower Keys Mangrove Terrapin,
Malaclemys terrapin rhizophorarum

151a Upper Keys Mangrove Terrapin,
Malaclemys terrapin ssp.

151b Upper Keys Mangrove Terrapin,
Malaclemys terrapin ssp., plastron

152 Florida East Coast Terrapin,
Malaclemys terrapin tequesta

153 Mobile Cooter, *Pseudemys concinna mobilensis*

154 Suwannee Cooter,
Pseudemys concinna suwanniensis, hatchling

155a Florida Cooter,
Pseudemys floridana floridana

155b Florida Cooter, *Pseudemys floridana floridana,*
hatchling

156a Peninsula Cooter,
Pseudemys floridana peninsularis, hatchling

156b Peninsula Cooter,
Pseudemys floridana
peninsularis, hatching

157a Florida Red-bellied Turtle, *Pseudemys nelsoni*

157b Florida Red-bellied Turtle, *Pseudemys nelsoni*

157c Florida Red-bellied Turtle, *Pseudemys nelsoni,* hatchling plastron

158a Florida Box Turtle, *Terrapene carolina bauri*

158b Florida Box Turtle, *Terrapene carolina bauri,* hatchling

159 Eastern Box Turtle, *Terrapene carolina carolina*

160 Gulf Coast Box Turtle,
Terrapene carolina major

161 Three-toed Box Turtle,
Terrapene carolina triunguis

162b Yellow-bellied Slider,
Trachemys scripta scripta

162a Yellow-bellied Slider,
Trachemys scripta scripta, juvenile

163 Red-eared Slider,
Trachemys scripta elegans

164a Striped Mud Turtle,
Kinosternon baurii, mainland

164b Striped Mud Turtle,
Kinosternon baurii, Lower Keys

165 Florida Mud Turtle,
Kinosternon subrubrum steindachneri

66 Mississippi Mud Turtle,
Kinosternon subrubrum hippocrepis

167 Eastern Mud Turtle,
Kinosternon subrubrum subrubrum

68 Loggerhead Musk Turtle,
Sternotherus minor minor

**169 Striped-necked Musk
Turtle,** *Sternotherus minor
peltifer,* juvenile

170 Common Musk Turtle, *Sternotherus odoratus*

171 East African Black Mud Turtle,
Pelusios subniger subniger

172a Gopher Tortoise,
Gopherus polyphemus

172b Gopher Tortoise,
Gopherus polyphemus, hatchling

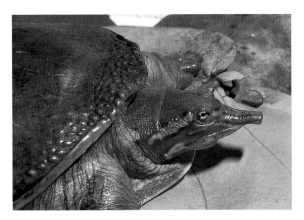

173a Florida Softshelled Turtle, *Trionyx ferox*

173b Florida Softshelled Turtle, *Trionyx ferox*
hatchling

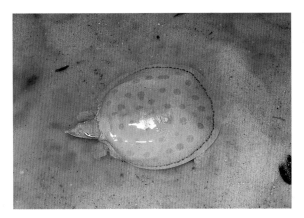

174   Gulf Coast Smooth Softshelled Turtle,
Trionyx muticus calvatus

175 Gulf Coast Spiny Softshelled Turtle,
Trionyx spiniferus asper, juvenile

176 Southern Painted Turtle,
Chrysemys picta dorsalis

177 Eastern Painted Turtle, *Chrysemys picta picta*

logs and other woodland litter. During dry periods, they seem to occur nearer the streams, dispersing more widely during wet periods.

Size This is a fairly robust salamander that commonly attains 4.5–5.5 in. in total length. They rarely exceed 6 in.

Reproduction The 3–7 dozen eggs are laid, probably in early winter, beneath rocks or logs in shallow, flowing water. Females have been found in the proximity of eggs, but it is not known whether they actually attend the clutches. Incubation seems to take from 6–9 weeks. The larvae are aquatic.

Coloration/pattern The southern red salamander is the dullest in color of the several races. This is especially true of old adults. The dorsal and lateral coloration is a pale reddish-brown to purplish-brown. There is a profusion of light flecks anteriorly and dark speckling posteriorly. The venter is lighter than the dorsum and is black-flecked. The iris may be gold or brassy in color, but some are dark. Larvae are similar to the adults in ground color but lack the light and dark flecking.

Similar species The races of the mud salamander in Florida are more slender, often have darker irises and lack the light flecking.

Behavior By day this is a secretive salamander. They emerge from their burrows to forage at night. This is especially true during rainy weather and when barometric pressure is falling. Little is known about the life history (including the reproductive biology) of the southern red salamander.

Comments As with most Florida salamanders, a comprehensive study of the wiles and ways of the southern red salamander is badly needed. The southern red salamander may not be as truly rare as just rarely seen.

58 MANY-LINED SALAMANDER

Stereochilus marginatus

Abundance This small salamander is rare in Florida, and occurs only in and near the drainage of Georgia's Okefenokee Swamp in Baker, Columbia, Nassau, and Union counties.

Habitat The primary habitat of this poorly known salamander is sphagnum mats growing in acidic backwaters and swamps. There, it may be found in standing water in the mats and by checking beneath the mats. It may also inhabit swamp- and seepage-edge leaf mats.

Size The many-lined salamander is small, slender, and attenuate. It is adult at about 2.5 in. and rarely attains a 4 in. overall length.

Reproduction Despite its primarily aquatic lifestyle both as an adult and larva, the eggs of many-lined salamanders have been found above the waterline in the decomposing logs that crisscross their swampland habitats. Females lay from 10 to 50+ eggs during the winter months. Incubation takes several weeks, during which the female remains in attendance of the eggs.

Coloration/pattern This is one of the most nondescript of Florida's salamanders. Despite the reference to many lines in the common name, the lines are obscure and difficult to perceive. A dark stripe from the eye to the back of the head, a dark vertebral line and dark (often broken) lines on the lower sides are usually the most discernible markings. The ground color of this small salamander is olive- to yellowish-brown dorsally and lighter ventrolaterally and ventrally. The belly has dark flecks. The tail *may* be a lighter gold-brown dorsally. The head is very slender. The larvae are colored similarly to the adults but have external gills.

Similar species The southern dusky salamanders (the only dusky found in the range of the many-lined salamander in Florida) lacks all traces of longitudinal lines, has a dark belly, hind legs that are stouter than the front legs, and has a proportionately broad head.

Behavior Many-lined salamanders are very secretive, often leaving the water only when the pond or slough dries. The salamanders then seek seclusion in and beneath rotting logs, and in moisture-holding mats of vegetation (including fallen leaves). In general, very little is known about this Florida salamander.

Comments This salamander is considered among the more primitive of the plethodontids. It is difficult to find in Florida.

WATERDOGS
Family Proteidae

There is probably only a single representative of this family in Florida. It is restricted to panhandle streams. It is usually referred to as a waterdog, but is occasionally called a mudpuppy.

At the moment, its taxonomy is askew, so future texts may refer to the same species under both a different common and scientific name.

Waterdogs have only four toes on each foot and, as permanent neotenes, retain external gills and lack eyelids throughout their lives.

59 EASTERN GULF COAST WATERDOG

Necturus species cf *beyeri*

Abundance Common, especially in smaller sizes, in the panhandle streams they inhabit. These waterdogs range from Leon and Wakulla counties westward.

Habitat These salamanders prefer streams of small to moderate size with a fair current. Waterdogs can be common where cover in the form of snags and leafbeds is adequate.

Size This is a small waterdog. Adults vary from 5–7 in. in total length, and rarely may exceed 8 in.

Reproduction Although by now this statement must sound like a broken record, we must again state that there is little known about the life history, including the reproductive biology, of this salamander. In Alabama, nests containing 37–67 eggs have been reported for the Alabama waterdog, a similarly sized species. It is probable that the Eastern Gulf Coast waterdog is a winter breeder that lays its clutch in the spring beneath tree roots, sunken logs, or in similarly protected areas.

Coloration/pattern The Eastern Gulf Coast Waterdog is clad in mud tones dorsally and laterally, and is profusely marked with obscure to well-defined rounded dark spots of moderate size. These are usually more visible on the sides than on the back. The venter is light and unspotted. The gills are bright red. Immatures are similar to the adults.

Similar species This is the only large, aquatic salamander in Florida with four legs and four toes on all feet.

Behavior This is a secretive *aquatic* species of salamander. They are stream dwellers and can be common in areas where bottom detritus accumulates. They are most often seen in the winter and early spring months.

Comments At present, the true identity of this Florida waterdog is unknown. It has only recently been determined to be different (Bart, Bailey, Ashton, Moler; 1997) from the Alabama waterdog, *Necturus alabamensis*. Now that this has been established, additional studies are needed to provide this salamander with a valid taxonomic status. As these studies ensue, it may be found that there is more than a single unidentified species requiring attention.

NEWTS
Family Salamandridae

Just as all toads are frogs, but not vice versa, all newts are salamanders, but not all salamanders are newts. In Florida this family of largely temperate salamanders is represented by only two species, one having two subspecies. The more specialized of the two, the striped newt [60] seems to have been declining in numbers for some period of time and is now uncommon. The two subspecies of the red-spotted newt (the Peninsula and the Central newts [61, 62]) are common to abundant.

Although as adults newts are capable of emerging from the water, in many areas of Florida they are aquatic for all of their long lives. In some areas, newts are neotenic, that is, they attain sexual maturity but fail to assume all adult characteristics. Perhaps the most noticeable of these characteristics are the retained external gills of neotenes.

Because they are rather easily found at all stages of their lives, the natural history of the peninsula and central newts (both subspecies of the more northerly red-spotted newt) is comparatively well known—at least in comparison to the lives of many other salamanders, including the congeneric striped newt.

Under ideal conditions the life of the eastern newts can be divided into four stages: the aquatic egg stage, the aquatic larval stage, the terrestrial eft stage (this may be skipped if terrestrial conditions are hostile), and the adult stage, which is aquatic in the subspecies of the red-spotted newt and either aquatic or terrestrial (depending on whether or not their ponds hold water) in the striped newt. Populations of newts of several species and subspecies are known to occasionally be neotenic.

Adult newts have rough skin; that of the larvae is smooth and slimy. During the breeding season, males develop heightened tailfins and black, roughened, excrescences on the innersides of the hind legs and on the toetips. These help the male retain a breeding embrace. The female is grasped around her neck or shoulders by the "non-skid" hind legs of the male. Tail undulations by the male apparently waft stimulatory pheromones to the female. After adequate stimulation she will pick up a sperm packet from the tip of a spermatophore with her cloacal labia. Following this, the eggs are laid singly and are often loosely wrapped in the leaf of an aquatic plant.

60 STRIPED NEWT

Notophthalmus perstriatus

Abundance This is the rarer (and apparently still declining) and more habitat restricted of Florida's two newt species. It may be found locally in the northern two fifths of the peninsula and the easternmost region of the panhandle.

Habitat The distribution of this pretty species is enigmatic even to researchers. It can be fairly common in one situation but rare or absent from several nearby areas that look virtually identical. Look for the striped newt in and near temporary ponds and cypress heads in pine flatwoods and the pine-dominated sandhill areas of north Florida.

Size This slender salamander is often less than 2.75 in., and rarely more than 3.5 in. in total length.

Reproduction Little is known with certainty about the reproductive biology of the striped newt. It is known to be a spring breeder. Newly hatched larvae have been found in late March and throughout April. It is thought that metamorphosis occurs in about 8 months. Where and when terrestrial conditions are hostile, the eft stage may be skipped over.

Coloration/pattern Adults are yellowish-green, olive, or nearly brown dorsally. Cold specimens are usually darker than warm ones. The red dorsolateral stripes that give this newt its name begin on the head and continue uninterrupted to about half way down the tail, where they then break into a series of dashes. There may be a series of poorly defined red dashes below the red stripe. The yellow-belly bears a few black spots. During the aquatic breeding season, a rather large tailfin and black excrescences on the innersides of the hindlegs develop.

Similar species No other newt or salamander in Florida has a continuous red stripe along each side.

Behavior Much of the life history of the striped newt remains steeped in mystery. Males have been seen amplexing gravid females in late March. Numbers of efts have been found near the breeding ponds during and following hard rains. Adults have been found beneath fallen limbs and logs near dried ponds. The strategy used by these newts to avoid desiccation in these well-drained habitats is not known.

Comments A study of the life history of the striped newt is badly needed. Before we can halt the decline in its numbers, we must know what it is that this species truly needs to thrive.

61 PENINSULA NEWT

Notophthalmus viridescens
piaropicola

Abundance This rough-skinned salamander is a common denizen of many heavily vegetated waterholes—lakes, ponds, oxbows, slow streams, and other such habitats—over virtually all of the southern four fifths of the Florida peninsula.

Habitat Peninsula newts can be found in most canals, lakes, ponds, and drainage ditches throughout central and southern Florida. They are also abundant in the backwaters and oxbows of rivers and creeks. This newt is often associated with areas of profuse aquatic growth. The terrestrial eft stage is usually foregone.

Size Although most peninsula newts are adult at 2.75–3.5 in., some may attain 4 in. in total length.

Reproduction Peninsula newts breed in the winter and spring months. Males develop a heightened tailfin and horny, black excrescences on the inner sides of their hind legs during the breeding season. With their hind legs males grasp females around their neck or shoulders. Undulations of the tailfin waft stimulating pheromones to the female. After sufficient stimulation the female picks up a sperm packet with her cloacal labia. The 50 to 150 (sometimes more) eggs are laid singly and are placed by the female on the stems and leaves (sometimes loosely wrapped in a leaf) of a submerged plant.

Coloration/pattern This is the darkest of the four races of the red-spotted newt. The dorsum is dark olive, olive-brown or nearly black. Small black spots, heaviest laterally, may be present. There are no red spots. The venter is dark olive-yellow, heavily peppered with fine black dots.

The larvae are dark dorsally, liberally peppered with darker spots dorsally and laterally, and pinkish-white ventrally. Dark ventral spots, while present, are not bold.

Similar species None. The striped newt has continuous red stripes from nose to tail.

Behavior Because of the excessive seasonal dryness throughout much of Florida, peninsula newts are often aquatic throughout their lives. Occasional adults may be found beneath moisture-retaining mats of wateredge vegetation or crossing roadways on rainy nights. Efts are dark-colored and rarely reported. This race of the eastern newt does not seem to wander far from permanent water sources, even during the rainy season. Unlike the striped newt, which preferentially chooses ephemeral ponds, the various races of the red spotted newt prefer permanent sources of water.

62 CENTRAL NEWT

N. v. louisianensis

The peninsula newt is replaced in the northern one fifth of the peninsula and the panhandle by the central Newt. This is a somewhat more brightly colored subspecies. The dorsum tends to be a little yellower or greener and a dorsolateral row of tiny red spots may be present on each side. If present, the red spots are not edged with black. The yellowish belly is heavily peppered with tiny black spots. This is the commonly seen race in northwestern Alachua County, whereas in the south and east of the county the peninsula newt is found.

This race seems to wander more extensively on rainy nights than the more southerly Peninsula newt.

SIRENS
Family Sirenidae

The salamanders in this family are so divergent from others that they were once placed in their own order, the Trachystomata.

All are fully aquatic, having three pairs of bushy external gills throughout their long lives. Hind limbs and pelvic girdle are lacking; only forelimbs are present. These, although small, are moved in a walking sequence when the siren is moving slowly on the pond or river bottom. They are folded along the side while the siren is swimming, but are brought forward into a "landing position" as the siren comes to rest.

The use of the colors and patterns described for the identification of the dwarf sirens may be inconclusive in some cases. Broad overlaps and variations have now been found.

Whether pale and difficult to see or bright and obvious, the striping of the three subspecies of *P. striatus* is precise and evenly edged, whereas the stripes of the two races of *P. axanthus* are rather ragged edged.

The dwarf sirens (*Pseudobranchus*) have only 3 toes on each forefoot and a single gill opening. The members of the genus *Siren* have 4 toes on each forefoot and 3 gill slits.

The breeding biology of the sirens remains nearly as muddy as the preferred habitats of most. It is thought that egg fertilization is external. External fertilization would certainly be workable in the members of the genus *Siren*, all of which apparently lay their eggs in clumps or clusters. It seems far less efficient—in fact, almost unworkable—in the case of the two species of *Pseudobranchus*, the dwarf sirens, which are, apparently, egg-scatterers.

All sirens of both genera survive the drying of their ponds by burrowing (sometimes rather deeply) into the mud, and forming cocoons of from one (short droughts) to many (lengthy droughts) layers of slime to conserve body moisture.

Speciation in both genera of this family is currently being addressed.

63 NARROW-STRIPED DWARF SIREN

*Pseudobranchus axanthus
axanthus*

Abundance This small sirenid seems to be common to abundant, but only seasonally available to "traditional" collecting methods. This siren occupies a range south of a line drawn from Jacksonville to Gulf Hammock and north of a line at the latitude of the northern edge of Lake Okeechobee.

Habitat The narrow-striped dwarf siren has found ready habitat with the proliferation of the introduced water hyacinth in Florida. For at least part of the year (spring, summer, and autumn) it is easily found by dredging hyacinths and carefully sorting through their root systems. Dredging at the same sites during the winter months has produced few of these salamanders. Moler and Kezer consider this a siren of open areas—ponds, marshes, and the like.

Size This is a tiny, slender salamander that is adult at 5–8 in. in length. Very occasional specimens may slightly exceed 9 in.

Reproduction Much regarding the reproductive biology of this siren remains conjectural. It is thought that this species scatters its dozen or so eggs singly through plant material. How fertilization is accomplished is unknown.

Coloration/pattern This is a dusky colored siren with obscure striping. There is a series of 4 dark dorsal stripes on a field of olive-gray to olive-green. The sides are somewhat lighter and there are two light lateral stripes. The venter has light spots. There are only 3 toes on each forefoot. The head is rather broad and the snout of this species is more rounded than that of *P. striatus*.

The juveniles seem similar to the adults in coloration.

Similar species The greater and lesser sirens have 4 toes on each hand. See also the account for the very similar *P. striatus* [65–67].

Behavior This is a very secretive, fully aquatic salamander. It seems inactive by day but does forage among the hyacinths, frogsbit, and water lettuce roots, or through the bottom detritus, by night. Additional studies into the life histories of all dwarf sirens are badly needed.

Comments Until critically looked at by Paul Moler and James Kezer in the early 1990s, the genus *Pseudobranchus* was thought to contain a single species with five subspecies. The Moler-Kezer work, based on chromosomal studies, disclosed that two species, one with two subspecies and the other with three, existed. Additional sampling and assessment of dwarf sirens on the southern peninsula is still needed.

64 THE EVERGLADES DWARF SIREN

Pseudobranchus a. belli

This is the more strongly patterned, smaller, southern subspecies. This 4–6 in. siren ranges southward from the latitude of northern Lake Okeechobee to the southern tip of the peninsula. Its venter is a nearly unicolored gray; the lateral stripe is buff, bordered on both top and bottom by a light stripe; the dorsum is dark (olive-black) and contains three lighter stripes. In our samplings, we have found this subspecies to be less easily found than the nominate form. Many hours of seining in the creeks and canals of southern Florida have produced only a couple of dozen specimens for us.

Dwarf sirens of both species were once coveted bass baits in central Florida. This use is seen less frequently today than only a decade ago.

65 SLENDER DWARF SIREN

Pseudobranchus striatus
spheniscus

Abundance Rather than rare, it seems probable that it is the secretive habits of this species that make it difficult to find. This subspecies ranges northward to southeastern Georgia from St. Lucie and Sarasota counties in Florida.

Habitat Acidic cypress pools and swamps in pine flatwoods are the preferred habitat of this salamander. It is found more often in the muck and detritus of pond bottoms than in floating vegetation.

Size At an adult length of 4–6 in., this diminutive subspecies vies for the title of smallest of the genus.

Reproduction This siren is believed to be an egg scatterer, but virtually nothing is known with certainty.

Coloration/pattern This is the most pallid of the *striatus* group. The dark middorsal field contains three rather poorly defined buff stripes. At each side of the dark vertebral area is a somewhat better defined light (yellowish) stripe, below which is an olive stripe, and below that a yellowish lateral stripe. The venter is gray(ish) with irregularly placed obscure light spots. There are only three toes on each forefoot. The head is narrow and the snout is wedge-shaped.

Similar species See the description of the very similar narrow-striped dwarf siren [63]. The lesser and greater sirens both have 4 toes on each forefoot.

Behavior The slender dwarf siren is an accomplished burrower in pond bottom detritus. Should its pond dry, it is capable of burrowing deeply and secreting a moisture-conserving, slime cocoon.

66 GULF HAMMOCK DWARF SIREN

Pseudobranchus s. lustricolus

Where is this salamander today?
Certainly it exists—or at least it existed until the
early 1950s. At that time both adult and hatchling
specimens were collected from hurricane-flooded
roadside ditches and overflow ponds in the Gulf
Hammock area (Citrus and Levy counties) of northwestern
peninsular Florida. It has not been found in more recent
decades, despite a precise knowledge of where it was found
and concerted efforts to locate it. This 8 in. long dwarf siren
is the most distinctively and contrastingly marked of the group. The
broad, dark dorsal stripe contains three precisely defined yellowish
stripes. In addition, there is an orange-buff dorsolateral and a silvery-
gray ventrolateral stripe on each side. The belly is dark. Other than a
precise appearance of both adults and hatchlings (the latter found in
mid-February in a cluster of more than 100 beneath a wateredge board
([Neill, 1951]), and the geographic area whence they came, we are left
with nothing but questions about the Gulf Hammock dwarf siren.

The illustration [66] depicts the pattern as it would be seen if
removed and flattened.

67 BROAD-STRIPED DWARF SIREN

Pseudobranchus s. striatus

This is the most northeasterly race.
It ranges southward from southeastern South
Carolina to extreme northeastern Florida. This race has
a dark back bordered by a rather broad, light line on
each side. A poorly defined, narrow, vertebral line is
present. An often difficult to discern, narrow, light, lateral
line is present on each side. The belly is rather prominently
reticulated or mottled. This dwarf siren is about 8 in. long.

The dwarf sirens are occasionally seen in aquarium
shops, but are more delicate than the members of the genus
Siren.

68 Eastern Lesser Siren

Siren intermedia intermedia

Abundance This is a common salamander that inhabits vegetation-choked waterways. It is found throughout most of mainland Florida, excluding the Everglades.

Habitat Slow rivers, ditches, canals, and cypress ponds are among the habitats of this eclectic salamander. Small specimens are often found in mats of hydrilla, hydrocotyl, frogsbit, and the roots of water lettuce and water hyacinth.

Size The eastern lesser siren is adult at 8–16 in. Although larger sizes are often mentioned, specimens of more than 12 in. are rare.

Reproduction The breeding biology of this and other sirens remains fraught with uncertainties. Godley (1983) reports the finding of two post-deposition female lesser sirens in a southwest Florida canal. One female was attending a nest of 206 eggs, the other guarded 381 eggs. The nests were about 12 ft from shore, on peat mats, beneath groupings of water hyacinths.

Coloration/pattern Only rarely is an adult eastern lesser siren olive or greenish in Florida. Rather, it is brown, bluish-brown, black or bluish-black. The spots, if present, are dark rather than light. The tailtip is rather narrowly pointed. Juveniles *may* be dark olive-green or olive-black but they also have dark spots. The hatchlings *may* have a red(dish) band on the sides of the head and across the top of the head. Lesser sirens have prominent external gills, 4 toes on the front feet, and the rear legs are lacking.

Similar species The greater siren has light (not dark) dorsal and lateral flecking. Dwarf sirens retain stripes throughout their lives and have only 3 toes on their forefeet.

Behavior This is a secretive burrower that seems to shun open-water situations. It is most commonly seen at night, particularly where aquatic vegetation is abundant and matted. It may occasionally be seen foraging at night in muddy and/or vegetated shallows. If the waterhole in which the lesser siren lives dries, the salamander burrows deeply into the mud and creates a multi-layered slime cocoon that prevents desiccation.

Comments The western lesser siren, *Siren i. nettingi,* is found almost to the Escambia River in eastern Alabama. This larger (to 20 in.) and

SALAMANDERS, NEWTS, AND SIRENS

125

more prominently spotted race may eventually be found in the Escambia drainage of Florida's western panhandle. The western lesser siren has light spots on its belly. Hatchling western lesser sirens have a light vertebral stripe and a light ventrolateral stripe on each side.

Lesser sirens live well in aquaria and are interesting, easily-cared-for creatures.

69 GREATER SIREN

Siren lacertina

Abundance The greater siren is common in rivers, canals, drainage ditches, and other such areas throughout the state of Florida.

Habitat The greater siren uses a variety of habitats. Although the adults may be residents of open-water situations, they are also found amid the snags, hydrilla, and spatterdock of Florida's drainage canals. Look for these salamanders in ponds, lakes, slow rivers, canals, water-filled ditches, and any other permanent or semi-permanent body of water. Hatchlings and juveniles are commonly found in mats of floating vegetation.

Size The greater siren is the second longest of Florida's salamanders, but may actually be the largest by weight. Adult greater sirens vary from 24–30 in. in length, and may occasionally exceed a yard. Although elongate, they are of robust build.

Reproduction Virtually nothing is known about the reproductive biology of this interesting salamander. It is thought that breeding occurs in late winter, that egg fertilization is external, and that the several hundred eggs are deposited in shallow-water situations. Greater sirens of less than 2 in. have been found in the early spring months in north Florida and in late winter in south Florida.

Coloration/pattern The ground color of the greater siren varies from brown to olive-green both dorsally and ventrally. The lower sides may be somewhat lighter than the dorsum. The back *may* be mottled with spots or bars of darker pigment. The sides are flecked with blue or green. Old, large specimens may be duller than younger animals. The external gills are prominent. The forelimbs are well-developed and used in a walking motion when the siren moves slowly. Each forefoot has 4 toes. The eyes lack lids. As with all sirens, rear limbs are lacking.

Hatchlings and juveniles have prominent light vertebral and lateral stripes, and a light chin, cheeks, and venter.

When non-regenerated, the compressed tailtip of the greater siren is rather bluntly rounded in profile.

Similar species The lesser siren tends to have a bluish cast to its brown body and has *dark* spots on the side and a much more sharply pointed tailtip.

Behavior This is a fully aquatic salamander that is often quiescent by day, but which forages actively under the cover of darkness. They may also be active on cloudy days and during periods of low barometric pressure. Greater sirens are often caught by fishermen and are generally, but unjustly, feared. Sirens bury deeply into the pond-bottom mud, create a moisture-retaining, multi-layered, slime cocoon, and become dormant when their ponds dry.

Comments This species reportedly makes "plaintive yelping sounds" when disturbed. If properly cared for, greater sirens will live for decades in an aquarium.

PERIPHERAL AMPHIBIANS

70 SPOTTED SALAMANDER

Ambystoma maculatum

Abundance The spotted salamander is a localized species that is usually seen only for the few days each year when it is on breeding migrations. It can be locally common. Known to occur a few miles north and/or west of the Florida state line in Alabama, this species will probably be found in Florida's northwestern panhandle.

Habitat The spotted salamander is associated with hardwood forests and woodlands. It breeds in ephemeral ponds and puddles.

Size Most adults are 5.5–7 in. long, with occasional specimens exceeding 8.5 in.

Reproduction The spotted salamander is a winter breeder. It is induced above ground and into breeding migrations by heavy rains (often of a warm front), which moderate winter temperatures. Males usually arrive at a pond first, and deposit spermatophores (stalked sperm packets) on pond-bottom litter such as leaves, sticks, and flat stones. Milling masses of males vie for the choicest deposition sites. The females, which arrive later, pick up the sperm packets with the cloacal labia, then deposit their egg masses on submerged sticks, heavy grasses, or other such sub-surface mounts. From 65 to more than 150 eggs are in a mass.

Depending on water temperature, eggs may take longer than a month to hatch. Again, varying by water temperature, development of the larvae can take from about 65 days to nearly twice that long.

Coloration/pattern The spotted salamander is black(ish) dorsally and gray ventrally. There is usually a double row of yellow to orange spots (sometimes orange on the head and yellow on the back) dorsally. Light blue flecks occur on the sides. Unspotted specimens have been found. The metamorphs have confusingly fragmented dorsal spots, but assume the normal markings within a few days.

Similar species The eastern tiger salamander, a rare species in Florida, has elongate or irregular spots and an irregular pattern. The lower sides and belly of the tiger salamander are often largely olive to yellowish.

Behavior Except during the few days of the year when they are in the breeding puddles, spotted salamanders are persistent burrowers. They may occasionally be found beneath ground litter (logs or rocks) during periods of wet weather when they are induced upwards. However, this is the exception rather than the norm.

Comments The spotted salamander is a member of the family Ambystomatidae. For general comments on this family, see page 89.

71 THREE-TOED AMPHIUMA

Amphiuma tridactylum

Abundance This species remains unknown in Florida but nears the state line both to the west and the north of the panhandle in Alabama.

Habitat This aquatic salamander occurs in a very wide range of aquatic habitats.

Size Slightly smaller than its two-toed relative, the three-toed amphiuma rarely exceeds 3 ft in length.

Reproduction The 150 or more eggs are laid beneath matted vegetation or other such material in a shallow-water depression. The nesting season for this species seems to be between mid-spring and late summer.

Coloration/pattern The dorsum of this large aquatic salamander is brown to brownish-gray. The venter is a light gray. There is a clear line of demarcation between the dorsal and the ventral colors. The snout is flattened, the eyes are lidless and non-protuberant, and there are 3 toes on each of the 4 tiny legs. The whole animal tends to dull for a few days prior to shedding. At that time the eyes appear bluish.

Similar species The two-toed amphiuma is very similar, but has only 2 toes on each foot and no clear line of demarcation between belly and dorsal colors. The one-toed amphiuma has a single toe on each foot and a convex, rather than concave, snout when seen in profile. Sirens lack rear legs and have external gills.

Behavior This is a secretive and nocturnal salamander that may be easily seen at night in shallow-water situations.

Comments For comments on the family Amphiumidae, see page 95.

REPTILES

It is believed that reptiles, of some obscure and poorly understood form, evolved from amphibian stock more than 315 million years ago, during the early Upper Carboniferous Period. The lineage of modern reptiles can be traced back some 280 million years to the Permian Era.

Extant today are some 6,600+ species belonging to more than 900+ genera, 48+ families, and 4 orders.

Reptiles, of course, include in their ranks species as diverse as 30-ft-long reticulated pythons, 20-ft-long salt-water crocodiles, 6-ft-long leatherback turtles, and 2-in.-long reef geckos.

Most reptiles are less dependent on moisture than amphibians, but all will dehydrate if sufficient moisture and/or humidity is not available to them. There are, though, those forms of reptiles that are entirely or mostly aquatic and cannot function out of water.

Reptiles are anatomically distinct from amphibians. They have scales (of some form) covering their skin, most have limbs, and if toes are present, claws usually are.

Of the four orders, three occur in Florida. One order, the Squamata, can be broken into three suborders, all of which have Floridian representatives.

Found in Florida are three species of crocodilians (order Crocodylia), 25 species of turtles and tortoises (order Chelonia), and 95 species of lizards, amphisbaenians, and snakes (order Squamata).

Squamata in Florida comprises the following three suborders:

44 species of snakes (suborder Serpentes)
50 species of lizards (suborder Sauria)
 1 species of worm lizard or amphisbaenid (suborder Amphisbaenia)

CROCODILIANS
Order Crocodylia—Alligators, Caiman, Crocodiles

The crocodilians are among the best known and most readily recognized of the reptiles. All, even the smallest, are comparatively immense, semi-aquatic creatures with osteoderm-protected backs and bony, broadly flattened, rounded (alligators and caiman) or variably pointed (crocodiles) snouts.

All are highly predaceous. American alligators and spectacled caiman are capable of overcoming and consuming sizable prey. American crocodiles prefer prey the size of a water bird or smaller. Male alligators and caiman are quite cannibalistic; females provide care and protection for nests and hatchlings. Vegetation is gathered by female American alligators and spectacled caiman into nest mounds; female American crocodiles dig a nest above the vegetation line in a low mound of scraped together sand and beach debris or merely in the beach sand. The female American crocodile provides less overall nest and hatchling protection, but does assist in the release of the hatchlings from the nest.

Alligators and caiman are more strongly dimorphic than crocodiles with the females the smaller sex.

Comparatively huge American alligators may survive in relatively small freshwater (usually) waterholes, which they sometimes widen and deepen. American crocodiles are creatures of tidally influenced estuarine areas. All crocodilians bask in the sunlight extensively. They are active both by day and after nightfall.

All have a strongly developed homing instinct. Relocated "problem" specimens will return time and again to their home territory.

Both the American alligator and the American crocodile are protected in Florida; the introduced spectacled caiman is not. American alligators have caused human fatalities in Florida. Extreme care should be used when you are near large specimens.

These reptiles all have voices. During the nesting season adults may be more irascible than at other times.

Representatives of two families occur in Florida. These are:

Family Alligatoridae—Alligators and Caiman

Family Crocodylidae—Crocodiles

How to Find Alligators, Caiman, and Crocodiles

All crocodilians are normally restricted to the vicinity of permanent water. Alligators are *abundant* in most state and federal parks in Florida. They can also be seen basking on sunny days on the sides of many, if not most, sizable road-paralleling canals, along rivers and near favored fishing holes. They can be dangerous. Do not approach large 'gators. At night, females may be unseen but in attendance of babies. Do not molest any alligator. Feeding or catching them is in violation of state and/or federal laws.

Caiman are secretive and difficult to find. They are established only along a few canals in Dade and Broward counties, but are reportedly expanding their range.

American crocodiles are occasionally seen in the Everglades National Park, Florida Bay, or Crocodile Lake National Wildlife Refuge, on northern Key Largo. Specimens are occasionally seen 100 (or more) miles farther northward.

Crocodilians may be found by their eyeshine at night. Look into swamps and rivers at night while holding a flashlight at eye level. You may be pleased to see the red reflections from their eyes shining back at you.

ALLIGATORS AND CAIMAN
Family Alligatoridae

These are the broad-snouted representatives of the order. The American alligator, once made uncommon by skin-trade hunting, is now common again in Florida.

72 AMERICAN ALLIGATOR

Alligator mississippiensis

Abundance The American alligator is now a common to abundant species that occurs in every county in Florida.

Habitat Although this is primarily a freshwater species, alligators are occasionally encountered in estuarine or saltwater habitats. It may be seen in and along ponds, canals, lakes, rivers, large streams, borrow pits, swamps, and marshes or virtually any other water-retaining habitat.

Size Females seldom exceed 8 ft; males attain 11 ft. The reported record size is 19 ft 2 in. (but this is now suspect). Hatchlings are about 9.5 in. A male measuring 14 ft was recently taken in central Florida by GFC permitted hunters.

Reproduction This is a mound-nesting crocodilian. From 20–50+ eggs are laid annually. Breeding males and nesting females can both be irascible and dangerous to approach. Hatching occurs after 65–75 days of incubation.

Coloration/pattern This is the darkest colored of our crocodilians. Babies are black with yellow crossbands. Adults are dull in color and contrast, often being largely or entirely a dusky olive-black. If yellow markings are retained, they will be most prominent on the sides. The snout is bluntly rounded.

Voice Babies produce a high-pitched grunt. Adults voice muffled, spluttering, roars.

Similar species Both the spectacled caiman and the American crocodile are olive-green or olive-gray with dark (not yellow) crossbands, have narrower snouts and are likely to be seen only in extreme southern Florida. American crocodiles are most apt to be encountered in brackish or saltwater habitats.

Behavior Shy when unfamiliar with humans, alligators accustomed to the presence of humans can become dangerous nuisances. During the breeding and nesting seasons, alligators of both sexes can be more adversarial than normal. Females may protect both the eggs and young. Normal prudence dictates steering clear of any large crocodilian. Household pets and small children are more at risk than an adult.

Comments Do not feed or otherwise "tame" these potentially dangerous creatures. Call the closest office of the Florida Game and Freshwater Fish Commission to report nuisance alligators.

ALLIGATORS AND CROCODILES

133

73 SPECTACLED CAIMAN

Caiman crocodilus crocodilus

Abundance Rare and of very localized
distribution in Florida. Breeding populations occur in
Dade County and possibly in Monroe County, Florida.
Feral, non-breeding specimens may occasionally be
encountered anywhere in South Florida. This race of the
spectacled caiman is native to much of northern South
America.

Habitat This is a secretive crocodilian of freshwater
marshes and heavily vegetated pond, lake, and canal edges.

Size Although in tropical America the spectacled caiman occasionally attains an 8-ft length, Florida specimens seldom exceed 6 ft. Hatchlings are about 8.5 in. long.

Reproduction In summer 10–40 eggs are laid in a temperature-stabilizing mound nest. Large females produce the largest clutches. Incubation is of variable duration but in south Florida seems in the 75–95-day range. Hatchlings are more contrastingly patterned than the adults.

Coloration/pattern Hatchlings of this "small" crocodilian are banded with very dark brown on a dark olive ground. The overall color darkens and the pattern obscures with advancing age and size. A curved ridge extends across the snout connecting the anterior extreme of both eyelids. The snout of the spectacled caiman is moderately sharp.

Voice Hatchlings produce a high-pitched grunt. This deepens in tone as the size of the caiman increases. Adult males produce a muffled, grunting roar.

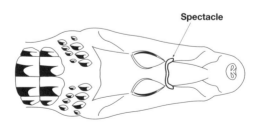

Spectacle

Of the Florida crocodilians, only the spectacled caiman has the ridge across the snout.

Similar species American alligators are black with yellow banding. American crocodiles are colored similarly to the caiman but have a sharper nose and are usually in estuarine habitats.

Behavior Although comparatively small and secretive, spectacled caiman are feisty if cornered. Even babies will bite sharply if molested.

Comments Following the protection of the American alligator, the spectacled caiman was imported in vast numbers for the pet trade.

"Specs" are a temperature-sensitive creature that, if caught away from relatively warm water, can be immobilized or killed by even a short freeze.

Many "pet" specimens have escaped and more have been deliberately released into Florida's canal systems. Obviously, some of these have acclimated and thrived.

CROCODILES
Family Crocodylidae

In general, these are the most narrow-snouted of the crocodilians. Although some of the world's crocodilians are confirmed maneaters (Africa's Nile and Australia's saltwater crocodiles, for example) the American crocodile in Florida is a shy creature that is usually difficult to find. The population in the state reportedly hovers at about 500 animals, and this species is protected by both state and federal legislation.

74 AMERICAN CROCODILE

Crocodylus acutus

Abundance Rare and local, this magnificent crocodilian occurs only in extreme southern Florida (Dade and Monroe counties, northward to Charlotte County on the Gulf Coast) including the Keys. This species may also be found in the West Indies, Mexico, Central America, and northwestern South America.

Habitat This is primarily a species of estuarine situations, brackish canals, mangrove flats, and saltwater habitats.

Size Hatchlings are about 10 in. in total length. Adults in Florida, the northernmost area of their range, attain 8–12 ft in total length. In South America, the American crocodile may attain a larger size than in Florida.

Reproduction Female American crocodiles may scrape together a nest mound of beach debris and sand or simply nest in a hole dug in the beach sand. From 20–50+ eggs are laid. Incubation takes about 3 months. Females assist in the escape of the young from the nest, may carry the young to the water, but offer no further maternal assistance.

Coloration/pattern The ground coloration of this crocodilian is olive-brown to dark olive-green. The cross bands are darker (not yellow). Small specimens are more contrastingly patterned than large ones. The snout is slender and tapering. The upper jaw is notched anteriorly, causing the fourth tooth of the lower jaw to be permanently visible.

Voice Recent hatchlings produce a high-pitched croaking grunt but specimens of more than a few weeks of age seldom vocalize.

Similar species The American alligator is black with yellow cross bands and has a bluntly rounded snout. The spectacled caiman is colored somewhat like the crocodile but occurs in freshwater habitats and has a more bluntly rounded snout.

Behavior This is a shy, quiet, and normally inoffensive crocodile. It seems less potentially aggressive toward humans than a similarly sized American alligator. But with that said, it is still prudent to avoid close contact with large crocodiles. This is a federally endangered reptile. Do not molest it.

Comments Studies into nesting successes and population stability in the state of Florida continue. Recently, one or more large crocodiles have begun wintering on Sanibel Island in Lee County. This is a fully protected reptile species.

AMPHISBAENIANS
Order Squamata; Suborder Amphisbaenia

WORM LIZARDS
Family Amphisbaenidae

Despite the fact that they are not true lizards, the amphisbaenians have long been referred to as such. These are specialized burrowers with the scales arranged in rings (annuli) that make the creatures look annulated like an earthworm. There are many representatives in the subtropical and tropical parts of the world, but (despite long-existing rumors of a second species) only a single *known* species in the United States.

Except for 3 Mexican species that have forelimbs, the amphisbaenians are limbless. None have functional eyes.

How to Find Worm Lizards

Unless driven from their burrows by heavy rains, worm lizards almost never come to the surface of the ground. They can be found by raking fallen leaves from atop a sandy substrate and by brushing sand and debris from near the base of sand-scrub plants. Worm lizards are often less than 1 in. beneath the surface of the soil.

LIZARDS

75 FLORIDA WORM LIZARD

Rhineura floridana

Abundance Because of its burrowing habits, the population statistics of this little creature are difficult to assess with accuracy. It is probably not rare, but is infrequently seen. Worm lizards occur in sandy habitats, throughout much of the Florida peninsula north of Lake Okeechobee. Because of the finding of a worm lizard in southern Georgia, this species can no longer be considered a Florida endemic.

Habitat Sandy, easily burrowed soils are preferred by this interesting species.

Size Most specimens range from 6–12 in. in length. Very occasional specimens of more than 14 in. have been reported.

Reproduction Little is known about the breeding biology of the worm lizard. Females with 1–3 fully formed oviducal eggs have been found in the summer. It is thought (but not confirmed) that from 60–90 days are required for incubation.

Coloration/pattern The worm lizard varies from pale sandy pink to a very bright pink. The nose and tail often appear the brightest. This species has no limbs and no functional eyes. The head is wedge-shaped, and the short tail is studded dorsally with conical tubercles. The lower jaw is countersunk, preventing sand from getting into the mouth.

Similar species This is the only annulated reptile in Florida.

Behavior The lifestyle and behavior of the worm lizard can be summed up in one short statement: "It is a persistent and obligate burrower."

Comments During the spring worm lizards are frequently found beneath leaf litter during gardening operations. They may be plowed to the surface during commercial planting activities. They also seem to near the surface when the weather begins to cool in the autumn. Burrow-innundating rains can force amphisbaenians to surface at any time of the year.

Rumors that the Baja two-footed worm lizard, *Bipes biporus*, has been released in Florida have long existed. Accounts of a two-legged lizard being occasionally found in central Florida have been recounted by gardeners and others. Thus far, no Florida specimens have reached museum collections or herpetologists.

LIZARDS
Suborder Sauria (Lacertilia)

Worldwide, the suborder sauria contains more than 3,800 species in about 400 genera and 24+ families.

They are all scaled, most have functional limbs with clawed feet (but some are legless), and many have functional eyes with lids. Others have functional eyes protected by a transparent, spectacle-like brille rather than by lids; yet others lack functional eyes.

Lizards vary in size from the massive 9 ft of the Komodo dragon to the minuteness and delicacy of some 1.5 in. geckos that dwell among the litter of forest floors in the neotropics.

In Florida there are 50 species in 6 families. These are

Family Agamidae—Agamids	(2 species)
Family Anguidae—Glass Lizards	(4 species)
Family Gekkonidae—Geckos	(13 species)
Family Iguanidae—Iguanas	(20 species)
Family Scincidae—Skinks	(7 species)
Family Teiidae—Racerunners and Whiptails	(4 species)

Counting all subspecies in these 6 diverse families, we learn that, at present, we have 57 varieties (species, subspecies, and distinct color phases). Of this number 17 species (22 subspecies) are native. The remaining 33 species (35 subspecies and morphs) are introduced, alien species. Most of the aliens are restricted to the southern peninsula, with Dade County being the epicenter. The native species range far more widely, with many being found over the entire peninsula and some being found over the entire state. Most are very typical in appearance, having fully functional legs, ears and eyes, and a long tail. However, the 4 species of glass lizards lack limbs. As an escape mechanism, the tail of most Florida lizards is easily broken. The tails of some actually have fracture planes in the caudal vertebrae to facilitate the breaking (termed autotomization). In most cases the tails quickly regrow, but the bone is replaced by cartilage and the shape and scalation differ from the original. Our native lizards are all diurnal to crepuscular. Several of the introduced gecko species are nocturnal.

How to Find Lizards in Florida

The lizard fauna of Florida may be conveniently divided into six non-technical groups. There are diurnal lizards and nocturnal lizards and of these there are those that inhabit natural areas and those that are more or less restricted to the vicinity of human habitations and arboreal or terrestrial forms.

The introduced geckos are all associated with dwellings or warehouse complexes. They may be found at night with the aid of a flashlight (get permission to prowl!). The introduced anoles are usually found in similar settings but are active on sunny days and are more apt than the geckos to colonize roadside trees. In most cases, permission should still be sought to prowl through suburban neighborhoods. Most of the introduced geckos and anoles are restricted in distribution to Dade, Monroe, and Lee counties.

All three species of introduced iguanas and the brown basilisk are also most common in Dade and Monroe counties, but are most often found in parks, fields, and along canals. Look for them on non-breezy, sunny days.

Most glass lizards and skinks are burrowers in open woodlands and sandhills. Raking the sand from around shrubs and turning debris may divulge some specimens. Our spiny lizards and racerunners also occur in these areas but will be seen either running on the surface of the sand or climbing in shrubs or trees.

Check piles of construction rubble in Dade County for curly-tails, brown anoles, and many geckos.

The following short list of selected terms may help when you read the lizard sections. Additional terms may be found in the glossary at the end of this guide.

Autotomize—having the ability to break off the tail with little or no external assistance.

Dichromatic—color differences in a species. Often sex linked.

Dimorphism—Color or morphological differences within the same species. Often sex linked.

Fracture planes—naturally weakened areas in the bones of the tail of some lizards that permit easy tail breakage.

Lamellae—the divided pads on the bottoms of the toes of geckos and anoles.

Ocelli—round or oval, eyelike spots.

Parthenogenesis—the ability to lay viable eggs without benefit of fertilization. Some geckos and whiptails are examples.

SVL—snout-vent length.

AGAMIDS
Family Agamidae

The family Agamidae contains myriad diverse Old World lizards that roughly parallel the old family Iguanidae (before its breakup) in habits and habitats. However, none of the agamids attain the large size of the true iguanas.

The two agamas now present in Florida are both pet trade species. One, the red-headed agama, dwells amidst rocky aridland habitats in Africa. The habitat of the second, the variable tree agama, is indicated by this lizard's common name. It is an Asian species.

When suitably warmed and if healthy, both species are very alert, very active, very fast, and very difficult to approach.

A third species of agama, the little spiny agama, *A. hispida,* from South Africa, has been found on a single vacant lot in Dade County. It has shown no evidence of expanding its range, hence it is not discussed further.

76 AFRICAN RED-HEADED AGAMA

Agama agama

Abundance An East African species, the red-headed agama is known from two suburban areas in Broward County, and one in Dade, Florida. There it is commonly seen within a several block radius of its release point. Whether it will spread farther or succumb to climatic conditions that are very different from its native habitat is unknown.

Habitat These lizards may be seen climbing trees, on the cinder block walls of houses and property barriers, amid rubble piles, and in similar habitats.

Size Males attain a foot in length, females are somewhat smaller.

Reproduction *Agama agama* routinely produces 2 or 3 clutches of up to 20 eggs each. Normal clutch size varies from 8–15. Hatchlings are only rarely seen in Florida.

Coloration/pattern This lizard is both geographically and populationally variable *and* dimorphic. At an optimum temperature, non-stressed males in nuptial coloring have brilliant orange heads, a bluish gray to charcoal dorsum, a vertebral keel, an orange vertebral stripe,

LIZARDS

and a light venter. Non-breeding, stressed, or cool males are paler and may lack the orange on the head. Females and juveniles are clad in yellows or earthen tones dorsally, are lighter beneath, and have at least traces of dorsal barring. Breeding females may have an orangish or a bluish blush to the head and a bluish blush on the limbs.

Red-headed agamas are slightly flattened, and heavily gravid females become enormously enlarged.

Similar species There are no similar lizards in Florida.

Behavior *A. agama* often thermoregulate while facing the sun. These lizards are active, agile, and wary. Sun-warmed lizards are more brightly colored than cool ones. These lizards are inactive on cloudy days but seem able to thermoregulate sufficiently to allow a normal lifestyle on cool but sunny days.

Comments The fact that both colonies of the red-headed agama are in close proximity to reptile dealerships discloses the lizard's origin.

77 INDOCHINESE TREE AGAMA

Calotes mystaceus

Abundance There seem to be at least two small colonies of this Asian agamid in Florida. One is in Okeechobee County, the other in Glades County.

Habitat Both in their natural habitat and in Florida, these are persistently arboreal lizards. They descend to fenceposts and even curbstones to sun and bask, but are alert and quick to dart to safety (often into the trees) when approached.

Size Because of their slenderness, these lizards tend to look smaller than their 15 in. overall length.

Reproduction Females lay 7–15+ eggs. They reportedly are able to double clutch. The incubation duration is in the vicinity of 70 days. Few hatchlings have been reported from Florida, but the colonies have been extant for several years, indicating at least some recruitment has occurred.

Coloration/pattern The color of these lizards varies geographically and populationally. Males of those in Florida have a grayish body and a variably blue head. During the breeding season the throat may become orangish. Females tend to be brownish with both darker crossbars and longitudinal dorsolateral stripes. A black shoulder spot is present, as is a prominent crest, strongest anteriorly.

Similar species In contrast to the rather stocky, depressed red-headed agama, the variable tree agama is a slender, attenuate species.

Behavior Although these lizards bask and forage close to the ground, they quickly ascend trees when frightened. They are alert, agile, and difficult to approach when suitably warm.

Comments Both known colonies of these lizards are in the proximity of pet dealerships. It is thought that escapees from the pet trade gave origin to both colonies. This species is also referred to in the pet trade as a "bloodsucker."

GLASS LIZARDS
Family Anguidae

The lizard family Anguidae is represented in Florida by four rather similar appearing legless species called glass lizards. It may be necessary to have the lizard in hand, where you can check the positioning of the dark lateral stripes to assure their identifications. Three of the four species are rather well known, the fourth, the mimic glass lizard, has only recently been described. Three of the four species occur over most of the state whereas one, again the mimic glass lizard, seems restricted to the panhandle and extreme northeastern Florida.

All of our glass lizards are oviparous. Females provide parental care throughout the incubation period.

The anguids are often referred to as lateral fold lizards, a reference to the longitudinal expansion fold found from nape to vent on most species.

Despite the superficial similarity of glass lizards to snakes, there are some important differences. Glass lizards have functional eyelids and ear openings (snakes have neither), and the glass lizards do not have the enlarged belly scales so characteristic of most snakes. Because of the presence of osteoderms (bony plates beneath each epidermal scale), the glass lizards lack the sinuosity and suppleness of snakes.

The glass lizards have very long tails, and three of the four species possess caudal fracture planes (a weakened area in a caudal vertebra to facilitate ready breakage). The island glass lizard lacks fracture planes. The tail of the three species with fracture planes regenerates well and almost fully. The tail of the island glass lizard does not.

Ophisaurus attenuatus longicaudus

Abundance Although the eastern slender glass lizard may be found nearly throughout the state of Florida, it is absent from wetlands, uncommon in some seemingly ideal habitats, but common to abundant in others.

Habitat This is a species of sandy pine and oak scrub woodlands, uplands with yielding soils, field edges, and other similar habitats. It does not prefer perpetually wet habitats. Although it is fully capable of burrowing, it does so less persistently than other glass lizards.

Size Adult eastern slender glass lizards range in size from 2–3 ft. The record size for this glass lizard is an even 3.5 ft.

Reproduction Between 5 (small females) and 20 (large females) eggs are laid. The nesting site chosen is often beneath clumps of field or

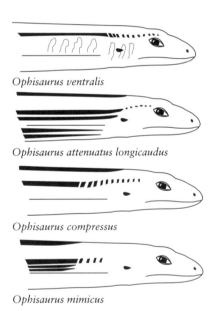

Ophisaurus ventralis

Ophisaurus attenuatus longicaudus

Ophisaurus compressus

Ophisaurus mimicus

Comparisons of the lateral striping of the glass lizards; eastern (top), eastern slender (center top), island (center bottom), mimic (bottom).

wire grass or beneath man-made debris. The female remains in attendance of the clutch throughout the 48–65-day incubation.

Coloration/pattern Similar to other Florida glass lizards in coloration, the slender glass lizard is the only one of the four to have dark ventrolateral stripes (stripes *below* the lateral groove). The uppermost and heaviest of the dorsolateral stripes may continue uninterruptedly onto the back of the head. If a vertebral stripe is present, it is best defined on young specimens. The ventrolateral stripes may be more poorly defined than those above the groove, but they are present. The dorsal color is a warm sandy brown, the venter is lighter. Some degree of ontogenetic changes occur. With advancing age the longitudinal pattern often fades and is replaced by anterior crossbarring and stippling. There is a series of dark outlined, light, vertical bars beginning beneath the eye and continuing onto the neck and anterior body. These often number from 7–9. The length of the tail is about twice that of the SVL.

Similar species See the following accounts for the other three species of glass lizards. The scales of the Florida worm lizard are in whorls and it lacks functional eyes.

Behavior This is an alert lizard that allows close approach but will thrash wildly if actually restrained. It is often seen crossing sandy country roadways in the late afternoon or early evening, or during or following daytime showers.

Comments Although once you have become familiar with the overall appearance of the different species of glass lizards you will probably become adept at separating them, initially a comparison of intensity, completeness, and positioning of the dark striping will be necessary.

79 ISLAND GLASS LIZARD

Ophisaurus compressus

Abundance Locally common, but seemingly uncommon overall, and easily overlooked. The island glass lizard occurs in suitable habitat throughout peninsular Florida. It appears to be absent west of the panhandle's Franklin County.

Habitat This is a resident of sandy habitats. It shuns perpetually wet situations but may be present in some numbers in the drier pine-oak scrubland above ephemeral ponds.

Size This is one of the two small species of glass lizards in Florida. The island glass lizard is adult at 16–22 in.

Reproduction Up to 12 eggs may be laid by large females in a moisture retaining nesting site. This may be amid the roots of bunch grasses or beneath debris or ground litter. The females remain with the clutch through the 45–65-day incubation period.

Coloration/pattern This species undergoes considerable age-related pattern change. Young specimens are prominently striped for their entire length. Anteriorly, older specimens become vaguely crossbarred and stippled. A vertebral stripe *may* be present. There is a single heavy lateral stripe. There are no stripes below the lateral groove. The unmarked venter is cream to white. Young specimens have a series of 7 to 10 prominent *dark* (not *dark-edged*) vertical markings posterior to the ear-opening. These obscure with advancing age. This species lacks caudal fracture planes. Although the tail will break, it does not readily do so and tail regeneration is comparatively imperfect.

Similar species See species accounts for the other three species of glass lizards. The legless Florida worm lizard has no functional eyes.

Behavior This is a nervous glass lizard that in warm weather may be seen crossing roadways in sandy areas in the late afternoon or at dusk. It is very difficult to find at other times.

Comments In one small area of inland Lee County, we found island glass lizards with regularity in the late spring and early summer between the evening hours of 7:30 and 8:30. Despite extensive searching in the area, we found none at other times. Had we not happened on the window of surface activity, we would not have suspected the presence of the lizards. This leads us to wonder about (but absolutely not discount) statements that the island glass lizard is an uncommon species.

80 Mimic Glass Lizard

Ophisaurus mimicus

Abundance This rather newly discovered, small, glass lizard is seemingly uncommon. It is known to range across much of Florida's panhandle and also occurs in Nassua County.

Habitat This is another of the glass lizards that prefers sandy habitats. Although much about it remains conjectural, it is thought to be a species of sandy but seasonally wet pine flatwoods as well as of open woodlands.

Size Most specimens seen are in the 16–20 in. range, but mimic glass lizards are known to slightly exceed 24 in. in total length.

Reproduction This is an oviparous species, but little else is known about its reproductive biology. It is probable that the clutch size does not exceed 12 and that the female remains in attendance throughout the incubation period. The life history of this species is badly in need of research.

Coloration/pattern The mimic glass lizard is clad dorsally in earthen tones and ventrally in an immaculate off-white. It has a dark vertebral stripe of variable definition (usually best-defined posteriorly) and a series of 3 or 4 dark side stripes—*above* the lateral groove. The uppermost of these is the most prominent. There are *no* stripes *below* the lateral fold. About 7 vertical bars occur posterior to the ear-opening. The bars are predominantly dark but may have narrow white centers. Indication of bars (or spots) between the eye and the ear-opening may be visible. The tail vertebrae have fracture planes. It is expected, therefore, that the tail autotomizes with comparative ease.

Similar species The slender glass lizard has stripes *below* the lateral groove. Besides its vertebral stripe, the island glass lizard has only *one* stripe on each side. Eastern glass lizards of all ages lack a well defined vertebral stripe. See the accounts for the three other species of glass lizards. Especially note the description of the eastern slender glass lizard [78]. The Florida worm lizard has no functional eyes.

Behavior Mimic glass lizards may be seen crossing roads in the early morning and late afternoon hours. They seem particularly visible on dirt country roads and may be seen in some numbers on hot afternoons following a shower. They allow close approach but not actual restraint.

Comments Many questions remain about this rather recently described species. Its existence was learned of when museum specimens of the genus were being examined. This species was so similar to the slender glass lizard in appearance that it had been overlooked. Because of this similarity, when described, it was given the specific name of *mimicus*—the mimic glass lizard.

81 Eastern Glass Lizard

Ophisaurus ventralis

Abundance This is the most abundant, least habitat specific, and commonest of the glass lizards. It occurs throughout Florida.

Habitat The eastern glass lizard may be found both in moist and dry habitats. It seems as abundant in grassy suburban yards as in the woodlands and wetlands with which it is often associated.

Size Most examples seen are in the 19–28 in. length range. Very occasional specimens near 36 in., and the record size is 42⅝ in.

Reproduction More than 15 eggs can be laid by large female eastern glass lizards. The incubation duration varies from 56–70 days, being the longest when temperatures are cool. The nesting site is beneath a log, trash, leaf mat, grass clump or some other moisture retaining debris. Females remain with the clutch until hatching.

Coloration/pattern Striking ontogenetic changes occur. Young specimens are often an olive tan with two prominent dark dorsolateral lines. The venter is yellowish. At adulthood the stripes fade, a suffusion of turquoise or green appears dorsally, and the venter turns a rather bright yellow. Dark spots develop on the rear of the dorsal scales and light spots on the lateral scales. At no stage in the life of this lizard are there dark lines below the lateral fold. The tail is very easily broken.

Similar species This is the only of our glass lizards to appear turquoise or greenish when adult. See the accounts for the three other species of glass lizard. The smaller, Florida worm lizard lacks functional eyes.

Behavior This big and pretty lizard is often seen poking its head up from beneath the recumbent stems of freshly watered lawn grasses or basking on sidewalks or road-edges on cool mornings. It is the only of the four glass lizards to be regularly associated with damp marsh, swamp, and canal edge situations. It also occurs in fairly dry, open woodlands, but usually seeks moister habitats than those sought by its congeners.

Comments This is the bulkiest and most commonly seen species of glass lizard in Florida. It may occasionally be seen in some numbers, late on summer afternoons, lying at pavement edge on rural roadways.

GECKOS
Family Gekkonidae

With a single exception, the geckos of Florida are of introduced status. The exception is the the Florida reef gecko, *Sphaerodactylus n. notatus,* one of the least conspicuous of species.

All that are commonly seen are house geckos (genus *Hemidactylus*) or wall geckos (genus *Tarentola*), and with increasing frequency, the gigantic tokay gecko, *Gekko gecko.*

Because the geckos of Florida are, with but two exceptions, nocturnal, they have essentially filled a niche unexploited by our native lizards. The two exceptions to the pattern of nocturnality are the diurnal yellow-headed gecko, *Gonatodes albigularis fuscus* and the giant day gecko, *Phelsuma madagascariensis grandis.* Many geckos are closely tied to human habitations, where they hunt insects in the glow of porch or street lights. All but one (again, the yellow-headed gecko) have distended toepads, which allow them to climb even smooth surfaces agilely. The toe pads are more complex than they might seem. The pads are transversely divided into a series of lamellae that contain vast numbers of tiny bristle-like setae. The setae are tipped with an equally vast number of microscopic, non-skid, suction cups. To fully appreciate the complexity of these climbing devices, simply watch the way a slowly moving gecko curls its toes upwards when disengaging a foot.

All Florida geckos lack functional eyelids, their eyes being instead protected with a clear spectacle (the brille).

All are cold-sensitive. Most are restricted to the southern half of the peninsula, but two species of house geckos are now found throughout the state.

Geckos are among the few lizards with a voice. These range in volume from the difficult to hear squeaks of the tiny house geckos to the loud, two-syllabled, advertisement calls of the foot-long tokay.

All geckos have an easily broken tail. Some species are capable of autotomizing their tail with little, if any, external help. A great many geckos seen in the field have a partially to fully regenerated tail. These always differ in scalation and appearance from the originals.

Male geckos are territorial at all times, but are especially so during the breeding season. Serious skirmishes can occur if two males meet and one does not quickly back down. A gecko's skin is thin and can be easily torn free, often permitting an attacked gecko to escape a predator. A gecko's skin also heals quickly.

Because they are the most visible, the geckos with which most Floridians are familiar are the various "house geckos" of the genus

Hemidactylus. Called "house geckos" because of their fondness for buildings, these little lizards become active at twilight and may gather around lit porch (or other) lights to prey on insects drawn to the glow. There are now four species (two warty and two smooth-scaled) of the genus *Hemidactylus* established in Florida. Two of these, *H. turcicus,* the Mediterranean gecko, and *H. garnotii,* the Indo-Pacific gecko, have now expanded their ranges to other southern states as well. The various *Hemidactylus* species seem to be successfully successful in their efforts at colonization, and where once the Mediterranean reigned supreme, it has now been replaced in many areas by the newer establishees. All of the "hemis" are quite capable of strong color changes. They are darker and (often) more heavily patterned by day, lighter and less contrastingly patterned by night.

82 ASIAN FLAT-TAILED GECKO

Cosymbotus platyurus

Abundance Rare. This gecko is known to occur only on a warehouse complex in Pinellas County, FL, and on two warehouse complexes in Lee County, FL.

Habitat In Florida, *C. platyurus* is very much a house gecko.

Size The flat-tailed gecko is adult at about 3.5 in. in overall length.

Reproduction Little is known about the reproductive biology of this gecko in Florida. Because eggs have not been found on the outer walls of the warehouse complexes these geckos populate, it is thought that these are deposited in protected areas inside the buildings. It is probable that adult females lay several clutches of two eggs each during the summer months. Extrapolating from house geckos of the genus *Hemidactylus,* we may guess that the incubation duration for *Cosymbotus platyurus* is between 40–50 days.

Coloration/pattern *C. platyurus* is a flattened (depressed) gecko. Its broad tail has serrate edges and there are skin flanges on the sides of its body and rear legs. When the lateral flanges are spread outward, this little lizard casts little if any shadow, hence is nearly invisible against many natural backgrounds. The toes are partially webbed and the digits greatly expanded distally. The pupils are vertically oriented. Like many geckos, *Cosymbotus* is quite capable of changing its color. They are often lighter at night, at times appearing a unicolored, pasty cream. By day, however, they may be quite dark with numerous even darker bands.

Voice Male *Cosymbotus* produce a series of clicks as "advertisement" calls or an easily heard, high-pitched squeak if distressed.

Similar species See the species accounts for the four species of house geckos (pages 153–158). *Cosymbotus platyurus* has more extensive webbing on the feet and a more flattened countenance than the house geckos. However, it is not an easily identified species.

Behavior *C. platyurus* is persistently arboreal. It easily colonizes disturbed areas and is quite common in areas with extensive human populations.

Comments Despite being established in Florida for a decade or more, this gecko's very limited distribution and failure to disperse prompt us to consider it a tenuous introduction at best.

83 TOKAY GECKO

Gekko gecko

Abundance This rather firmly established species occurs in many areas of southern Florida. Tokays have been found in Lee, Hillsborough, Palm Beach, Broward, Collier, Dade, and Monroe counties.

Habitat In southern Florida, where the benign, subtropical climate allows the species to survive in the wild, tokays have expanded their ranges from the original points of release to neighboring structures. In urban areas they may now be seen and heard in shade trees and palms, power poles, and other such habitats.

Size Not only is the tokay gecko the largest gecko species in Florida, it is one of the largest species in the world. Although often smaller, specimens nearing a foot in length are frequently encountered.

Reproduction The hard-shelled, paired, adhesive-shelled eggs are deposited in secluded areas of buildings, tree hollows, or other like spots. With her hind feet the female manipulates the eggs into the spot she has chosen. Wet and pliable when laid, the calcareous, moderately adhesive eggshell soon dries, holding the eggs in the desired spot. Each female may lay several clutches annually. The young exceed 3 in. at hatching. Communal nestings occur.

GECKOS

Coloration/pattern These predaceous lizards are unmistakably colored, having orange and white markings against a gray or blue-gray ground color. The protuberant eyes may vary from yellow-green to orange. The pupils are complex and vertically elliptical. The toepads are large and easily visible.

Voice The loud, sharp "geck-o, geck-o, geck-o-o-ooo" calls of the males of the Tokay gecko resound on warm spring and summer nights from areas of seclusion in and on buildings, shade trees, and other such locations. Their two-syllabled calls begin with a chuckle, evolve into a series of "geck-os" or "to-kays," and end in lengthened, slurred notes.

Behavior These big geckos are primarily nocturnal, but may thermoregulate in sunny areas on mornings following cool nights. Tokays are well able to overpower and consume other lizards, frogs, insects, and other arthropods, but may also accept nestling birds and rodents as well. If threatened with capture, tokays open their mouths widely, "growl" with a drawn out "Gecccck" and, if hard pressed, will jump towards the offending object and bite. They often retain their grip with a bulldog-like tenacity, tightening up at intervals to convince you that they're still there. Although the consequences of a tokay bite are not serious (hardly more than any other prolonged pinch), it can be a frightening encounter for an unsuspecting person.

Comments For years tokays have been a mainstay of the pet industry. In the usually misguided assumption that they will rid their dwellings of roaches, people have released the big geckos in residences and office complexes throughout much of the USA. Such free-ranging indoor tokays often succumb to a lack of available water.

84 Yellow-Headed Gecko

Gonatodes albogularis fuscus

Abundance A native of the West Indies and Latin America, the yellow-headed gecko was introduced both in and near Miami and on the Keys. They were once quite common in both areas. However, they now seem uncommon in most of their mainland range and seem increasingly so on the Florida Keys

Habitat These geckos are often seen hanging from the underside of low, large diameter, rough-barked, horizontal limbs. They are also found in rock and rubble piles and behind exfoliating tree bark.

Size This is one of the smallest of geckos. Adults attain a length of only 3.25 in.

Reproduction Unlike most other geckos, which produce eggs in pairs, the yellow-head lays only a single egg at a time. Each reproductively active female can produce several eggs annually. Incubation duration is a few days more than two months. Hatchlings are about 1.25 in. long.

Coloration/pattern The yellow-head has round pupils and lacks toepads. Very dimorphic, it is only the dark-bodied males (with a bluish sheen, especially at night) that have the yellow (or yellowish) head. A dark shoulder spot, sometimes outlined with blue, is also borne by males. The male's tail may also be yellow and if not regenerated will have a white tip. The colors are heightened during the breeding season. The females are little grayish lizards that often display a rather pronounced lighter collar. Hatchlings are banded with yellow on a gray ground.

Voice None.

Behavior The yellow-head also differs from other Florida geckos by being almost exclusively diurnal in its activity patterns.

Comments Although the yellow-headed gecko is known to have been present in Florida for nearly 60 years, it was once more common than it now is. A major population in Coconut Grove (Dade County) seems extirpated. Although it is still present on Key West and Stock Island, these populations, too, seem reduced. Although if we make a concerted effort we can usually still see these beautiful West Indian lizards, we no longer feel their continued presence in Florida assured.

These little geckos are extremely wary and difficult to approach.

85 COMMON HOUSE GECKO

Hemidactylus frenatus

Abundance Unknown. It is *thought* at the moment that this gecko is restricted in distribution to a few spots on Key West and Stock Island in the Lower Florida Keys and to a few warehouse complexes in Lee County.

Habitat The walls of buildings.

Size Although most are in the 3–4 in. size range, this gecko is known to attain a length of 4.5 in.

GECKOS

Reproduction Little is known about the reproductive biology of this gecko in Florida. This is not a parthenogenetic species. Captive animals have disclosed that the eggs are only weakly adhesive and are usually placed in crevices or beneath loose ground debris. Several clutches are produced by a female annually. Communal nesting is known. The 2-in.-long hatchlings emerge after about 48 days of incubation.

Coloration/pattern Dorsally this species is ashy gray with an irregular pattern of obscure darker pigment. It becomes very light at night. Ventrally it is nearly white. A gray lateral line *may* be present. The scales of the body are mostly smooth, but there are six rows of rather pronounced spinous scales on its tail.

Voice A barely audible squeak is voiced by restrained or combating males.

Similar species The ease with which the common house gecko may be confused with the more widely ranging Indopacific gecko may partially account for the paucity of records. *Hemidactylus frenatus* has a white or whitish (sometimes just on the yellowish side of white) belly while the venter of *H. garnotii* is always of some shade of yellow (often lemon). Both the tropical and Mediterranean house geckos are strongly tuberculate. The flat-tailed gecko has more extensive webbing between the toes and is of more depressed body conformation.

Comments This is the most recently found established member of this genus in Florida. In other areas of the world, the common house gecko has proven to be prolific and aggressive to other gecko species.

86 INDOPACIFIC GECKO

Hemidactylus garnotii

Abundance This species is widespread, but spottily distributed, in many urban and suburban areas of Florida. It continues to expand its range.

Habitat Buildings, trees, fences and similar structures are all suitable habitat for the Indopacific gecko. In the Florida Keys this species is abundant in mangrove forests and, bridge abutments, and cement power poles.

Size This interesting gecko is adult at 3.75–5 in.

Reproduction *H. garnotii* is, so far, unique among the geckos of Florida in that it is a parthenogenetic (unisexual—all female) species. Even though unisexual, motions of courtship are indulged in and may, in fact, be necessary to stimulate egg development. Several sets of two eggs are produced annually by each breeding individual. In the warmest areas of Florida this species breeds year-round. The eggs are placed in crevices, on windowsills, or beneath ground debris. The 2-in.-long hatchlings emerge after about 7 weeks of incubation.

Coloration/pattern Dorsally, this delicate appearing gecko varies from a rather dark grayish-brown (days) to a translucent flesh-white (nights). There may or may not be indications of darker or lighter spotting. If present, the spotting is often strongest on the dorsal surface of the tail. The belly is yellowish and the underside of the tail is often a rich orange. The body is covered with tiny non-tuberculate scales. The sides of the tail appear vaguely flanged.

Voice This is a vocal species, but the squeaking sounds they produce may be easily overlooked.

Similar species No other gecko of Florida has a yellowish to orange venter.

Behavior If you hope to see this gecko, choose a still, humid night to look for them. They will be most easily found on the walls of dwellings and warehouse complexes. On breezy or cool nights they often remain near cover. Be keenly observant as you approach the outer perimeters of the halos surrounding lit porchlights or other sources of outdoor illumination. Indopacific geckos are vigilant and often quick to seek cover.

Comments Of Florida lizards only this species and (possibly) some individuals of the introduced rainbow whiptail are known to be parthenogenetic.

Despite its delicate appearance, this is a hardy and successful gecko.

87 TROPICAL HOUSE GECKO

Hemidactylus mabouia

Abundance This prolific gecko is aggressive towards other gecko species. It is rapidly expanding its range in Florida. It is now known to occur with regularity as far north as Palm Beach (east coast) and Collier (west coast) counties.

Habitat Of our four house gecko species, the tropical seems the most willing to expand its sphere of activity to tree trunks and debris piles well away from human habitation.

GECKOS

Size This is marginally the largest of our four introduced hemis. It commonly attains a robust 4 in. in total length and may occasionally attain 5 in.

Reproduction Eggs and hatchlings have been found year-round in southern Florida. The tropical house gecko is a communal nester. Incubation varies from 45–55 days. Females produce several sets of two eggs each. Hatchlings are about 2 in long.

Coloration/pattern By day the dorsal color of this gecko is darker than by night. Day colors may vary from tan to gray or olive-brown. There are usually several darker, backward pointing, chevron-like dorsal markings. Tuberculate scales are liberally scattered over the dorsum and are especially abundant laterally. The venter is light. At night, if on white walls, tropical house geckos often appear an unpatterned, ghostly white.

Voice This is a garrulous species. Males squeak quite audibly if restrained or when involved in territorial disputes.

Similar species Neither the Indopacific nor the common house geckos have tuberculate scales. The Mediterranean gecko has tuberculate scales, but they are less numerous and proportionately larger. The dorsal markings of the Mediterranean gecko are less precisely defined and *never* chevron-shaped.

Behavior These robust geckos may be seen at night clinging tightly to the trunks of trees or high on the walls of dwellings and other buildings. They often assume a head down position. They are wary and easily frightened.

Comments For a house gecko, this is a rather predacious species. Adults are fully able to overcome hatchlings of anoles and other small geckos as well as the more usual invertebrate prey. Because of this potential for predatory behavior, it is unknown whether this species will adversely affect any native Florida fauna.

Hemidactylus turcicus

Abundance This species is widespread but of
patchy distribution in the Florida peninsula.
It seems to be losing ground in south Florida
where more aggressive congeners are now present.

Habitat This gecko is strongly tied to human habitations.
It is seldom seen on trees or other such natural vantage
points.

Size Although most are smaller, this species occasionally
nears 5 in. in total length.

Reproduction Unlike its congeners, which breed year-round (at least
in southern Florida), the Mediterranean gecko breeds only during the
warmer months of the year. Females lay several sets of two eggs
each. Incubation takes about 48 days, and the hatchlings are nearly 2
in. long.

Coloration/pattern The dorsal tubercles are prominently large and most
abundant on the upper sides. Those on the tail are conical. Mediterranean geckos are darker by day (brownish to gray) than by night (light
gray to pasty-white). Somewhat darker, irregular dorsal markings are
usually visible but may disappear at night. The venter is white.

Voice The males of this species make weak squeaking sounds. They
may vocalize during territorial scuffles or when captured by human
or other predators.

Similar species Of the two warty species in Florida, the Mediterranean gecko is the more strongly tuberculate, but the tropical house
gecko has more tubercles. The dorsal markings of the tropical house
gecko are chevron-like in form, while those of the Mediterranean
gecko are less precisely defined and never chevron-shaped.

Comments Once *the* common *Hemidactylus* of the United States, the
Mediterranean (also called "warty" or "Turkish") gecko, now seems
to have been displaced over much of its south Florida range by one
or more of the three newer interloping species. Look for these geckos
on still, humid nights near the outer perimeter of the halos produced
by porch lights. They are less active and more difficult to approach
on breezy or cool nights.

GECKOS

89 BIBRON'S GECKO

Pachydactylus bibroni

Abundance This Southern African species is commonly seen at its small Manatee County introduction site.

Habitat In Florida, Bibron's gecko is usually seen on the outer walls of dwellings. It occasionally moves from houses to nearby power poles and trees.

Size Specimens in the Florida population seem to top out at about 5.5 in. in total length. This species is known to attain 8 in. in Africa.

Reproduction Nothing is known of the reproductive biology of this species in Florida. Female captives in Florida produce several sets of two eggs each during the summer months. Incubation takes up to 74 days. Hatchlings are about 2.5 in. long.

Coloration/pattern This robust gecko has a tuberculate, tan to buff or light brown dorsum. Transverse dark bars are usually present and scattered tubercles are white. The venter is white. These geckos are lighter in color at night when they are active than when at rest during the day.

Voice Squeaking-clicks are produced by males both when it is restrained and during territorial combat. Vocalizations have been heard when there seem to be no other geckos in view, indicating that the calls may be used as an advertisement mechanism also.

Similar species Young Moorish geckos have a scalation and pattern very similar to that of Bibron's gecko. However, the ranges of the two in Florida are widely separated at present. The white spotted wall gecko has smoother scales and four white spots on the shoulder.

Behavior These hefty geckos are seldom seen before nightfall. They position themselves head down on walls near the eaves. This robust species is able to eat both small vertebrate and the more normal invertebrate prey.

Comments Feral specimens of this gecko were first seen in Florida in the early 1970s. The continued existence of the colony was recently confirmed. This species is a popular item in Florida's pet trade. It seems likely that the Manatee County population is the result of a deliberate introduction.

Phelsuma madagascariensis grandis

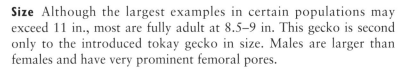

Abundance This impressively beautiful lizard has been found on several occasions in Lee County, and a seemingly well established breeding colony was recently found in Broward County. Reports that it is also established in Dade County have not been verified.

Habitat At the moment, this gecko seems restricted to palms and other trees near buildings, and the buildings themselves.

Size Although the largest examples in certain populations may exceed 11 in., most are fully adult at 8.5–9 in. This gecko is second only to the introduced tokay gecko in size. Males are larger than females and have very prominent femoral pores.

Reproduction Adult, sexually active female giant day geckos have an endolymphatic (chalk) sac on each side of the neck. It is thought that the calcareous material contained therein is important to the formation of the egg shells. Nothing is known about the breeding biology of this species in Florida. However, in both their native Madagascar and captivity, adult females deposit several clutches of eggs during the warm months of the year. Duration between clutches varies from somewhat more than two weeks to more than a month. The adherent, hard-shelled eggs are laid in pairs in secluded, protected areas. We recently found several hatched eggs of this species in frond axils of palm trees. Several hatchlings and two adults were also seen. The 2.5-in.-long hatchlings emerge after a 50–70-day period of incubation.

Coloration/pattern When healthy and unstressed, adults of this lizard are bright Kelly green both dorsally and laterally. Spots or blotches of brilliant orange are often present dorsally. An orange stripe extends on each side of the snout from nostril to eye and an anteriorly directed orange V may extend from above each eye onto the top of the snout. An orange spot is usually present posterior to each eye and several similarly colored spots are present on the rear of the head. Except for the stripes from the nostril to the eye (which are invariable), the amount of orange is very variable and may be lacking entirely. Bruises and tears in the skin will show dull green until fully healed. The belly is whitish. Fright or cold temperatures will cause the lizard to assume a much darker, less pleasant, green coloration on the back and sides. The scales of the back and sides are granular.

GECKOS

The large, lidless, eyes have round pupils. The toes are broadly expanded and this gecko is an agile and persistent climber.

Hatchlings are usually a dull olive-green.

Voice Although the giant day gecko can vocalize, it does not seem as prone to do so as many other gecko species.

Similar species This is the only large, bright green lizard with lidless eyes and expanded toes known to be established in Florida.

Behavior This highly arboreal gecko darts with great ease over the walls of dwellings and on the trunks of trees. Those seen on palms were near the frond axils and quickly darted into the "boots" and living fronds when approached. Besides eating insects, day geckos lick pollen, exudate from overripe fruit, and fresh, sweet sap.

Males are strongly and aggressively territorial. Although females are less so, hierarchies (pecking-orders) are often established. If stylized head-nodding and tail-wagging does not dissuade an encroaching male from additional overtures, fierce skirmishes will follow. As do many geckos, the tail of this species is easily autotomized and the delicate skin may be torn even during gentle handling.

Comments When temperatures are suitably warm and food is plentiful, this gecko can attain sexually maturity in considerably less than a year's time. The presence of this species in Florida may be traced to escaped pet trade animals. Other members of this genus are imported in large numbers for the pet trade and it is expected that additional species may eventually become established in the southern peninsula.

91 OCELLATED GECKO

Sphaerodactylus argus argus

Abundance The population statistics of this Antillean species in Florida are fraught with uncertainty. It is unquestionably the most infrequently seen of any gecko species. Ocellated geckos are apparently restricted to Key West and Stock Island.

Habitat Although well able to climb, *S. argus* seems to prefer terrestrial situations where, like its congeners, it can take advantage of leaf litter and other ground debris.

Size This species is adult at 2–2.5 in.

Reproduction The breeding biology of this species in Florida is unknown. It is surmised that like other sphaerodactylines the ocellated gecko lays a single egg at intervals during the summer months and that it is a communal nester.

Coloration/pattern The ocellated gecko takes its name from the several pairs of dark-edged light nape and shoulder ocelli that are usually present on both sexes. Some specimens may have the ocelli rather indiscriminately arranged, or fused into longitudinal stripes. The tail is reddish, the body darker. Light lines are usually present on the head. The dorsal scales are smaller than the lateral scales and both are keeled. A supraocular projection is present above each eye. Toepads are present.

Voice None.

Similar species The ashy gecko has non-keeled body scales, and the reef gecko has large, heavily keeled dorsal scales and only dark lines on the head. Female reef geckos usually have a pair of relatively large, light ocelli, on the posterior nape.

Behavior Virtually nothing is known with certainty about the habits and behavior of this ground-litter-dwelling gecko in Florida.

Comments At present, documented sightings of this 2.25-in. sprite seem to number no more than one or two a decade. Because of the ease with which ocellated geckos may be confused with reef geckos, this may be an artificial rarity. Additionally, ocellated geckos were known to be very localized in distribution. Occasionally, we try to explain away the seeming rarity of ocellated geckos by posing the question "how much cover does it take to conceal a 2-in.-long lizard that has long since perfected its skulking techniques?" Well, truthfully, not much. But ashy and reef geckos, neither of which is substantially larger, and both of which are skulkers par excellence, are turned up by the hundreds. It takes no more cover to conceal either of them, but *they* are found. Where then, are the ocellated geckos?

This gecko was probably accidentally introduced to Florida in commerce.

92 Ashy Gecko

Sphaerodactylus elegans elegans

Abundance This Cuban native is restricted in distribution to the lower Keys. Once common, its numbers seem to be depleted in recent years.

Habitat The ashy gecko is the most arboreal of Florida's sphaerodactylines. They climb well and often ascend trees, buildings, and other structures in search of insects. On warm, humid, summer evenings, we have found ashy geckos to be abundant on the walls of motels and other such structures as well as behind the loosened bark of Australian pines and other trees. They also seek shelter beneath moisture-holding ground debris.

Size At 2.75 in., the ashy gecko is the largest (by nearly half an inch) of the three Floridian sphaerodactylines. Males are the larger sex.

Reproduction A single egg is laid at intervals throughout the summer months. Incubation (in captivity) is 55–70 days. Hatchlings are more than 1 in. long.

Coloration/pattern Considerable ontogenetic color change occurs during the life of this species. Adults are dark with irregular light spots and dots and streaks. Hatchlings are pale green with dark crossbands and brilliant orange tails. The color change from that of the juvenile to that of the adult is gradual. However, even the darkest of adults are apt to be a pasty-white at night. The body scales are non-keeled. Toepads are present.

Voice None.

Similar species Both the reef and ocellated geckos have keeled dorsal and lateral scales.

Behavior Although they are reportedly diurnal and crepuscular, the ashy geckos we have seen in the Florida Keys have been active until long past midnight.

Comments On the Lower Keys, ashy geckos were once commonly seen in the company of Mediterranean geckos on the walls of dwellings. However, with the now burgeoning population of the more predaceous tropical house gecko, both ashys and Mediterraneans are less often seen. The ashy gecko was probably introduced to Florida in commerce.

Sphaerodactylus notatus notatus

Abundance This elfin gecko is abundant in leaf
litter and debris in Dade and Monroe counties.

Habitat Reef geckos are particularly abundant (or at
least are most easily found) beneath tidal wrack. On
some of Florida's lower keys it is not uncommon to find
three or four of these minuscule lizards beneath a board or
bit of flotsam just above the high-tide line.

Size The snout-vent length of this species is barely over
1 in. Total length is about 2 in.

Reproduction A single egg is laid at intervals during the hot summer
months. Incubation takes somewhat more than 2 months. Hatchlings
are more than 1 in. long.

Coloration/pattern Both sexes of this dimorphic species are darker by
day than night. The males are a study of dark on dark . . . deep
brown specks against a slightly lighter ground color. Very old males
may be nearly or entirely deep brown. Females are also dark flecked,
but have dark stripes on the head and usually a pair of light ocelli in
a dark shoulder spot. The tails of both sexes may be just on the
orange side of brown. Both dorsal and lateral scales are large and
keeled. This species has well developed toepads.

Voice None.

Similar species The ocellated gecko has small dorsal scales, usually
several pairs of light ocelli on the nape, *light* lines on the head, and
an orangish tail. The ashy gecko has non-keeled scales.

Behavior Reef geckos are amazingly fast and adept at instantaneous-
ly disappearing into the tiniest of fissures or openings. Reef geckos
are also commonly found under human debris in the ubiquitous
roadside dumping areas so prevalent on the keys. They are principal-
ly terrestrial.

Comments Finding one of these geckos does not necessarily equate
with having time to positively identify it. When disclosed, they are
amazingly adept at instantly finding cover.

GECKOS

94 WHITE-SPOTTED WALL GECKO

Tarentola annularis

Abundance Unknown. This is a newly established species about which little is known in Florida. It occurs in Lee and Dade counties.

Habitat This species does not yet seem to have spread beyond the environs of 3 or 4 warehouse complexes. It is seen on the outside walls on warm evenings.

Size This robust gecko attains a 6-in. total length.

Reproduction Details are unknown in Florida. Hatchlings have not yet been reported. It is known that females of this northern African gecko produce several sets of 2 eggs in a season. Hatchlings are about 2 in. long.

Coloration/pattern This is a grayish or sand-colored gecko with 4 discrete white, tuberculate, spots on its shoulders. Males are the larger sex. Although rough, the dorsal scales are not as rugose and tubercular as those of the Moorish wall gecko. Belly scales are smoother than dorsal scales. Elongate toepads are present.

Voice An audible squeak is voiced when these geckos are restrained or indulging in territorial disputes. It is not known whether the voice is used as an advertisement call.

Similar species Neither Bibron's nor Moorish wall geckos have white shoulder spots.

Behavior In Florida this species is seemingly restricted to the walls of warehouse complexes and nearby dwellings. Its potential for dispersal in the state is not yet known.

Comments This is a heavy-jowled predacious gecko that may well prey on other lizards as well as invertebrates. Pet trade escapees or releases are responsible for the presence of this gecko in Florida.

95 MOORISH WALL GECKO

Tarentola mauritanica

Abundance Unknown. This is a rather newly established species that is still restricted to two small areas in Lee County, and a second slightly larger area in Dade County.

Habitat Moorish wall geckos are now seen on the outside walls of dwellings, warehouses, and stone (cinderblock) fences.

Size About 6 in. long.

Reproduction Unknown in Florida. In Old World populations, 2 semi-adhesive eggs are laid in rock crevices or amid ground litter. A female can produce several clutches annually. Incubation duration is about 50 days. Hatchlings are about 2 in. long.

Coloration/pattern Adults are uniformly sand-colored dorsally with both granular and tubercular scales. The overall appearance is of a very rough-scaled gecko. The venter is smoother. Young specimens have dark transverse bands. At night these geckos pale considerably from their daytime color. Elongate toe pads are present.

Voice Males emit audible squeaks during territorial disputes.

Similar species Bibron's gecko has a scalation and pattern very similar to those of young Moorish geckos. However, Bibron's geckos are currently known only from Manatee County. The white-spotted wall gecko has smoother scales and 4 white spots on the shoulder.

Behavior Unknown in Florida. This is a strong-jawed predacious gecko that is known to eat both invertebrate and small vertebrate prey.

Comments The presence of this gecko in Florida can be traced to the pet trade. Hatchlings were first reported in 1996.

GECKOS

165

ANOLES, IGUANAS, AND RELATED LIZARDS
Family Iguanidae

As used in this book, the family Iguanidae contains several divergent groups of lizards. In Florida these are anoles, the basilisks, iguanas, swifts and horned lizards, and curly-tailed lizards. All, except iguanas, have been contained in other families. We have provided a general description of each group, and mentioned the family in which each was contained at the beginning of each group discussion.

Anoline Iguanids

These lizards have been variously contained in the family Polychrotidae or Iguanidae. We are using the conservative family designation of Iguanidae and the equally conservative generic classification of *Anolis* for all. Of the 10 species now established in Florida, only one (possibly two, depending on perspectives), the green anole, is considered a true native. The second *possibility* is one subspecies of the little bark anole, *A. distichus*. This, the Florida bark anole, *A. d. floridanus,* assuredly arrived on our shores long ago. It is considered by some researchers to be a true native. Sadly, it has now been overrun and intergraded by the introduced green bark anole, *A. d. dominicensis.*

The remaining 8 species of anoles have been either deliberately introduced, escaped from captivity, or arrived as stowaways. Males of all are territorial and aggressive, especially during the spring and summer breeding season. Territorial and breeding displays are species specific. These displays include dewlap distension, lateral body flattening, pushups, temporary erection of glandular nape and vertebral crests, and intimidating sidles.

Dewlap coloration is often species-diagnostic for human observers. It is, apparently, even more so for the lizards themselves, which perceive and respond to ultraviolet reflections from the dewlaps.

Anoles are oviparous. Reproduction is stimulated by the increasing daylengths of spring and terminates in late summer when daylengths have again diminished. After an initial annual breeding, sperm retention results in fertile eggs when the female is stimulated solely by courtship displays. From one (smaller anole species) to several (larger anole species) eggs may be laid at 2-week or somewhat longer intervals. Many anoles prepare no actual nest, instead nudging their eggs into the protection of a grass clump, bromeliad leaf axil, or between fallen leaves with their snout. Incubation varies between 35–65 days.

Although color changing ability is well developed in many primarily arboreal anoles, it is not at all well developed in others and is nearly lacking in many primarily terrestrial species. Those that change color do so in response to temperature and attitude rather than as camouflage, although remarkable camouflage may result.

Distended, elongate (teardrop-shaped) toepads are characteristic.

96, 97 GREEN ANOLE

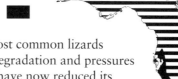

Anolis carolinensis carolinensis

Anolis carolinensis seminolus

Abundance Once one of the most common lizards throughout its range, habitat degradation and pressures from introduced anole species have now reduced its numbers in central and southern Florida. Green anoles continue to be a common backyard, canopy, and hammock species in undisturbed areas in the northern third of the state.

Size Large males may attain a total length of 8 in. The tail is nearly twice as long as the SVL. Females are noticeably the smaller sex.

Habitat This species is strongly arboreal. It favors tall native grasses, shrubs, and trees and was once abundant in cypress heads, pine-palmetto scrublands, and even in shrubs along prairie edges. It often hangs head-down on trunks, wooden fence posts, and other such vantage points. Green anoles diminish in numbers in seriously disturbed habitats and where native plants are replaced by ornamentals.

Reproduction A single egg is laid at 14–17-day intervals throughout the warm months of the year. Depending on temperature and moisture, incubation can vary from just over a month to nearly two months.

Coloration/pattern Green anoles have the ability to change color. Resting and content anoles tend to be of some shade of brown, but may be bright green. They are darker when cold, and turn a pasty-gray when overly warm. Disturbed anoles may be patchy brown and green. Males involved in aggression are often bright green with a nearly black ear-patch. Breeding males are often green but lack the dark ear-patch. In south Florida indications of darker dorsal and dorsolateral streaking may be present. Female green anoles have a light vertebral line. Displaying males can erect a low vertebral crest on the nape and anterior trunk. Throughout most of its range male green anoles have a decidedly red to pink dewlap. However, in south

Florida the dewlap may be pink, gray, nearly white, or even a very pale green. Whether this is merely individual variation or has greater significance is not yet known.

Similar species Throughout most of its range, this is the only small color-changing anole. If in extreme south Florida, see also the species account for the Haitian [98] and the Cuban green anoles [106].

Behavior These are shy lizards that will sidle to the far side of a tree trunk or post or dart upwards into the canopy if approached by day. They are more easily approached at night, when they sleep soundly.

Comments Research has rather conclusively disclosed that where the two are sympatric, the native green anole is being seriously outcompeted by the introduced brown anole. Adult male brown anoles are not only fully capable of eating hatchling green anoles, but the aggressiveness and high population density of the ground-hugging browns frequently drives the green anoles from low-level shrubs into the treetops and seems to eventually decimate the populations of the latter. Additionally, the introduced Haitian green anole and the Cuban green anole, both highly arboreal species, may prove to be effective competitors for habitat in southeastern Florida, while the equally arboreal and much larger knight anole is almost certainly a predator deserving consideration.

In 1991 the subspecific designation of *Anolis carolinensis seminolus* was erected for the gray, white, or greenish dewlapped green anoles of southern and southwestern peninsular Florida. We call these the pale-throated green anole [97]. Often, these specimens have an elongate dark shoulder spot on each side. The subspecific designation has not yet been widely accepted.

98 HAITIAN GREEN ANOLE

Anolis chlorocyanus

Abundance This species is now restricted to two colonies in Broward and Dade counties, where they are not uncommon but do not seem to be expanding their range. Other Miami populations, known a decade ago, are apparently now extirpated.

Size Males attain a total length of 8.5 in. but are often smaller. Females are normally the smaller sex. The tail is about 190% that of the SVL.

Habitat Primarily a canopy species, these wary anoles occasionally descend low on trunks to bask in the sun.

Reproduction Captives have produced single eggs at 14–20-day intervals during the summer months. The eggs were scattered in the leaf litter on the cage floor. Incubation duration varied, but averaged about 50 days.

Coloration/pattern In body color and color changes, this species closely parallels our native green anole, *A. carolinensis*. However, males have a large, and females a small *blue* dewlap. Whorls of enlarged scales are interspersed between several rows of small scales on the tail. The nose of the Haitian green anole is proportionately longer than that of the native green anole.

Similar species See the species accounts for the green anole, *A. carolinensis*, and the Cuban green anole, *A. porcatus* [106].

Behavior This is a wary canopy anole that quickly retreats high in the trees at the slightest disturbance.

Comments The presence of this species in Florida is directly attributable to pet trade escapees. It is no longer found at several initial points of introduction. This seems to be a temperature-sensitive species that expands range slowly and fares poorly during Florida's occasional freezes.

99 PUERTO RICAN CRESTED ANOLE

Anolis cristatellus cristatellus

Abundance This is an introduced species that has become locally common in Dade County.

Habitat Although somewhat arboreal, the crested anole is usually seen fairly close to the ground. It perches, often head downward, low on treetrunks, fences, rock piles, house walls, and other vantage points. Although it may descend to a rock pile or other ground cover when threatened, if possible it usually moves to a higher perch.

Size Males occasionally attain 7.5 in. The tail is about 150% of the SVL. Females are noticeably smaller.

Reproduction Captive females produce an egg (one female routinely produced two) at roughly 2-week intervals throughout the summer months. Incubation duration varied, but averaged about 50 days.

Coloration/pattern This olive-tan to almost black anole, reverses the anole-trend of being darkest when cold and lightest when warm. Warm, basking crested anoles, that appear at peace with the world, are often nearly black in coloration. When the ground color of this anole is light enough, dark bars (often broken into spots), variable both in length and contrast, may be present on both trunk and tail. The dewlap of the males may vary individually from olive-green through various yellows to pale orange, usually with a darker border. Most males have a wavy crest on the tail. This may be nearly entirely absent or conspicuously high. A vertebral and nape crest can be raised by muscular contraction. Females and juveniles have a dark bordered light vertebral stripe and lack the tail crest.

Similar species Puerto Rican crested anoles with the lowest tail crests can be easily mistaken for the more common and widely spread brown anole, *A. sagrei* [107]. Please compare photos and species accounts.

Behavior If approached slowly, this anole will allow close observation, but it darts quickly away when it feels its space is truly violated. It is more apt to seek safety by dashing upwards than by descending. Males indulge in intricate sidling displays.

Comments The crested anole was introduced to Florida either deliberately or in produce and ornamental plantings brought from Puerto Rico. Its presence seemed tenuous for the first decade, but it is now a commonly seen species. Crested anoles include blossoms and fruits from the various fig trees (*Ficus*) in an otherwise insect diet.

100 LARGE-HEADED ANOLE

Anolis cybotes cybotes

Abundance This species is known from only two small areas in Broward and Dade counties. It is moderately common within these small pockets, but does not seem to be expanding its range quickly.

Habitat This robust anole displays from low on treetrunks, fence posts, building walls, and concrete block fences. When frightened it is as apt to run downward and seek refuge in ground debris as upward. The crested anole seems most abundant in disturbed areas with well separated trees.

Size The large-headed anole is noticeably dimorphic, with males being much the larger sex. Males to 9 in. (often smaller); tail more than 200% of SVL.

Reproduction Captive females have produced 1 or 2 eggs at 2–3-week intervals. Incubation duration was not specifically noted, but was probably about 6 weeks.

Coloration/pattern The dorsal color is usually of some shade of brown (varies from pale reddish-brown to nearly gray) and the flanks are lighter. Broad dorsal bands and a light (bluish, greenish, or cream) lateral stripe are often present. Males are proportionately stocky. Females have a dark-bordered (often scalloped), light vertebral stripe, a light lateral stripe, and a light spot on each shoulder. The dewlap is huge and variably cream to yellow or yellow-gray and may be pale orange-yellow centrally. Through muscular contractions, males can erect both a vertebral and a nuchal crest.

Similar species The enlarged head of adult males is diagnostic. Females have a rather well defined light lateral stripe and a light spot on each shoulder. Also see crested (*A. c. cristatellus*) [99] and brown (*A. sagrei*) [107] anoles.

Behavior Males of this hefty anole display constantly during the warm hours of the day and are very territorial. Females are less confrontational.

Comments This is an Hispaniolan species. The questionably viable colony in eastern Broward County is the result of pet trade escapees. The well established (but static) population in Dade County is the result of deliberate introduction. Besides insects and some small vertebrates, snails and ficus fruits are eaten.

101 BARK ANOLE

Anolis distichus

Abundance In certain areas of Dade and Broward counties this West Indian anole is common to abundant. The Bimini subspecies, *A. d. biminiensis,* was released 20 years ago in Lake Worth, but no information is available on its status. A fair number of bark anoles were seen in our Lee County garden after planting heliconias and gingers brought from Miami nurseries. We saw no evidence of reproduction in Lee County.

Habitat Bark anoles seek their prey of ants and aphids while low on the trunks of ornamental trees, vines, and herbaceous plantings. They often sleep, with tail tightly coiled, on the upper surface of low, broad-leafed ornamental plants. In south Florida the bark anole readily colonizes urban gardens and seems most common near dwellings and lushly planted office complexes.

Size With a total length of only 4.5–5 in., this is the smallest anole now found in Florida. Sexes are about equally sized.

Reproduction A single egg is laid at approximately 2-week intervals throughout the warm months of the year. Incubation duration is about 2 months.

Coloration/pattern Because of the intergradation of 2 (possibly 3) subspecies, the dorsal coloration of the bark anoles of south Florida is extremely variable. This may vary from brown through gray to pea green. Cold or frightened lizards are darker than warm or content ones. Sleeping lizards are lighter than active ones. There are often 2 small ocelli on the rear of the head, a dark interorbital bar, a series of dark posteriorly directed chevrons on the back, and the limbs and tail are banded, the latter prominently so.

Similar species There is no other anole species in Florida with dorsal chevrons and a skittering gait.

Behavior This little spraddle-legged anole skitters more like a house gecko than like other anoles. It is nervous and wary, usually skittering around to the far side of a trunk, then ascending when approached.

Comments The bark anoles of south Florida were long considered two subspecies; *A. d. floridanus* and *A. d. dominicensis*. The former was a grayish lizard with a pale yellow dewlap. The latter varied from greenish-gray to pea green and had a very pale orange dewlap. Because the two races have now interbred throughout the greater portion of the Florida range, subspecific identifications are next to impossible. For this reason most researchers no longer attempt to designate a race. However, because *A. d. floridanus* is *never* green, when yellow-green to pea-green bark anoles are found, they can be rather reliably designated a *A. d. dominicensis*.

This lizard feeds largely on ants.

102 KNIGHT ANOLE

Anolis equestris equestris

Abundance Although very territorial, this largest of all anole species is now a common denizen in much of Dade County and has recently been seen in the Naples area of Collier County as well. Reports of knight anoles being in Lee County have so far proven erroneous. In all known cases the large anoles seen in Lee County have been Jamaican giant anoles, *A. garmani*.

Habitat Knight anoles use different habitats at different times of year. During the cool nights and short days of late autumn, winter and early spring, knight anoles are primarily canopy denizens. As the weather warms and the hours of daylight lengthen, knight anoles descend from the canopy and station themselves, usually head lowermost, low on the trunks of ornamental trees. Conspicuous in this position, they become even more so when the males fan their immense pink dewlaps like semaphores.

Size Although usually somewhat smaller, male knight anoles occasionally exceed a total length of 18 in. The tail is about 150% of the SVL.

Reproduction Little is known about the reproductive potential of wild knight anoles in Florida. However, captive females in large walk-in cages produced 2–4 eggs several times each summer. Hatching took about 60 days.

Coloration/pattern Like most canopy species, the knight anole can change color extensively. Although its usual color is bright green with yellow flash marks below each eye and on each shoulder, cold or frightened knight anoles can darken their color to chocolate brown or almost black. In most cases the flash markings are lighter and remain visible. Yellow bands may show on the tail, and light (cream to yellow) interstitial (between scales) skin may be visible. Through muscle contractions, the knight anole can raise a low vertebral and a much more prominent nuchal crest. The head is large and bony. Both sexes have dewlaps, but that of the male is proportionately immense. Both sexes are territorial and display, but the displays of the males are more energetic and lengthy.

Some long-term captives turn blue, rather than green. This is probably due to missing components (perhaps beta carotene) in the diet. It is not known whether a blue knight anole returned to the wild will eventually turn green again.

Similar species No other U.S. anole has as large and bony a head, nor do any attain as great a size as adult knight anoles. The yellow to white flash marks are diagnostic. See also the account for the Jamaican giant anole, *A. garmani* [105].

Behavior This is an alert lizard that can be aggressive and that will bite strongly if restrained. It generally gapes widely, distends its dewlap, and turns its laterally flattened body towards a threat. The knight anole is slower than many other anoles and is more prone to stand its ground if disturbed.

Comments Native to Cuba, the knight anole was deliberately introduced to Florida more than 40 years ago. Additional accidental introductions have occurred. This immense lizard, often referred to as "iguana" or "iguanito" by the Miamians, is now a familiar sight in much of balmy Dade County. It is known to eat fruits (being particularly partial to the various ficus fruits) as well as insects and small vertebrates. Despite being a cold sensitive species, populations of knight anoles seem stable or expanding.

103 BARBADOS ANOLE

Anolis extremus

Abundance Fewer than a half dozen specimens of this little anole were seen over a 3-year period in Lee County. Its existence in Florida is tenuous at best.

Habitat The first two specimens were seen in ornamental palms on the west side of the Ft. Myers Country Club. In mid-1994 two males and two females appeared atop my outside anole cages (we lived then on the east side of the Ft. Myers Country Club) and were seen until that autumn when we moved. They were frequently seen in that time period in our citrus trees as well.

Size Males attain 7.5 in., females are smaller.

Reproduction Unknown, but probably similar to the native green anole.

Coloration/pattern This is an olive-brown to olive-green anole, darker dorsally, and patterned with dark blotches and light spots. It is greenest on the sides and posterior dorsum. The venter is a sunny yellow and the head is gray to gray-brown. Females are less colorful and smaller than the males.

Similar species This anole is distinctively colored. It is not apt to be confused with other small green anoles.

Behavior Nothing is known of this anole's habits in Florida. It is said to be abundant and ubiquitous in Barbados, but more sparsely populated on St. Lucia.

Comments The presence of this anole in Lee County can be traced to the pet trade.

104 MARIE GALLANT SAIL-TAILED ANOLE

Anolis ferreus

Abundance Unknown, but probably rare.

Habitat One immature specimen was captured in 1990 from high in a tree near a Lee County reptile dealer. In 1992 an adult male and a juvenile were seen near the Ft. Myers Country Club in ficus trees. In 1993 an adult pair and three juveniles were seen in the same area. In 1994 several adults and juveniles were seen on our outside anole cages and in our citrus trees, probably drawn by the crickets that were always available. We moved in 1994, terminating the study.

Size Males attain 12 in. or slightly more in total length. Females are smaller.

Reproduction Unknown in Florida. See previous comments.

Coloration/pattern Bluish gray to grayish brown with some yellowish to yellow-green overtones dorsally and laterally. Some dark spots are occasionally seen. The eye turrets are cobalt. Females have a light lateral stripe that is best defined anteriorly. The head is large, but not distinctly bony such as that of the knight anole. Males have a high caudal crest. The dewlap is gray at the throat and pale yellow distally.

Similar species None.

Behavior Except for the above comments, unknown in Florida. Males displayed while hanging head downward on the uprights of our anole cages.

Comments This anole is a pet trade escapee in Florida. Despite its subdued coloration, it is an impressively beautiful lizard.

105 JAMAICAN GIANT ANOLE

Anolis garmani

Abundance This is now a commonly seen anole in Ft. Myers (Lee County) and Miami (Dade County).

Habitat In Lee County this species is much like the knight anole in its seasonal habitat variance. During cooler weather (mid-autumn to mid-spring, inclusive), the Jamaican giant anole is a canopy species. It descends to the lower levels and is often seen only 3–5 feet above the ground on the trunks of shade trees in summer. It is most often seen in a head-down position. Hatchlings use ferns and such plants as heliconia, dracaena, and ginger as their preferred habitat.

Size Males occasionally exceed 12 in. in total length, females are smaller and less robust. The tail is about 200% of the SVL.

Reproduction *A. garmani* is a prolific anole. Females produce up to 4 eggs per clutch at intervals during the summer. Incubation duration nears 2 months.

Coloration/pattern This canopy species is able to change color quickly and completely. When content they are often bright green, but may be brown. When cold they are dark and very wary. When suitably warm they are lighter and allow rather close approach. The male of a breeding pair was brilliant green while the female was a warm brown. A well defined crest of enlarged scales extends from the back of the head to about a third of the way down the tail. The crest is best defined anteriorly. This is a beautiful anole that, compared to the voracious knight anole, is a gentle giant. Males do display but seldom spar. The large dewlap is pale to bright orange with a yellow border.

Similar species Only the knight anole equals or exceeds the Jamaican giant in size. The knight anole has an angular bony head and yellow flash markings. The Jamaican giant anole has a normal appearing head and lacks flash marks. The very rare *A. ferreus* is nearly as large as *A. garmani* but is never green and males have a very high sail-like crest on the tail.

Behavior This is a rather quiet and unobtrusive anole that is seldom seen, even where common, during the winter months. It becomes more conspicuous during warm weather when it hangs head-downward low on the trunks of sizable trees. We have watched this species, positioned near an arboreal carpenter ant trail, eat several dozen ants in an afternoon. It completely ignored a small bark anole that sat near it. We have seen wild specimens eat ficus fruit and hibiscus petals, and captives have eaten many other types of fruit.

Comments We first saw this species at a Miami reptile dealer's in the early 1980s. Soon after we learned of a small feral colony in Miami. It was not until the late '80s that we began seeing this species in Ft. Myers. Like most large green lizards in southern Florida, *A. garmani* is often referred to as either iguana or iguanito. It seems to be a hardy and tolerant anole.

106 CUBAN GREEN ANOLE

Anolis porcatus

Abundance This species seems rather firmly established, but occurs in only a few known colonies in Miami. Apparently, hobbyists have known of the presence of this population for years, but biologists had not learned of its existence until 1996.

Habitat This anole closely resembles the Haitian green anole [98] in habitat preferences. It frequents ornamental trees (including ficus and palms), fences, yards, and the walls of houses. It is primarily arboreal, often ascending to the canopy, but may also descend to rock piles and piles of rubble.

Size To 8.5 in. (males); females are smaller.

Reproduction Nothing seems known about the reproductive biology of this species in Florida, but it is thought to be a summer breeder. It is likely that comments pertaining to the reproduction of the Haitian green anole, *A. chlorocyanus*, would apply equally to *A. porcatus*.

Coloration/pattern Like most arboreal anoles, this species is capable of undergoing extensive color changes. Content specimens are often a very intense green, disturbed examples may be brown or patchy brown and green. White(ish) spots *may* occur randomly on the body and neck. Ill defined dark markings may be present on the dorsum. When bright green, males usually have some striping (interstitially) of robins-egg blue on the nape, have a dark bordered light vertebral stripe, and *may* have a dark spot on each shoulder. Females usually lack the dark dorsal splotches. When clad in brown the males often have a series of even darker brown lines laterally and females have a cinnamon vertebral stripe. The dewlap of this species is quite red and its nose is proportionately long and very pointed.

Similar species Were the shoulder spots always present, this would be an easy anole to identify in Florida. It is best to check several specimens (if necessary) until one with the shoulder spots is found. *A. porcatus* seems to be slightly bulkier and more intensely colored than either *A. carolinensis* [96, 97] or *A. chlorocyanus* [98] (also see the species accounts for these latter two species and compare photos of all). Male green anoles lack the robins-egg blue striping on the nape (visible only when the lizard is in hand).

Behavior Little is known with certainty about this anole in Florida. It is expected that most of the comments made for *A. chlorocyanus* will apply equally here.

Comments The population of *A. porcatus* in Florida is badly in need of study. Other than the fact that it exists here in what seems to be burgeoning numbers, we know little about its life history in the Sunshine State.

107 BROWN ANOLE

Anolis sagrei

Abundance In the last three decades, this lizard has gone from comparative rarity to being one of the best-known lizards in Florida. It varies from common to abundant over the southern four fifths of the peninsula. It works its way farther northward each year.

Habitat This is a lizard that thrives in disturbed habitats and among ornamental plantings. It inhabits virtually every kind of inland and coastal habitat available in the state. Although often seen low in trees and shrubs, this lizard is quite terrestrial. If frightened it will more often than not dart to cover on the ground.

Size Males attain a total length of about 8 in. Females are substantially smaller.

Reproduction This is a prolific anole species. Males strut, bob, and display from mid spring to late summer. Although only a single egg is laid at a given time, most seem viable and several eggs are laid each summer at roughly 14-day intervals. Incubation is rapid, taking only about one month. Although territorial, populations of brown anoles can be immensely dense.

Coloration/pattern The brown anole is aptly named. Both males and females are of some shade of brown. The males often have bands of light (yellowish) spots and are darkest dorsally. Males can erect a nuchal, vertebral, and anterior caudal ridge. This is best developed on the nape and anterior trunk. Because of extensive intergradation of two subspecies, the dewlap of the brown anole may vary from quite a bright red-orange to a rather pale yellow. The edge of the dewlap is white. When the dewlap is not distended, the white edging is visible as a white stripe on the throat. Female and juvenile brown anoles have a dark, scalloped-edged, light vertebral stripe.

Similar species Of the several brown colored anoles found in Florida, only the brown anole has a white stripe on the throat when the dewlap is not distended.

Behavior These are feisty anoles that bluff and display throughout each of the warm days of the year. They are somewhat less aggressive (but far from benign) during the non-reproductive winter days. Brown anoles will even distend their dewlaps and indulge in agonistic behavior if a human makes eye-contact and bobs his/her head at the lizard. These are now the most abundant anole over the southern half of the Florida peninsula, and population densities are increasing as far north as Alachua and Duval counties.

Comments Because of decades of extensive intergradation in Florida, the characteristics that separated the two races of brown anoles have been blended.

In earlier years, the two could be rather easily identified as the Bahaman brown anole, *A. s. ordinatus,* a race with a yellow or red-blotched yellow dewlap, and the Cuban brown anole, *A. s. sagrei,* with a bright red-orange dewlap. Because of the intergradation, biologists no longer assign a subspecific status to the Florida populations of these lizards.

Although studies continue, it becomes more apparent that the brown anole figures prominently in reducing the populations of the native green anole in Florida.

BASILISKS

The impressive lizards in this genus may be classified in the family Corytophanidae by some researchers. Only one species is known with certainty to be established in south Florida. This is the northern brown basilisk, *Basiliscus vittatus*. It lacks well defined vertebral and caudal crests.

Rumors of the establishment of the very beautiful green basilisk, *B. plumifrons*, in the canals of Miami are being heard with increasing frequency. We are aware that several adults of this latter species have been captured by collectors in Miami. So far, though, we have seen no evidence that the green basilisk is reproducing in the wild. However, because it is currently being imported in large numbers for the pet trade, its establishment in Miami may be only a matter of time.

Male basilisks are much larger than the females. Males may exceed 24 in. in total length. The very long tail may be twice to thrice as long as the lizard's head and body length.

Basilisks have fringed rear toes. Buoyed by the surface tension and the great toe surface area, basilisks are able to run quickly across the surface of quiet water.

108 NORTHERN BROWN BASILISK

Basiliscus vittatus

Abundance Still local in the vicinity of canals in Dade and southern Broward counties, but common and apparently increasing in numbers where found. This lizard is native to a vast region of Latin America. It is found from Central Mexico southward to northern Colombia.

Habitat Although it may wander into fields and brushlands, in Florida basilisks are traditionally associated with canal-edge situations.

Size Males may slightly exceed 2 feet in total length, females are considerably smaller.

Reproduction This oviparous lizard lays 3–12 eggs. A secluded, moisture retaining nesting site is chosen. This is often in a hole along a canal bank. Eggs hatch in 55–65 days. Hatchlings are about 6 in. in total length.

Coloration/pattern This is an unmistakable, gangly (long-limbed, long-toed), brown lizard. Basilisks can both hop and run swiftly. When running, a bipedal stance is usually assumed. They are capable of swift movement and are able to run over the surface of quiet water when startled. If the running basilisk slows, it sinks. The males have a prominent crest on the back of the head; a low, serrate vertebral crest extends onto the tail. Females have a folded "hood" outlining the back of the head and a lower vertebral crest than the males. Both sexes are dark-barred dorsally and have variably distinct yellowish dorsolateral lines. The lips and venter are light. Young specimens are particularly prominently patterned.

Similar species No other lizard in Florida has the suite of characteristics that identifies the basilisk.

Behavior This is an alert, agile, speed-demon of a lizard. They are difficult to approach. Brown basilisks are capable of climbing, running, and swimming, all with equal facility. Adult males are particularly wary and may often be heard crashing to safety through the underbrush.

Comments These are remarkable lizards that catch the attention of nearly everyone who sees them. They are prominent in the pet trade, once being imported from Colombia in large numbers. Now, however, most northern brown basilisks seen in the pet trade are captured from the feral south Florida populations.

TRUE IGUANAS

The numerous species of true iguanas (3 species now established in Florida) and chuckwallas (none in Florida) have always been classified in the family Iguanidae. The 3 Florida "establishees" are all large (to 4 ft or more), and are mainstays of the pet trade.

While the green iguana is readily recognizable to most folks, the two, very difficult to distinguish, species of spiny-tailed iguana are less well known. Of the 3, the green iguana and the Mexican spiny-tailed iguana are firmly established. The black spiny-tail seems somewhat less so.

109 MEXICAN SPINY-TAILED IGUANA

Ctenosaura pectinata

Abundance Common in many areas of Dade County including the streets and trees of metropolitan Miami, this species is now also common on Gasparilla Island (Charlotte County), and may be present on other Gulf Coast islands as well. This species is native to the Pacific drainages and slopes of southern Mexico.

Habitat Like the green iguana, this lizard is indiscriminate in its choice of habitats. However, it swims less readily than the green iguana.

Size Hatchlings are about 7 in. long. Adult females commonly attain a total length of 3 ft; adult males may near or slightly exceed 4 ft.

Reproduction From 12–30 eggs are deposited in the late spring. Large healthy females deposit more and larger eggs than smaller specimens.

Coloration/pattern Hatchlings are grayish but change to a pale green within just a few days. With growth they gradually assume the adult coloration of black bars on a tan ground. Breeding adults may assume an overall orange lateral color and be banded with jet black across the dorsum. After the breeding season is over, the orange fades to tan or buff. Females are always less colorful than males. A prominent vertebral crest is present. The scales of the crest are longest in adult males. There are more than 2 rows of small scales between the whorls of spiny scales on the tail.

Similar species In Florida, the two species of spiny-tailed iguanas, which could be identified by range alone in their natural habitats, are *extremely* difficult to distinguish. *C. similis* tends to be darker (hence the name black spiny-tail) but also becomes suffused with orange during the breeding season. The babies of *C. similis* tend to be a more brilliant green than those of *C. pectinata* and are more heavily marked with black. *C. similis* usually has only 2 rows of small scales separating the whorls of spiny scales on the tail.

Behavior This is an alert and wary lizard, which knows its home territory well. They are often seen basking, head raised well away from the ground, on piles of rubble and building materials. They retire to burrows at night and in inclement weather and dart to the burrows if frightened during the day.

Comments Like the larger green iguana, the presence of this spiny-tail in Florida results from pet trade escapees or discards. They are not as frequently imported from the wild now as once, but there is little likelihood that this will affect wild populations at all. If carelessly restrained, these lizards will scratch, bite, and swat with their spine-studded tail. Singly, any of these can be painful. Together they will make anyone wonder why he or she chose to bother this lacertilian buzzsaw.

110 BLACK SPINY-TAILED IGUANA

Ctenosaura similis

Abundance Unknown. It has only recently been discovered that this species exists in Florida. At the moment, it seems restricted to Dade County. It is native to both drainages of southern Mexico, from the Isthmus of Tehuantepec and Veracruz southward.

Habitat This lizard apparently uses a wide variety of habitats but seldom enters water, even when hard pressed.

Size Hatchlings are about 7 in. long. Adult females near 3 ft; adult males may near 4 ft.

Reproduction From 10–28 eggs have been laid by captive females. Breeding biology of feral specimens in Florida remains unknown. Incubation duration is 75–95 days.

Coloration/pattern In general, the hatchlings of this species are a pale gray marked with a variable amount of darker gray to black. The gray ground color soon turns to a bright green. When not in breeding color, the adults are quite dark both dorsally and laterally. Adult, non-breeding males can be jet black. Breeding adults can be strongly suffused with orange. There are usually only 2 (rarely 3) rows of small scales between the whorls of enlarged spiny ones on the tail. A prominent vertebral crest, best developed on adult males, is present.

Similar species Positive identification of the black spiny-tailed iguana can be difficult. Juveniles of the Mexican spiny-tailed iguana tend to be a paler green and to have less black. Adults of the Mexican spiny-tail tend to be less heavily suffused with black laterally than the adults of the black spiny-tail and there are usually 3 or more rows of small scales separating the whorls of spiny tails on the tail. At best, these differences are all merely comparisons, and variable comparisons, at that. Green iguanas have no enlarged spiny scales on the tail.

Behavior Even when comfortably basking, these wary lizards immediately notice a human intruder or other predator and immediately dash to their burrows. They often bask while sitting on the alert, head well raised from the substrate. If unable to reach their burrow they climb agilely. Be careful when handling large specimens. Scratches, bites, and tail-lashes are all painful.

Comments Because of the ease with which this species and *C. pectinata* are confused, the true extent of the range of *C. similis* in Florida is not yet known. However, there seems little doubt that it is the less common of the 2 species in south Florida.

111 Great Green Iguana

Iguana iguana

Abundance This huge green lizard is now quite common and well-established throughout much of south Florida. Escapees and releases are also seen in other areas of the state during the warm months of the year. This species is native to most of the neotropics.

Habitat In south Florida the green iguana uses every imaginable habitat except the air and the sea. They may be found foraging in tree canopy, hiding beneath canalside debris, thermoregulating on downtown sidewalks or in urban backyards. Iguanas swim as well as they climb and run.

Size Hatchlings are about 7 in. long. Adult females may attain 4.5 ft+; adult males may attain more than 6 ft in total length.

Reproduction This is an egg-laying species. Large, healthy green iguanas can have 35 or more eggs. They usually dig an extensive nesting chamber, often angling downward from against ground debris. However, some females merely scoop a sizable chamber directly beneath debris (such as a piece of discarded plywood, a large rock, or an old mattress), and lay their eggs almost in contact with this cover. This happens frequently where the soil is difficult to dig (such as in the surface limestone areas of Dade County).

Coloration/pattern Healthy babies are bright green, ill ones may be brownish or yellow. Some (especially those from Peru) have dark bars across the back and sides. Adults tend to fade, retaining a green suffusion over grayish scales. Some individually suffuse anteriorly with orange during the breeding season. A huge dewlap and vertebral crest are present. These are larger on males than on females. A large rounded scale is present on the jowls. There are no enlarged, spiny scales on the tail.

Similar species Both species of spiny-tailed iguanas have whorls of spines interspersed between non-spinous whorls on the tail. The knight anole, often referred to as an iguana, has no dorsal crest and has a yellow(ish) jaw and shoulder stripe.

Behavior Both males and females are territorial and will indulge in pushups, tail-slapping, and actual skirmishing to rout interloping iguanas. If threatened with capture and not able to escape, adults will slap with the tail. If actually captured their scratching and biting will quickly open wounds. Babies are very fast and dart quickly to safety when threatened. These lizards will drop considerable distances from the limbs of trees, hit the ground or water with a resounding thud, and either run or swim quickly away.

Comments These are magnificent lizards that are able to tolerate the vagaries of south Florida's weather, but which die in the winter farther to the north. Florida populations include a hodge-podge of genes from Peruvian, Surinam, Guatemalan, Honduran, and Colombian iguanas. Pet trade escapees and unwanted releasees account for the presence of this species in Florida.

CURLY-TAILED LIZARDS

The members of this group were once classified in the family Tropiduridae. The 3 members of this family now found in Florida are all alien species. In general conformation these lizards look much like robust swifts, from which they may be immediately distinguished by their lack of femoral pores. Curly-tails may or may not have a fold of skin (a lateral fold) on their sides.

The common name comes from the habit of some species curling the tip of their tail upwards when they are foraging. This serves males both as a sexual attractant and a territorial mechanism. When the lizard gets excited (such as when it is stalking an insect), the tail waves back and forth.

Leiocephalus carinatus armouri

Abundance This is a common lizard in its rather small range in Florida's east coast counties of Dade, Broward, and Palm Beach. It has been introduced from the Bahama Islands.

Habitat This curly-tail has populated parks, agricultural lands, canal edges, and myriad other equally diverse habitats. They are abundant near areas of ground rubble and climb agilely as well. Ocean and river-edge seawalls are especially favored.

Size These robust lizards range from 7.5–11 in. in total length. Females are the smaller sex.

Reproduction This species is a spring breeder and females have been known to double-clutch. From 7–12 eggs are laid and incubation lasts for somewhat more than 2 months. Hatchlings are about 3 in. long.

Coloration/pattern Dorsally this lizard is gray to tan. Light nape stripes may be present as may light dorsolateral stripes and a variable amount of light stippling and dark spotting. The tail is rather prominently dark banded, and the venter is light. The dorsal scales are strongly keeled, and a low but noticeable vertebral crest is present. Hatchlings are similarly colored but have an orangish throat. This species has no lateral fold.

Similar species Swifts (scrub and fence lizards) have prominent femoral pores and lack a vertebral crest.

Behavior These are active and alert lizards, which dart about, tail curved above the back, in pursuit of their insect repast. They are most at home in terrestrial settings, but seem to readily exploit some arboreal habitats in Florida.

Comments Northern curly-tails were first introduced to Florida nearly 60 years ago in an attempt to rid sugarcane of insect pests. Since then, additional releases have assured the continuance of the species. It is also a popular pet trade lizard.

113 GREEN-LEGGED CURLY-TAILED LIZARD

Leiocephalus personatus scalaris

Abundance At best, this Hispaniolan species is tenuously established in Florida. It is known from several areas in Dade County.

Habitat The green-legged curly-tail seems more terrestrial than the northern species, and is less able to tolerate our occasional freezes. It prefers lightly wooded areas to open expanses of land.

Size Although most males and all females are smaller, occasional male green-legged curly-tails attain 8 in.

Reproduction An oviparous species, females may lay 2 clutches of up to 6 eggs. The 2.75-in.-long hatchlings emerge after some 9 weeks of incubation.

Coloration/pattern Males of this pretty, rough-scaled, red-sided curly-tail have a brownish dorsum and a greenish venter, green hind limbs, and a dark mask. A low medial crest is present. Females are less brilliantly colored and tend to retain the juvenile pattern of prominent dorsolateral stripes. Females have a speckled belly. Juveniles are strongly patterned with dorsolateral and lateral stripes, but are not brilliantly colored. The tail of this species curls, but not as tightly as that of the northern curly-tail. This species has no lateral fold.

Similar species The red-sided curly-tail is larger, has smoother scales, and has a lateral skin fold.

Behavior Although this is an alert lizard, it often allows quite close approach. It is most frequently seen in terrestrial positions, often sitting on a sidewalk, curbstone, or pile of rubble.

Comments This species, thought to have been established in southern Florida in the 1970s, seems to have disappeared during the 1980s when lizard imports from Haiti temporarily ceased. Imports began again in the mid 1990s, and once again this lizard is seen in fields and parks in the vicinity of reptile importers. Whether these current populations will actually become truly established is questionable. The green-legged curly-tail does not seem able to weather Florida's occasional periods of cold weather.

Leiocephalus schreibersi schreibersi

Abundance A native of Hispaniola, this beautiful lizard is present in small numbers in Broward and Dade counties.

Habitat This aridland curly-tail prefers open expanses such as in fields, the edges of parking lots, and particularly in piles of building or other rubble. It is active even on the hottest of days.

Size Adult males are occasionally 10 in. long. Females top out at about 8.5 in.

Reproduction From 2–7 eggs are laid in the early summer. Incubation lasts for about 65 days. The hatchlings are about 3 in. long.

Coloration/pattern Males are the more brightly colored sex. They are pale brown dorsally with a low yellowish vertebral keel and yellowish dorsolateral stripes. Red vertical bars occur on the flanks. Between the bars are patches of the palest blue. Turquoise may be present over the fore and rear limbs. The dark banded tail is brown dorsally but often flecked with red ventrally. Females and juveniles are paler and have about 8 dark transverse bars crossing the dorsum. This species curls its tail, but not as tightly as the northern curly-tail. A prominent lateral fold is present.

Similar species Neither the northern nor the green-legged curly-tails have lateral skin folds.

Behavior This is a wary lizard, but if it is approached slowly, it will often allow an observer quite near. It is robust and not as prone to curl its tail as some other members of the genus.

Comments This species seems less hardy than the northern curly-tail but hardier than the green-legged species. It has been present in Dade County for more than 20 years and in Broward County for about 10 years. It is a favored pet trade species.

Spiny Lizards and Relatives

The spiny lizards of Florida are often referred to as swifts or fence lizards. Both species are native. One, the appropriately named scrub lizard, is restricted in distribution to rapidly disappearing sandy scrub areas, now largely in the center of the state. The remaining species, the southern fence lizard, accepts a greater variety of habitats.

The third member of this family needs virtually no introduction. It is the ant-eating Texas horned lizard, a species that was introduced decades ago to the northeastern section of the state and which still, despite insecticides and other pressures, persists in low numbers. After having been classified for a short time in their own family, the Phrynosomatidae, the horned lizards, swifts, and their relatives, are again considered iguanid lizards.

115 Texas Horned Lizard

Phrynosoma cornutum

Abundance Rare and probably declining in numbers. In Duval County the Texas horned lizard seems to be now restricted to a few dune areas and seaside developments. It also occurs in littoral areas of Santa Rosa County and on parts of the gigantic Eglin Air Force Base (Santa Rosa, Okaloosa, and Walton counties).

Habitat In Florida, this remarkable little lizard has colonized sandy fields, dunes, and other such habitats.

Size Most specimens of the Texas horned lizard range are 3.5–6 in. long.

Reproduction This is an oviparous species. The 10–30+ eggs are buried in moisture retaining sandy areas. The 1.25 in.-long hatchlings emerge after some 45–55 days of incubation.

Coloration/pattern This is a reddish, tan, or buff lizard dorsally. The venter is white. From nape to hips there are 5 pairs of light-edged, irregular, dark spots. When undisturbed, this is a flattened lizard that is rounded (when viewed from above). When frightened it may inflate itself prodigiously. The two center horns are elongated.

Similar species None.

Behavior If startled, the Texas horned lizard can move with rather unexpected speed. They often sun while sitting on open ground or in areas vegetated with low herbs and grasses. Remarkably little is known about the life history of this species in Florida.

Comments The Texas horned lizard is an ant-eating specialist. In its natural home on the Great Plains, it may often be found near the trails of harvester ants where it picks off straggling ants, one by one. It often sidles beneath the surface of the sand, then sits quietly with only its eyes, horns, and nostrils visible. At night it may go entirely beneath the sand—eyes, horns, and all.

116 SOUTHERN FENCE LIZARD

Sceloporus undulatus undulatus

Abundance This is a common lizard throughout the northern half of the state, including the panhandle.

Habitat Sandy pinewoods and mixed woodlands are preferred habitats, but these little lizards colonize oaks in yards and are often seen sunning on fallen trees and wooden fences as well.

Size Adults of this alert lizard vary from 5–6.5 in. in total length. The sexes are quite similar in length.

Reproduction Adult, healthy females may lay several clutches of 5–12 eggs during the summer months. Incubation duration varies from 6–8 weeks. Hatchlings are about 1.75 in. long.

Coloration/pattern Southern fence lizards are dichromatic—that is, the sexes are colored differently.

Females are the darker with a gray to gray-brown dorsum that contains about 8 dark, irregular transverse bars. There is usually at least an indication of a dark dorsolateral stripe on each side. Females have a dark flecked white venter that *may* have a little blue to each side.

Although males have a grayish dorsal ground color, both the dorsal markings and sides are brownish to terra-cotta. Males have a grayish midventral area and large bright blue ventrolateral patches that are bordered with black centrally. One or two black edged blue spots are on the throat. The black edging from the throat spot broadens posteriorly and continues upwards onto the shoulder as a black wedge.

Hatchlings are colored like the females.

Similar species The Florida scrub lizard [117] is very similar in appearance but have broad, well-defined dorsolateral stripes.

Behavior This is an alert lizard that skitters to the far side of a trunk or log when approached. When clinging to a tree, they usually do so oriented head up, ready to ascend if frightened. They may occasionally sun on the ground near the base of a tree but dart upwards at the slightest disturbance.

Comments These pretty lizards are often seen on old fences and buildings and fallen trees in much of rural northern Florida. Considerable populations persist in many state and federal parks and refuges.

117 FLORIDA SCRUB LIZARD

Sceloporus woodi

Abundance This species is common but localized in distribution. It was once far more widespread along Florida's now largely developed sandy ridges. It now occurs sparingly in Collier County on the southwest coast and in the scrub along the sandy southeastern coastline. It is more abundant in suitable habitat on the Lake Wales Ridge and in the scrublands of Lake and Marion counties.

Habitat Although this lizard climbs agilely, it is often seen foraging on the ground some distance from the nearest tree. Its common name aptly describes this lizard's preferred habitat.

Size Scrub lizards attain 3.5–5 in. in total length. Females are slightly the larger sex.

Reproduction Healthy, fully adult females may lay several (3–5) clutches of 2–6 eggs each summer. The 2-in.-long babies hatch after 60–75 days of incubation.

Coloration/pattern Females and juveniles are gray dorsally with a broad dark dorsolateral stripe and dark, wavy, transverse markings on the back. Males tend to lack the dorsal barring, are of a browner color dorsally than the females, and have brownish dorsolateral striping. The large turquoise ventrolateral patches are *narrowly* bordered in black. The chin is largely black but has a white median stripe and two small blue patches.

Similar species The southern fence lizard lacks well defined dorsolateral stripes.

Behavior This lizard has well-defined terrestrial tendencies. If surprised while on the ground, the scrub lizard may either quickly dart across the sand to safety of ground cover, or ascend the nearest tree. It is adept at keeping a trunk or branch between it and its pursuer.

Comments This is a beautiful lizard that is a joy to watch. If secure, it basks in abandon and when hungry either awaits the arrival of an arthropod at its resting spot or, more rarely, darts to, and consumes, nearby insects that it sees. The continuing transformation of scrub habitats to golf courses and orange groves has accounted for the extirpation of many populations of this species.

FLORIDA SKINKS
Family Scincidae

The 7 species of skinks in Florida are contained in 3 genera, *Eumeces,* with 5 species, and *Neoseps* and *Scincella,* each with a single species. Of the 7 species, 3 are adult at 6 in. or less in total length, 3 may push 8 in., and one may near, or slightly exceed, a foot.

In general, skinks are elongate lizards with long, easily autotomized tails, short to diminutive legs, and shiny scales. Most have some degree of striping on either (or both) the dorsal and lateral surface(s). Many species undergo extensive ontogenetic (age related) color and pattern changes, some (especially the males) develop brilliant orange heads or cheeks during the breeding season, and many of the species are sexually dimorphic (the sexes vary in appearance). All Florida skinks are oviparous (egg-layers), and the females of the 5 species of *Eumeces* usually remain in attendance of the eggs throughout the incubation period. All are wary and secretive. Two species are persistent burrowers in sandy scrubby areas, one is rather arboreal, one is associated with streamedge situations and readily dives into the water to escape threat, and the remaining 3 are habitat generalists.

Skinks often make a very audible rustling when darting away from danger.

The smooth scales make these lizards difficult to grasp. Most will bite if carelessly restrained; the bite of the large species can be painful.

One species, the specialized sand skink, *Neoseps reynoldsi,* lacks ear openings. Two, the aforementioned sand skink and the ground skink, *Scincella laterale,* have transparent areas in their lower eyelids.

Eumeces anthracinus pluvialis

Abundance Although little is known about the population statistics of this skink in its limited Florida range, it seems to be rare or uncommon.

Habitat In Florida, at least, the southern coal skink is associated with pine-woodland brooksides and cool, moist, inclines which drain through sphagnaceous seepages and ultimately into brooks. Although other skink species swim and dive, *E. a. pluvialis* seems the most prone to take to the water to escape a threat. It hides beneath stream-bottom debris and in submerged vegetation. The southern coal skink is secretive and shelters in moisture-retaining areas such as beneath sphagnum mats and fallen trunks.

Size 6.5–7.5 in. Males may be marginally larger than females. The tail is 180–200% of the SVL.

Reproduction Other than the fact that it is oviparous, virtually nothing is known about the reproductive biology of the southern coal skink in Florida. It is supposed that the eggs number between 4 and 10, are deposited in mid- to late-spring, and that the female southern coal skink remains in attendance of the clutch throughout the incubation period.

Coloration/pattern This is an attractive *four*-lined skink (a *weak* vertebral stripe may be present) of moderately heavy build. The males are most brightly colored when in breeding condition. The dorsum is tan to olive-tan, the sides are dark brown, and a well defined off-white to yellow(ish) dorsolateral and ventrolateral line is present on each side. Counting towards the side from the middle of the back, the dorsolateral stripe is on scale row 3 and 4. These light stripes, which extend well onto the tail, separate the dorsal and ventral colors from the side color. If a vertebral stripe is present, it is only weakly defined, broken and strongest anteriorly. Variably distinct light spots may be present on the supralabials from beneath the eye to the rear of the mouth. There are no stripes on the top of the head. Reproductively active males become suffused with pale orange on the sides of the head and chin. The mental scale (the anteriormost chin scale) is not divided.

Hatchlings of the southern coal skink in Florida are black with light anterior supralabials and prominent white spots on the posterior supralabials. The white spots often continue onto the sides of the neck.

Similar species The mole (*E. egregius* ssp.), ground (*Scincella laterale*) and sand skinks (*Neoseps reynoldsi*) are tiny and proportionately slender. The three remaining species (*E. fasciatus, E. inexpectatus* and *E. laticeps*) have 5 (to 7) lines when young, but dull with age. These 3 have divided mental scales.

Behavior The southern coal skink is secretive and more aquatic than other Florida members of this family. Adults can sometimes be found beneath logs or other forest litter, or may be surprised as they forage for arthropods. Behavioral studies of this skink in Florida are badly needed.

Comments This is the most poorly understood of the 7 species of Florida skinks.

MOLE SKINKS

Eumeces egregius ssp.

Abundance When taken as a group, it may be said that mole skinks are fairly common where suitable habitat remains intact. However, with that said, we hasten to admit that all are very secretive, hence seldom seen, and they dive back beneath the sand so quickly when unearthed that one is often left wondering whether they have really seen a lizard. Some races of the mole skink are more abundant and widely distributed than others. Mole skinks are currently divided into 5 subspecies (see comments), all of which occur in Florida. Because of habitat degradation, one, the blue-tailed mole skink, *E. e. lividus,* of the central peninsula, is listed by both federal and state regulatory agencies as a threatened species.

Habitat All subspecies of the mole skink are persistent burrowers in sandy habitats. In such areas, mole skinks may be found beneath surface debris (papers, boards, discarded appliances, fallen leaves, and lichens) and may be plentiful on the beach side of tidal dunes, near the base of shrubs. These lizards seem to dig more deeply when the weather is cold but thermoregulate very effectively. On cool but clear winter days, when the sand-surface is sun-warmed, mole skinks may be very near the surface and the lizards are then very agile. Mole skinks are occasionally found in the sandy mounds of the pocket gopher or in other exposed patches. Three of the five subspecies of the mole skink have restricted ranges (see Comments).

Size Although mole skinks up to 6.5 in. long have been found (the blue-tailed mole skink is marginally the largest of the 5 races), most specimens seen are 4–5 in. Males may be slightly larger than females. The tail is about 180% of the SVL.

Reproduction Although up to 11 eggs have been recorded, we have found most clutches to contain between 3 and 5, and a few to contain only 2 eggs. In their quick-draining habitats, wild females must choose nesting sites that retain sufficient moisture to prevent egg-desiccation. Nests have been reported from near surface level beneath debris to a depth of several feet. Females reportedly remain with their clutches. Captive females have chosen moisture retaining areas of their terraria (beneath water dishes, partially buried limbs or against the stems of succulent plants) to nest and have remained curled around their clutch for the entire incubation period. We have not seen them eat during this period, but because termites and pinhead crickets often also congregate in moisture retaining areas, it is possible that the lizards eat occasionally while never leaving their nest.

Coloration/pattern Mole skinks of all races can be of variable body and tail color. They are attractive, shiny, agile, and fast. The intensity and length of the body stripes (if present) are also variable. Each dorsal and lateral scale (including scales on the top and sides of the tail) may be outlined with dark. The lighter scale centers give the appearance of light striping on the body, while the brighter tails appear dark-striped. A light line is present above each eye and the labial (lip) scales are often of a light color. The body color varies from tan to a rather deep brown. This may or may not be darkest on the sides. The tail is heavy and is particularly so when moisture and food are abundant. Tail color varies from pale cream and brownish-red, through red and purple to bright blue (see Comments). Hind limbs *may* be nearly as brightly hued as the tail. Regenerated tails are not distinctively colored. Sexually active males usually develop an orange blush ventrally. This may carry over to the sides of the face and fades after the breeding season. The legs are tiny but fully developed and entirely functional. Five toes are present on each foot. Of the 5 races of mole skinks, the hatchlings of 3 (the northern, the peninsula, and the Florida Keys) are paler diminutives of the adults. However, hatchlings of the Cedar Key race are black, and hatchlings of the blue-tailed mole skink usually have the definitive blue tails from which the name is derived (adults may have brownish to reddish tails).

Similar species The ground skink, *Scincella laterale,* is of very similar body shape. It has a long and slender brown tail and a broad, dark dorsolateral stripe on each side and preferentially chooses more heavily wooded and damper habitats than those preferred by the mole skinks. The sand skink, *Neoseps reynoldsi,* is very pale, has a sloping shovel-like snout and degenerate legs with only one (forefeet) or two (hind feet) toes. Hatchling southeastern five-lined skinks, *Eumeces inexpectatus,* have a blue tail, similar to, but somewhat more of an electric blue, than that of the blue-tailed mole skink, and have 5 prominent yellow lines on the body.

Behavior Mole skinks (long called red-tailed skinks, until the discovery of the blue-tailed subspecies *lividus* dictated a change in common names) are agile and difficult to capture. Indeed, they are even difficult to see, and are so secretive that considerable numbers may be present yet unsuspected. The name of mole skink rather graphically describes the propensities of this species. However, it implies nothing about its remarkable agility.

Comments The 5 subspecies of mole skinks are difficult to identify if a geographic origin of the specimen(s) in question is not known. Tail color differs on some, striping differs on others, but both characteristics are variable and may overlap broadly. While counting the scales around the trunk at midbody and the number of labial (lip) scales is difficult, it may help to confirm a subspecific identification.

- Usually 22 or more scale rows at midbody: *E. e. egregius*
- Usually fewer than 22 scale rows at midbody: All races except the above.
- Usually 6 supralabials: *E. e. similis*
- Usually 7 supralabials: All races but the above.

119 FLORIDA KEYS MOLE SKINK

E. e. egregius

This race occurs only on the Florida Keys and is the only race *on* the Florida Keys. The tail is dull to bright red. Most texts state that this race has 8 light lines on the body. This is not invariably so. However, when present, the striping is of uniform width and lateral stripes are often longer than the dorsal stripes.

120 CEDAR KEY MOLE SKINK

E. e. insularis

This skink is restricted in distribution to Cedar Key and surrounding Keys (including, among others Seahorse, North, and Atsena Otie Keys) in Florida's Gulf Hammock area. The body stripes, if present, are inconspicuous; the tail is orange to orange red, brightest on moderately large adults. Hatchlings and juveniles of this race are primarily black in color.

121 BLUE-TAILED MOLE SKINK

E. e. lividus

This skink is the only of the 5 races to ever have a truly blue tail (even if only on the distal half), but not all specimens actually have a tail of blue. Thus, tail color alone is not always diagnostic. It seems that young adult specimens of the blue-tailed mole skink often do have the bluest tails, while the tails of aging adults may be purplish to red. The range of this imperiled race follows the yielding white sand habitat of the Lake Wales Ridge northward from southern Highlands County to northern Polk County. During studies of the reptile and amphibian populations of Ocala National Forest, Steve Johnson found a mole skink with a bright blue tail where only purplish-tailed peninsula mole skinks should be found.

122 PENINSULA MOLE SKINK

E. e. onocrepis

Still found over much of the Florida peninsula, because of habitat degradation the peninsula mole skink is no longer as common as it once was. Despite areas of suitable habitat, this skink may be uncommon or absent from many areas of central and southwest Florida. The tail of this race may vary from whitish to nearly red, rarely to blue, to purplish or purplish-red. The tail color may become less brilliantly contrasting with age.

123 Northern Mole Skink

E. e. similis

This is another red or red-orange tailed race. It is the only of the 5 races to occur beyond the Florida state line (it ranges eastward from central Alabama through much of southern Georgia). Although the range of this skink parallels the Georgia-South Carolina state line, it has not yet been recorded from South Carolina. In Florida the northern mole skink ranges as far southward as Dixie, Union, and Clay counties and is present throughout most of the panhandle.

Florida's Five-Lined Skinks

Although distinguishing the 3 species of five-lined skink (*Eumeces fasciatus, E. inexpectatus* and *E. laticeps*) may seem intimidating at first, once you have become familiar with them the task is not difficult.

Let's first mention some obvious similarities:

- All undergo similar age related (ontogenetic) changes.
- At hatching they are black lizards with 5 (sometimes 7) white to yellow stripes and electric-blue tails. With advancing age, the tail and body colors fade, and the lines become more obscure. Males may lose all vestiges of the lines. Reproductively active males develop widened temporal areas and an orange(ish) head. Females often retain at least some indications of the juvenile striping.

Now for some obvious differences:

- Of the 3, the five-lined skink, *E. fasciatus*, (which is not particularly common over most of its Florida range) has the broadest stripes.
- Adults of the broad-headed skink, *E. laticeps*, exceed the adult size of the other 2 species by 3–4 in. Broad-headed skinks usually take to the trees if frightened. The other two are more inclined to seek ground cover.

The three species of five-lined skinks can be difficult to identify. Compare the relative size of the subcaudal scales (broadheaded and five-lined [left] and southeastern five-lined [right]), and the number of labial scales (broad-headed [top], five-lined [bottom]).

- Only the southeastern five-lined skink, *E. inexpectatus,* occurs in the lower one half of the state.

And, finally, on to some not-so-obvious differences (from this point on, it may be necessary to have the skink in hand).

- Subcaudal scale size: The median row of scales beneath the tail of *E. inexpectatus* are about the same size as those above them. The subcaudal scales of the broad-headed and the five-lined skink are noticeably wider than those above them.
- Ear opening: If only 2 small scales touch the anterior edge of the ear opening the skink is *E. fasciatus;* if four small scales touch the anterior edge of the ear opening the skink is *E. laticeps.*
- Supralabial (upper lip scale) count: Variable, but *E. fasciatus* *usually* has 4 supralabials whereas *E. laticeps* usually has 5.

124 FIVE-LINED SKINK

Eumeces fasciatus

Abundance Although present in the northern one third of the state, this seems to be the least common of the 3 species of five-lined skink in Florida. Accurate population statistics are badly needed.

Habitat A basically terrestrial species, the five-lined skink is well able to swim, climb, and burrow. It seems most common at the edges of damp woodland openings, in logged areas where decomposing stumps and fallen trunks remain, and amid debris at the yard peripheries of rural dwellings. It may be particularly common in seasonally flooded lowlands.

Size This moderately robust skink attains a length of slightly more than 8 in. Males may be marginally larger than females. The tail is about 150% of the SVL.

Reproduction Females create a nesting chamber beneath ground litter and remain with the 3–12+ eggs throughout the 55–65-day incubation period.

Coloration/pattern Ontogenetic changes are marked. Juveniles are black with 5 *broad* white to yellow(ish) lines and an electric blue tail. Females fade to brown or olive-brown but usually retain at least a vestige of the striping. A dark lateral color is separated from the lighter dorsum and venter by a light dorsolateral and a light ventrolateral line. The vertebral stripe is the most poorly defined. Males are like the females but have a somewhat broader head with an orangish blush on the jaws. The jaws, sides of the face, and temporal areas become more intensely orange during the spring and early summer breeding period.

Similar species See comments regarding the 3 species of five-lined skink on page 198. Also see all pertinent species accounts. Southern coal skinks have only four light lines.

Behavior This is an alert and wary lizard that quickly hides when approached. They usually seek to hide in ground cover, but occasionally may climb a tree to escape. Five-lined skinks thermoregulate in patches of sun, but usually remain quite close to cover. Males tend to move about more openly in the spring when seeking mates.

Comments Unless actually in hand, females of the five-lined skink can be very difficult to differentiate from females of the southeastern five-lined skink. At the normal 5.5–7 in. adult size of the female five-lined skink, females of the broad-headed skink are usually still rather prominently striped.

125 SOUTHEASTERN FIVE-LINED SKINK

Eumeces inexpectatus

Abundance This is a common to abundant species over most of its range. This species occurs throughout the state of Florida.

Habitat This species is rather a habitat generalist, being found in pinewoods, humid hammocks, and most habitats between these extremes. This is the most terrestrial of the 3 five-lined skinks, but often basks atop inclined and fallen trees, cement walls or piles of rubble. It is often a common lizard in dumps and trash piles. It can swim and climb but usually seeks cover beneath logs, rocks, leaf litter, or debris. This species may be encountered in tidal wrack.

Size This common skink is adult at 5.5–8 in. (rarely to 8.5 in.). The tail is somewhat more than 150% of the SVL.

Reproduction Females produce 3–7 eggs (rarely to a dozen). Females construct a suitable nesting chamber and remain with the eggs during the two month incubation period.

Coloration/pattern Except that the 5 lines are *narrow* (with the vertebral line being particularly so), yellow to orange, and brightest anteriorly, all comments regarding color and pattern made in the species account for the five-lined skink [124] apply. Breeding males may or may not develop an *extensive* orange wash on the sides of the face.

Similar species See the accounts for the five-lined and the broad-headed skinks as well as the lead-in on page 198. The southern coal skink has only 4 body lines.

Behavior Like most skinks, the southeastern five-line is alert, wary and difficult to approach closely. If on an inclined or fallen tree it will often seek cover beneath exfoliating bark or by moving to the far side of the trunk. This species readily darts beneath logs, rocks, and debris. Some may climb trees to escape a threat.

Comments This, slender-lined skink is the most abundant of the five-lined skink species in Florida. It may be encountered from backyard habitats to open woodlands far from human habitation.

Eumeces laticeps

Abundance This largest of our skinks remains common to abundant in suitable habitat in the northern one half of the state.

Habitat This is one of the most frequently seen lizards in many areas on university campuses, is a common resident of the many altered habitats in yards, and is common in most city and state parks as well as in the wilds of moist deciduous and mixed hammocks and woodlands. *E. laticeps* is the most arboreal of our southeastern skinks. If frightened it often scampers up a tree or may be seen just sunning or foraging on high limbs amid the resurrection ferns and poison ivy vines.

Size With the occasional male reaching 12.5 in., this is our most spectacular skink. The tail of an adult is about 120% of the SVL; tails of younger individuals are proportionately longer.

Reproduction The 5–15 eggs can be laid in moisture retaining piles of ground debris, under fallen logs, or in secure, damp, leaf-filled crotches of large trees. The female usually remains in attendance of the clutch throughout the 55–65 day incubation period. I (RDB) have found huge clutches of 30 or more eggs (apparently the result of communal nestings) in sawdust piles and in the low, decomposing, leaf-filled crotch of an ancient live oak. In only one case was a female present.

Coloration/pattern The yellow to orange lines of the juveniles of this large skink are usually better defined and more precise than those of *E. inexpectatus,* but narrower than those of *E. fasciatus.* See the discussion in the lead-in (page 198) for the comparison of this species with the other 2 five-lined species of Florida. The normal ontogenetic changes that broad-headed skinks undergo are also discussed in that section. Juvenile broad-headed skinks often have a rather prominent ventrolateral stripe on each side, giving them 7 rather than 5 lines. Adult broad-headed skinks of both sexes lose most of the striping. Except for the orange blush of their head, males become a uniform warm brown. During the spring breeding season the head widens posteriorly and becomes an intense fiery-orange.

Similar species Size alone will identify the adults of this skink. There is no other species that even approaches it in size. Also see the species accounts for *E. fasciatus* [124] and *E. inexpectatus* [125]. The southern coal skink is smaller and has only 4 body stripes.

Behavior In urban settings and busy parks, this normally alert and wary lizard can become rather accustomed to humans. If we move slowly and do not approach them too closely, those that sun on our deck will remain watchfully in place. While they may tolerate us, the presence of a dog sends the lizards quickly scrambling for cover. To escape some retreat to ground cover while the largest males usually move to and ascend the nearby live oaks.

Comments Broad-headed skinks are occasionally collected from the wild for the pet trade. They are favored terrarium lizards and live for a decade or more if properly cared for.

127 SAND SKINK

Neoseps reynoldsi

Abundance Although both a federally and state threatened species, the sand skink can be locally common in suitable habitat.

Habitat This wonderfully adapted "sand-swimming" skink is endemic to white-sand habitats in several central Florida counties. They continue to occur in some numbers on the Lake Wales and Winter Haven Ridges and are only rarely found on the Mt. Dora Ridge. Sand skinks are most common in the low rolling, sparsely vegetated scrubs that host plant communities of lichens, rosemary, turkey oak, saw palmetto, and sand pines. In such habitats, the sand surface dries quickly into the yielding consistency needed by this specialized skink, but moisture may usually be encountered from one to several inches below the surface. Sand skinks may be found by raking through the surface sand with your fingers, and are most common near the base of plants, beneath fallen leaves, and under patches of lichens or man-made debris. On the hottest days they are seldom seen, apparently burrowing more deeply.

Size At 3.5–5 in., this skink is one of the smallest skinks of the southeast. The rather heavy tail is 90–100% of the SVL.

Reproduction The reproductive strategies of the sand skink are poorly known. Female sand skinks are known to deposit clutches of 2 eggs in the late spring or early summer. Hatchlings have been found in July and August. Incubation is thought to take approximately 45 days. The deposition sites are unknown, but it is thought that the females choose moisture retentive sites such as beneath logs, fallen palmetto fronds, or other such ground debris. Additional research on this species is badly needed.

Coloration/pattern This is a silvery to buff-colored skink. Tiny darker dots are present on most scales, imparting a vague lineate pattern which may be strongest laterally. A dark bar (mask) runs from the snout, through the eye, to where the ear opening would be—if an ear opening were present. All legs are greatly reduced, but the forelegs are especially so. Each hind foot bears 2 toes, the forefeet only one toe each. The eyes are small, the lower lid has a transparent window, the snout is wedge-shaped and the lower jaw is countersunk.

Similar species There are no other skinks in Florida with such reduced limbs or the dark mask.

Behavior This is a persistent burrower that is usually seen only when dug up or disclosed when surface debris is moved. Even then it again squirms beneath the sand-surface so quickly that one is left wondering what, exactly, they have seen? Tiny insects and other arthropods often abound in the protection of fallen palm fronds or other moisture retaining plant material and it is thought that the sand skink preys extensively on these.

Comments It is illegal to take or restrain this federally protected species without a permit.

128 GROUND SKINK

Scincella lateralis

Abundance This is one of Florida's most common lizard species. It may be seen in urban, suburban, and woodland habitats.

Habitat This secretive little skink may be seen in woodlands darting from the cover of one leaf to another, gliding in serpentine manner amid the grasses of a well manicured lawn, or hunting tiny insects in relatively dry scrub. It occurs in dry upland woodlands as well as along stream and pond edges. The ground skink may take to the water if threatened. The ground skink seems absent from the Everglades south of Lake Okeechobee. They often hide beneath logs, boards, and other man-made and natural ground litter.

Size *Scincella lateralis* occasionally attains a slender 5.5-in. length (of which two thirds is tail) but is usually about an inch shorter.

Reproduction This little terrestrial skink does not remain with its eggs through incubation. It is the only of Florida's skinks known to regularly multi-clutch. Although up to 7 eggs are reported, most clutches contain from 2–5. A healthy female may lay several clutches of eggs at 4–5-week intervals throughout the late spring and summer. Incubation duration is in the 50–60-day range.

Coloration/pattern This active little lizard, once called the brown-backed skink, is of an overall dark coloration. The broad, dark brown dorsolateral stripes, which extend from the snout to well on to the tail, separate the light brown dorsum from the even lighter sides. There is no light striping. The top of the head may be coppery colored, especially on juveniles. The tail is not contrastingly colored. The legs are tiny but fully functional and bear 5 toes each. Although it is not easily seen, there is a transparent area (often referred to as a window) in the lower eyelid.

Similar species The other 2 small skink species of Florida are either light colored with a reduced number of toes (sand skink, *Neoseps reynoldsi*) or have a contrasting tail color and (often) light lines (mole skink, *Eumeces egregius* ssp.).

Behavior Although this tiny skink is often seen on top of or next to leaves, it is seldom more than one quick squirm away from cover. It is alert and rarely allows close approach.

Comments Although the legs are fully functional and used when the ground skink is moving slowly, the legs are folded against its body and the lizard relies on serpentine squirming when haste is required. Juveniles are especially pretty, and gleam in the sunshine like burnished copper.

RACERUNNERS AND WHIPTAILS
Family Teiidae

The teiids are far better represented in our western states than in Florida. In fact, of the 4 species that occur in Florida, only one, the six-lined racerunner is native. The others, all of prominent importance in the pet industry, are of neotropical origin.

All teiids are fast, nervous lizards. They routinely move in short bursts of speed. Most either construct burrows or use burrows made by other animals.

All teiids are active foragers that scratch through ground litter and loose sand to find their insect repast. Some readily eat plant materials. The lizards are confirmed heliotherms, basking between bouts of foraging. They tend to be most active from 9 o'clock in the morning to noontime but may forage well into the afternoon. All Florida species are terrestrial.

The dorsal and lateral scales of all racerunners and whiptails are small and evenly granular. The ventral scales are large and platelike and arranged in 8 (*Cnemidophorus*) or 12 (*Ameiva*) parallel rows.

129, 130 GIANT AMEIVA

Ameiva ameiva

Abundance This variable species is locally common in several sections of Dade County. They are of neotropical origin.

Habitat It prefers open areas such as fields, parklands, weedy canal banks, and among the low shrubs at the edges of office complexes. Trash piles and rubble are especially favored.

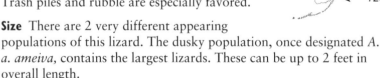

Size There are 2 very different appearing populations of this lizard. The dusky population, once designated *A. a. ameiva*, contains the largest lizards. These can be up to 2 feet in overall length.

The populations of green-rumped lizards (once designated *A. a. petersi*) contain lizards that seldom exceed 18 in.

Reproduction Little is known with certainty about the breeding biology of this lizard in Florida. We have observed them breeding in October. They are thought to lay single (rarely two) clutches of up to four eggs in the early summer. The eggs hatch in somewhat more than two months. Hatchlings are nearly 5 in. long.

Coloration/pattern The hatchlings of both phases are prominently striped with green against a body color of light gray, tan or brown.

Dusky phase [129] The color of this phase changes dramatically with the age of the lizard, and males are always the darker sex. Adult females are dusky olive-gray posteriorly, but may retain some evidence of striping or greenish coloration anteriorly. A broad buff vertebral stripe may be present and light ventrolateral spangling is prominent. The dorsum of adult males is charcoal to bluish-gray with rather regular crossrows of pale blue to yellowish or whitish spots. The belly has numerous blue spots on the outer several rows of scales. Blue to whitish-blue spots also appear on the limbs.

Green-rumped phase [130] Some have a dorsum of warm tan anteriorly shading to brilliant green posteriorly. Others are entirely green dorsally. In both cases, the upper sides are darker and liberally patterned with prominent dark-edged white spots. These spots shade to blue ventrolaterally. The belly has brilliant blue spots on the outermost rows of ventral scales.

There are 12 rows of large belly scales.

Similar species Only the giant whiptail [132] approaches these lizards in size. It is has a blue or bluish spangled, brownish dorsum.

Behavior Remarkably pretty and remarkably fast most concisely describes these lizards. Ameivas are alert lizards that nervously move between patches of cover. They dig burrows to which they return at night and, if possible, if frightened while basking. Once up to speed, they are capable of bipedal movement.

Comments These two very different-appearing lizards were once given subspecific status. In some areas of the tropical American range there appears to be a great overlap of characteristics. The two races are no longer considered of subspecific status. Escapees from the pet industry account for the presence of this lizard in Florida.

Cnemidophorus lemniscatus complex

Abundance These are common lizards within their very circumscribed range behind two or three warehouse complexes in Dade County. They occur widely in the neotropics.

Habitat Rainbow whiptails are found in heavily pebbled expanses of sandy soil on which grows a sparse cover of low, mostly exotic, weeds.

Size Usually in the 9–10-in. range, some large males may exceed 12 in. Females are the smaller sex.

Reproduction This species is actually a species complex—a number of externally similar but genetically different (sibling) species. Some members of this complex are parthenogenic. Others are bisexual. It appears as if those in the Dade County populations are of this latter form.

No studies have been conducted on the life history (including the reproductive biology) of this whiptail in Florida. Captive females have laid two clutches of up to 4 eggs (usually 2 or 3) during the summer months. These have hatched after some 47–55 days of incubation. Hatchlings are about 3.5 in. long.

Coloration/pattern This is one of the most beautiful of the lizards in Florida. Males are warm brown dorsally. This is bordered with a thin yellow stripe below which is a lime-green stripe. Another thin yellow stripe separates the green stripe from a broad, yellow spangled, golden lateral area. The face, throat, and anterior surface of all limbs is turquoise or robin's-egg blue. The tail is green. A white-spangled purplish shoulder spot is often present. Venter is grayish. Females lack much of the pattern complexity, having instead 7–9 yellow stripes on a field of greenish-brown. The head is orange(ish), the lower sides, hindlimbs and tail are a rather bright green. The venter is white.

Similar species No other lizard in Florida has the combination of colors of the male rainbow lizard. Six-lined racerunners superficially resemble female rainbow lizards but have only 6 yellow lines.

Behavior This lizard skitters and probes over and among the sand and pebbles of which its home consists. When sufficiently hot they either retire to their burrows or to the shade of a plant or building.

Rainbow lizards feed not only on insects and other arthropods, but on the leaves and flowers of the toxic (to endotherms, anyway) European punctureweed.

Comments The Florida population of this pet trade favorite is badly in need of comprehensive study. It has been established here for more than 30 years but, despite being locally abundant, virtually nothing is yet known of its life history.

132 GIANT WHIPTAIL

Cnemidophorus motaguae

Abundance Unknown. Construction has driven these lizards farther from the epicenter of their Dade County introduction site, but population statistics are scant. They are of northern Central American origin.

Habitat Open fields, canal banks, grassy parking lot edges, and road shoulders are all favored habitats.

Size Males of this rather large lizard grow to 13 in. Females are smaller.

Reproduction Nothing is known about this species in its Florida habitat. Precious little is known about it in its natural range. A captive female had 4 eggs, which hatched after 54 days of incubation. Hatchlings were 4.25 in. long.

Coloration/pattern This whiptail has a golden brown vertebral area that gently shades into tan or golden spangled deeper brown sides. The lower sides are the darkest and are spangles with white spots. The venter is gray with bright blue spangle ventrolaterally. Females are somewhat paler than the males. The tail is brown anteriorly, shading to reddish-brown terminally.

Similar species Giant ameivas have either a darker (blue-black) or a green dorsum.

Behavior Like all whiptails this is an alert and active species. They are adept at evading enemies, including human captors. It will be interesting to see whether feral populations of this species will remain in Florida in ten years' time.

Comments Comprehensive studies are needed on the feral populations of this pet trade species in Florida.

133 Six-Lined Racerunner

Cnemidophorus sexlineatus sexlineatus

Abundance This is a common lizard throughout all of Florida.

Habitat Like its congeners, the six-lined racerunner inhabits well drained sandy fields, rosemary scrub, sandy parking lot edges, and myriad other such habitats.

Size This is a small teiid. Adult males attain 7–8½ in. in total length; females are an inch or so smaller.

Reproduction Females lay two clutches of 1–6 eggs. Incubation takes about 48 days. Hatchlings are nearly 3 in. long.

Coloration/pattern This a beautiful but rather subtly colored lizard. Males, females and juveniles have 6 yellow lines against a ground color of variable brown. The ground color is lighter middorsally and darkest low on the sides. Males have a suffusion of light blue over their entire bellies. Females have almost white bellies. Juveniles have light bellies and bluish tails.

Similar species Female rainbow whiptails have orangish faces, more than 6 lines and greenish tails. Immature skinks have shiny mirror-like scales.

Behavior Alert, agile, and remarkably fast are adjectives which apply well to this lizard. They are active in the morning and early afternoon, often siesta during the hottest part of a summer day, but become active again in the late afternoon. On cool days the lizards bask more extensively but remain active longer.

Comments This is the only native teiid found in Florida. It remains common in sparsely developed and undeveloped areas where the soils are sandy and sharply drained.

TURTLES AND TORTOISES
Order Chelonia

These groups of shelled reptiles are easily recognized as such, but specific identification can be a lot harder.

Despite their similarities, turtles and tortoises are a diverse lot with widely varying needs and lifestyles. Contained in the 13 families are some 75+ genera and about 250 species.

Of these, 8 families are represented in Florida by a total of 26 species (41 subspecies).

Family Cheloniidae—Typical Sea Turtles	(4 species)
Family Chelydridae—Snapping Turtles	(2 species)
Family Dermochelyidae—Leatherback Sea Turtle	(1 species)
Family Emydidae—Basking and Box Turtles	(10 species)
Family Kinosternidae—Musk and Mud Turtles	(4 species)
Family Pelomedusidae—Sidenecked Turtles	(1 species)
Family Testudinidae—Tortoises	(1 species)
Family Trionychidae—Softshelled Turtles	(3 species)

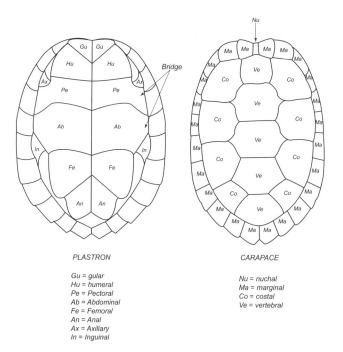

PLASTRON

CARAPACE

Gu = gular
Hu = humeral
Pe = Pectoral
Ab = Abdominal
Fe = Femoral
An = Anal
Ax = Axillary
In = Inguinal

Nu = nuchal
Ma = marginal
Co = costal
Ve = vertebral

The shields of a turtle's plastron (left) and carapace (right) are specifically named.

The terms "turtle" and "terrapin" are used differently by different folks and in different parts of the world. In the United States the term "turtle" is used for both freshwater and marine species. The terms "cooter" (of African derivation) and "slider" are also used for some of the big basking emydines. "Terrapin" is reserved by Americans for the brackish and saltwater emydines known commonly as diamond-backs. "Tortoise" is applied to only the exclusively terrestrial species.

It is often thought that the shell makes turtles impervious to attacks and predation. Certainly the shell helps protect these creatures, but does not always succeed.

Alligators routinely dine on their freshwater chelonian neighbors, and terrestrial box turtles are seemingly being adversely impacted by an introduced scourge, the tiny fire ants. Besides this, predation by raccoons, opossums, dogs, and cats occurs on eggs and hatchling specimens. The highest toll, though, is taken by vehicles when turtles cross roadways.

How to Find Turtles and Tortoises

As with all other reptiles and amphibians, to find turtles (except by accident) you must travel to and carefully search through their habitats.

Sea turtles, of course, are restricted to marine environments, but are usually encountered only when females come ashore at night in the late spring, summer, and early autumn to lay their eggs. Be aware, though, that all marine turtles of Florida are endangered or threatened, hence protected by federal and state regulations. Their nesting activities are often monitored by watchdog groups that prohibit close approach by observers. Sea turtles are most commonly encountered on the southern three fourths of Florida's Atlantic coast and on the beaches of Lee and Collier counties on the Gulf Coast.

Box turtles are open meadow and woodland animals that may be active by day during or following showers and are especially so in the spring and early summer months. They often cross rural roadways that traverse their habitats.

Gopher tortoises are creatures of the sandy ridges that support the grasses and herbs on which they feed. Their burrows are tell-tale signs of the tortoises' presence.

Diamond-backed terrapins are now uncommon throughout the state. They may occasionally be seen at low tide in brackish marshes as they swim or walk in water-retaining channels.

The big basking turtles are commonly seen in canals, ditches, lakes, and rivers throughout the state. They are wary where persecuted for food or other reason, but are often accustomed to rather close approach in state and federal parks where they are protected.

The following short list of selected terms and their definitions may help you understand our turtle and tortoise fauna more easily. Additional terms are defined in the glossary, pages 266–269.

Barbels—downward projecting papillae on the chins and/or throats of turtles. Commonly seen on musk and mud turtles.

Bridge—the area of a turtle's shell that connects the carapace to the plastron.

Carapace—the top shell of a turtle.

Cusp—downward projections, at both sides of a medial notch, from the upper mandible of red-bellied turtles.

Interorbital—on the top of the head between the eyes.

Papillae—fleshy, nipple like projections on the necks of some turtles.

Plastron—the bottom shell of a turtle

Pores—a circular or oval opening at the rear of the bridge scutes of certain sea turtles.

Postocular—behind the eyes.

Scute (or plate)—the large scales of a turtle's shell.

MARINE TURTLES
Family Cheloniidae

There are 4 beleaguered members of this family in Florida's waters: the loggerhead and the green turtle nest here in some numbers, and the hawksbill and the Atlantic Ridley are accidental in their occurrence.

All of these turtles have flipperlike limbs.

All, except the threatened loggerhead, are federally endangered.

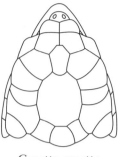

Caretta caretta   *Chelonia mydas*

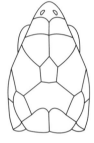
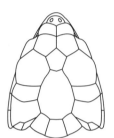

Eretmochelys imbricata   *Lepidochelys kempii*

Comparative head scalation of the sea turtles; loggerhead (upper left), green (upper right), Atlantic hawksbill (lower left), Atlantic ridley (lower right).

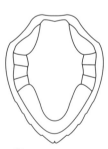
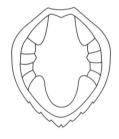

Caretta caretta   *Lepidochelys kempii*

Comparative bridge scalation of the loggerhead (left; 3 scutes) and the Atlantic ridley (right; 4 scutes) sea turtles.

134 LOGGERHEAD TURTLE

Caretta caretta

Abundance Relatively common but still considered a threatened species. This turtle may be seen anywhere along Florida's coastline.

Habitat Tropical and subtropical oceans.

Size The loggerhead follows the leatherback and the green turtle in size. Large adults attain a carapace length of more than 3.5 ft and have been known to weigh more than 400 lb.

Reproduction Females nest bi- or triennially, but in breeding years lay several clutches of 100 or more eggs at intervals through the summer. Prior to the actual nesting, a body pit is dug with the forelimbs. That done, the egg-chamber is dug with the hind limbs. Incubation lasts for 2–3 months. Hatchlings have a carapace length of 1.75 in.

Coloration/pattern Once past its deep brown hatchling stage, this becomes a reddish-brown turtle with tan highlights. Because their color is often obliterated by beach sand, the true colors of this attractive turtle are the easiest to determine when the turtle is in the water. Additional clues to help you identify this species are:

- There are always 5 costal scutes on each side.
- The first costal scute always touches the nuchal scute.
- There are usually 3 non-pored scutes on the bridge.
- There are 2 pairs of prefrontal scales (between the eyes).

Similar species No other marine turtle is a warm reddish brown.
Hawksbills are darker brown or have calico carapacial scutes and have only 4 costal scutes.
Green turtles have only a single pair of prefrontal scales and only 4 costals.
Ridleys are comparatively small, olive-gray or gray in color, and have 4 *pored* bridge scutes.

Behavior Hatchlings emerging from the nest can become confused by bright lights on or behind the beach and may crawl away from the water. Although numbers are now depleted, this remains the most commonly seen marine turtle in Florida. Besides turtle grasses (Zostera, etc.) loggerheads consume shellfish, crustaceans, coelenterates, fish, and myriad other marine creatures.

TURTLES AND TORTOISES

215

Comments This turtle, considered threatened by both federal and state conservation agencies, is completely protected in the United States by the provisions of the Endangered Species Act. Neither they, nor their eggs, should be bothered in any way.

135 GREEN TURTLE

Chelonia mydas

Abundance Fairly common in some tropical areas. This is the second most commonly encountered marine turtle species in Florida.

Habitat This is a species of open tropical and subtropical oceans that is often seen feeding on shallow eelgrass flats.

Size This gigantic marine turtle is exceeded in maximum size only by the leatherback. Green turtles are adult at from 3–4.5 ft and have been known to attain 5 ft in carapace length.

Reproduction Female green turtles nest only every 2–3 years. A body pit is first made with the front flippers, then the nest is dug with the rear flippers. During her nesting year, a female green turtle may lay 1–6 times, depositing about 100 eggs at each laying. Incubation takes about 2 months. Hatchlings average 2 in. in carapace length.

Coloration/pattern Adults of this turtle are basically a light to dark brown carapacially. Radiating dark lines may be visible on some of the lighter specimens. There are 4 costal scutes on each side. The first costal is not in contact with the nuchal scale. The venter is light. Hatchlings are dark brown to nearly black with the flippers edged neatly in white.

This species has only a single pair of prefrontal scales (the scales between the eyes).

Similar species All other sea turtles of this family found in Florida have *2 pairs* of prefrontal scales.

Behavior This large turtle can be common in shallow bays and estuaries where the various eel-grasses—its principal food—grow. Researchers now estimate that more than 200 females are nesting annually on Florida's beaches. This number is a bare remnant of the number that nested here in historic times. However, there are indications that the number that do nest here is growing slowly again. Green turtles are more common on the Atlantic than on the Gulf Coast.

Comments In recent years green turtle populations have been plagued by rapidly developing viral fibropapillomas. It is thought that susceptability to these viral growths may be enhanced by various pollutants. A great deal of research is now directed towards this problem. Florida populations are federally endangered.

136 ATLANTIC HAWKSBILL

Eretmochelys imbricata imbricata

Abundance Rarely seen in Florida, this species nests only infrequently on the state's beaches

Habitat Open ocean. The hawksbill is more frequently seen in the Atlantic than in the Gulf.

Size This is a rather small sea turtle. Adults range from 28 to 32 in. The record size is only 36 in. Most hawksbills weigh 100–175 lb.

Reproduction A body pit is dug, primarily with the foreflippers and then the nest is prepared with the rear flippers. Females nest bi- or triennially. Several clutches are laid in nesting years. The clutch size varies from 50 to more than 150 eggs. The 1.5-in.-long hatchlings emerge after about 60 days of incubation.

Coloration/pattern The carapace of the hawksbill is brown(ish), often with a prominent tortoise-shell pattern. The carapacial scutes are usually imbricate (overlapping). The plastron is light yellow in color. Young are quite similar to the adults in color but usually have a more vividly contrasting pattern. Hatchlings are very dark brown and lack a carapacial pattern. This species has a narrow hawklike beak. Yellow interstitial skin is visible between the head scales.

Similar species This is the only sea turtle of Florida with 4 costal scutes on each side *and* 4 prefrontal scales.

Behavior Because it is so solitary and so seldom seen, little is known about this turtle in Florida. Outside of Florida's waters, hawksbills feed on algae and other vegetation as well as on sponges, molluscs, crustacea, and myriad other marine creatures.

Comments Like most other sea turtles, the Atlantic hawksbill is considered endangered and is fully protected. The carapacial scutes were once used extensively in the manufacture of tortoise-shell for glasses frames and other items. Fortunately for these beleaguered turtles, plastic has largely taken the place of real tortoise-shell.

TURTLES AND TORTOISES

217

137 ATLANTIC RIDLEY

Lepidochelys kempii

Abundance Very rare and apparently declining.

Habitat This is an ocean-going species that was once common in the Gulf of Mexico.

Size The Atlantic ridley is the smallest of Florida's sea turtles. It is adult at 20–25 in.; its record size is only 29.5 in. Its average weight is about 90 lb.

Reproduction This species once appeared in vast nesting arribadas on the Gulf coast of northern Mexico. These congregations have been greatly reduced. Atlantic ridleys continue to breed in small numbers on the Mexican coast, the Texas coast, and rarely on both coasts of Florida.

Females nest only every second or third year. First a body pit is dug, then the egg-chamber. Seventy to 100 eggs are laid. Females may nest several times during each breeding season. The 1.5-in. hatchlings emerge after an incubation period of about 2 months.

Coloration/pattern Hatchlings are a rather uniform gray with a lighter stripe on the trailing edge of each front flipper. Adults are olive green to gray above and yellowish ventrally. There are 5 costals, 2 pairs of prefrontal scales and either 4 (usually) or 5 (rarely) pored scutes on the bridge.

Similar species Green turtles have only one pair of prefrontal scales. The Atlantic hawksbill has 4 costals on each side. Loggerhead has only 3 scutes (non-pored) on the bridge.

Behavior This is a communally breeding species, that because of serious depleted populations, is now forced to nest singly or in very small numbers. Headstart programs have been in place for some time now, but their actual benefit to the species remains uncertain.

Comments This is the most seriously endangered of the Florida sea turtles. It is encouraging that a few females have begun nesting on our beaches but the number seems far less than what is needed to assure the species' survival.

SNAPPING TURTLES
Family Chelydridae

Adult males of the alligator snapping turtle are among the world's largest freshwater turtles. Several specimens of more than 200 lb have been found and believable anecdotal reports exist of at least one 'gator snapper that exceeded 300 lb.

The common snappers are much smaller, but still well worthy of extreme care when approached on land. In the water they are much more benign. All of the snapping turtles have long tails, and the 2 races of the common snapper have long necks. The brown carapaces of all are very rough and prominently keeled, at least when the turtles are young.

138 FLORIDA SNAPPING TURTLE

Chelydra serpentina osceola

Abundance Despite its large size and the bad press that accompanies it, the Florida snapping turtle continues to be one of the most common turtles on the Florida peninsula. It is found from the southernmost tip of the mainland northward to the Georgia state line.

Habitat Nearly any quiet or slowly flowing and heavily vegetated body of freshwater and weakly brackish waters are acceptable homesites to this adaptable turtle.

Size Of the 2 subspecies found in Florida, this is slightly the smaller. It tops out at a 17-in. carapace length, which with tail extended and neck only partially so would add up to a turtle with a length of well over a yard! The weight of an adult wild specimen can be up to 25+ lb.

Reproduction These are fecund turtles that often dig first a body pit and then the nest. More than 50 eggs can be laid. Females nest annually. Depending on nest temperature and soil conditions, hatchlings can emerge after slightly less than two months or more than four months of incubation. Hatchlings have a carapacial length of about 1 in.

Coloration/pattern Hatchlings are rugose and chestnut to dark brown. They have a light spot on the outer edge of each marginal. Adults are somewhat smoother and olive-brown to dark-brown. The plastron is very small and pliable. The tail is longer than the cara-

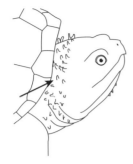
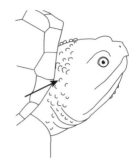

Chelydra serpentina osceola   *Chelydra serpentina serpentina*

The tubercles on the neck of the Florida snapping turtle (left) are long and papillate; those of the common snapping turtle (right) are shorter and rounded.

pace, and the neck, when fully extended in a snap, is nearly as long. The tail has a strongly serrate dorsal crest.

Adults are proportioned like the juveniles, but are less rugose. The posterior edge of the carapace is strongly serrate. This subspecies has conical papillae on the head and neck.

Specimens in water that is high in sulphur or iron may appear whitish or rusty. If algae are growing on the carapace, the turtle can appear green.

Similar species The alligator snapper has a more massive head with a strongly down-hooked beak, a shorter neck, and it lacks a strongly serrated dorsal tail crest.

Behavior When in its aquatic element, the Florida snapping turtle is usually quiet and relatively benign. When on land, it can be savagely defensive. Do not approach this turtle carelessly. It may elevate its hind quarters prior to snapping, but this is not an invariable.

Comments Snapping turtles continue to be a food source for many people. They are also indiscriminately killed by fishermen who erroneously blame the beasts for depleted stocks of game fish.

139 COMMON SNAPPING TURTLE

Chelydra serpentina serpentina

This replaces the Florida race in the entire panhandle and in Nassau County. It is a larger race, which may exceed 35 lb and have a carapace length of 19 in. or more. It is often of lighter color than the Florida race. A carapacial color of horn or olive-gray is not unusual. Light colored examples may have darker radiating markings on the costal scutes. The papillae on the neck of this race are rounded—not pointed cones. However, if you are close enough to a large specimen to determine the shape of the papillae, you may be *too* close to assure the safety of a finger or nose.

140 ALLIGATOR SNAPPING TURTLE

Macrochelys temminckii

Abundance This gigantic turtle is uncommon throughout its Florida range. It is found from Gilchrist and Alachua counties westward throughout the panhandle.

Habitat This is a turtle of big rivers, big creeks, backwaters, and reservoirs.

Size Males are by far the larger sex. They occasionally exceed 175 lb and rarely attain 250 lb (or more). Carapace length of a big male is 20–24 in. Adult females usually weigh less than 55 lb and are correspondingly smaller.

Reproduction Breeding occurs in the early spring, and egg laying begins a month or so later. In a site above the high water line, the female alligator snapper digs first a body pit and then the nest. An accessible bank or island is often chosen. Up to 50 eggs are laid. Incubation duration is somewhat more than 3 months. Hatchlings have a carapace length of about 1.5 in.

Coloration/pattern This is a brown turtle at all stages of its life. Hatchlings are mud-brown, dorsally and ventrally. Adults may darken or pale. On pale specimens there may be an indication of radiating dark lines on the costal scutes. Hatchlings are extremely rugose. With growth the carapace smooths somewhat and the rugosities of the head and neck become less accentuated. The plastron is very small. Although they are not easily seen, there is an extra row of scutes, the supramarginals, between the costals and the marginal scutes. The large head can not be withdrawn entirely within the shell. The dorsal surface of the tail is weakly serrate.

This turtle has a white (when at rest) to red (when in use) tongue appendage that resembles a worm. When hunting, the mouth is opened widely, the appendage is flicked, and when a passing fish swims into the mouth to investigate, the jaws snap shut. Dinner is served.

Similar species Common snappers have very long necks and strongly serrate tails.

Behavior Rather placid when in the water, this turtle can be aggressively defensive when on land. Because its neck is not as long, it is not quite as dangerous as a common snapper, but extreme care is still in order. Alligator snappers are persistently aquatic and only seldom wander on land.

Comments Larger specimens are eaten by humans. The hatchlings, perennial favorites in the pet trade, may no longer be commercialized in Florida.

LEATHERBACK
Family Dermochelyidae

This ocean-going behemoth is the largest turtle still extant. A carapace length of more than 6 ft and a weight of more than a ton have been recorded. This family has been erected solely for this divergent turtle.

Like all marine turtles, the leatherback has flipper-like limbs.

141 LEATHERBACK

Dermochelys coriacea

Abundance This is a rare and endangered turtle. It is occasionally seen in Florida's Atlantic and Gulf Coast waters. The occasional nestings have occured most frequently in the Brevard County region.

Habitat This is a pelagic marine species about which very little is known.

Size Most specimens seen are in the 3.5–4.5-ft carapace range, but 74.25 in. is the record carapace length.

Reproduction This immense turtle first digs a body pit with the fore-flippers, then a nesting cavity with the rear flippers. They nest above the tideline on open beaches. Several clutches of 150+ eggs are laid by a given female. The same female does not lay every year. Incubation takes from 2½–3½ months. Hatchlings are about 2.75 in. long.

Coloration/pattern The carapace and skin are slate blue to black. There are no plates on the carapace. There are scattered white, yellowish or pinkish markings. There are seven pronounced longitudinal keels on the carapace. The plastron is lighter than the carapace in color. Males have variably concave plastrons. Adult females tend to have pinkish markings on the top of the head. These may or may not be present on males. The front flippers are proportionately immense. Hatchlings, which are shaped much like a keeled torpedo (the immense foreflippers being the "stabilizers"), have a ground color quite like the adults but have numerous small (often white) scales (which are later shed), white keels, and white coloration outlining both front and rear flippers.

Voice Leatherbacks are capable of emitting sounds that are reminiscent of a human belch.

Similar species None.

Behavior This is a wide ranging turtle that is capable, because of circulatory modifications, of sustaining a warm body temperature in very cold waters. When disturbed or injured, leatherbacks have been known to attack boats. They are immensely powerful and extreme care should be used when observing them.

TURTLES AND TORTOISES

Comments Strangely, this, the largest turtle in today's world, is adapted to eat jellyfish. Deaths of even large individuals have occurred after the turtles mistakenly ingested discarded clear plastic bags.

BASKING AND BOX TURTLES
Family Emydidae

The emydine turtles are well represented in Florida. There are 10 species containing 21 subspecies. With the exception of the 4 subspecies of terrestrial box turtles, all of the Florida emydines are primarily aquatic.

Some, such as the spotted turtle, are rarely encountered in Florida. Others such as the various cooters and sliders are so common that it is sometimes difficult to complete a day in the field without seeing from one to several. Most of the basking turtles are freshwater species. However, the diamondbacked terrapins (one species with five described and one undescribed Florida races) are creatures of brackish and saltwater habitats, and several of the cooters are also regularly encountered in estuarine situations.

The loggerhead musk turtle, box turtles, river cooters, diamondbacked terrapins, and map turtles are protected or otherwise regulated by state laws.

142 SPOTTED TURTLE

Clemmys guttata

Abundance The population statistics of the spotted turtle in Florida are basically unknown, but the species is probably uncommon to rare. Some (many? most?) of the specimens found in Florida may have been escapees or deliberate releases. Occasional specimens have been found from northern Polk County northward to (and beyond) the Georgia line. Wakulla is thought to be the most westerly county of occurrence for the spotted turtle.

Habitat Few specimens have been field collected in Florida. Most that have been found are crossing roadways in the vicinity of periodically flooded pine flatwoods or sphagnum swamps. In some areas of their range spotted turtles periodically wander far away from their water sources. It is unknown to what extent this occurs in Florida.

Size This is the smallest of Florida's turtles. Adults of both sexes are 3.5–4.25 in. long (rarely to 4.75 in.).

Reproduction Nothing is known with certainty about the breeding biology of the Florida populations of the spotted turtle. Specimens from north of Florida breed in the rather early spring and females lay their small clutch of eggs (as few as 2, often 3 to 5, rarely 6 or 7) in the early summer. Captive spotted turtles can double clutch. Because of their normal period of summer inactivity, multiple clutches may not occur in the wild.

Coloration/pattern The black head of both sexes is spotted with yellow dorsally. The mandibular area, nose and chin of females are yellowish or orange. The corresponding facial areas of adult males are suffused with dark pigment. Spots on the sides of the head, neck and legs are usually distinctly orange. The skin at the apices of all limbs and the neck is orange. Males usually have brown eyes; females have yellow or orange irises (irides). The plastron is a dark-smudged orange. The carapace is very deep brownish-black to black with from one (hatchlings) to one or several (adults) yellow(ish) spots on each of the scutes (plates), including marginals. The spots are often the least precisely delineated on hatchlings.

Similar species There are no other Florida turtles with the yellow-spotted black carapace of the spotted turtle.

Behavior The spotted turtle is most common in heavily vegetated (often sphagnaceous) ponds with occasional small to extensive open swimming areas. Unless hard pressed, spotted turtles as often as not walk and burrow through and into the herbaceous aquatic vegetation. Northern populations of spotted turtles are most active in cool weather (spring and autumn) and are primarily diurnal in their activity patterns. By virtue of existing ambient temperatures in their Florida range, these southernmost spotted turtles are necessarily more tolerant of heat than their northern counterparts. However, it is possible that in Florida spotted turtles are active primarily during the comparative coolness of late autumn, winter, and spring.

Comments Every aspect of the life history of the spotted turtle in Florida is badly in need of study. Virtually everything stated about the behavior and needs of the spotted turtle in Florida is conjectural. Most definitive comments are based on the knowledge gathered about more northerly populations. Spotted turtles are seldom seen in Florida.

This species is an often kept "pet" turtle, and is now being bred in some numbers in captivity.

TURTLES AND TORTOISES

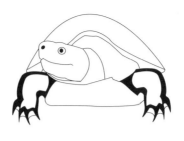

Comparative foreleg striping of the chicken turtles (top) and the yellow-bellied slider (bottom).

143 FLORIDA CHICKEN TURTLE

Deirochelys reticularia chrysea

Abundance This is a fairly common turtle species, but it is less frequently seen than many other aquatic species. It may be found statewide from the southern tip of the Florida peninsula to the latitude of central Alachua County.

Habitat Chicken turtles are typically associated with quiet, heavily vegetated bodies of water. Such habitats as grassy ditches, shallow canals, weedy ponds and equally weedy lake edges are among the preferred habitats of this turtle.

Size Although most specimens are adult at 5–7 in., occasional examples may slightly exceed 9 in.

Reproduction The chicken turtle is a fecund species that breeds throughout most of the year in southern Florida, but which may be more restricted to a late winter to autumn breeding season in the northern one quarter of its Florida range. Clutch sizes of as many as 15 eggs have been reported, but most clutches are 5–10 eggs. Females are known to multi-clutch. The eggs of the chicken turtle undergo a short-to-lengthy diapause (a temporary cessation of embryonic development) at some point. Diapause may be caused by various external stimuli. Because of the diapause the incubation period is variable, and may last 90–120 days.

Coloration/pattern Hatchlings and juveniles are more brightly colored and strongly patterned than adults. In all sizes the plastron is a rather bright, unmarked yellow. The carapace varies from olive-drab (especially if coated with mud or dried algae) to olive-green. There is a busy reticulum of rather broad, dark-edged, yellow carapacial stripes plus thin, dark circles and lines. Fine lineate rugosities exist on all carapacial scutes and to a lesser degree near the midline of the plastral scutes. These rugosities are roughly longitudinal on the marginals and costals, but are arranged in a radiating manner on the vertebrals. The slightest coating of algae will obscure these diagnostic markings. If viewed from above, the carapace will be seen to be edged in yellow. The elongate, smooth-edged carapace is narrowest anteriorly and broadest above the rear legs.

The neck of the chicken turtle is long and the head is narrow. Both are green(ish) brightly striped with yellow. The anterior of each forelimb bears a *broad* yellow stripe. The skin posterior to the shoulder and to each side of the tail bears *bright* yellow vertical markings.

Similar species The various sliders all have proportionately shorter necks and broader heads. Only the chicken turtle has a combination of a *single broad stripe* on the anterior of the forelimbs, vertical barring on each side of the tail, and no large yellow blotch or broad red(dish) stripe on the side of the head.

Behavior Chicken turtles bask extensively atop water-surface vegetation and exposed snags. They occasionally bask on the bank but are very wary and dive at the slightest disturbance. They wander far afield during the spring and summer months and may dig down into the dirt of litter to await a rainy-day-continuance of their journey. In south Florida, Florida chicken turtles are active year-round. In the more northerly sections of their range they may become inactive during the passage of cold fronts.

TURTLES AND TORTOISES

144 EASTERN CHICKEN TURTLE

Deirochelys r. reticularia

The Florida chicken turtle is replaced by the eastern chicken turtle from northern Alachua County northward. This race is also found across the entire panhandle.

The eastern chicken turtle is similar in most respects to its more southerly relative. However, its carapace is darker and is patterned with narrower, less contrasting, markings that are often greenish in color. Chicken turtles will bite readily if molested.

MAP TURTLES
Genus Graptemys

As a group, the map turtles are riverine species with fully webbed hind feet. They are among the wariest of turtles and are best watched and identified with binoculars.

There are 2 groups—the narrow-headed insect eaters (both male and females of this group are insect eaters; none occur in Florida) and the broad-headed species (adult females of this group develop enormously enlarged heads and are mollusc eaters, males have normally sized heads and are insect eaters; two species occur in Florida).

Females of the larger species are slow maturing, apparently requiring 14 or more years to attain sexual maturity. On the other hand, males reach sexual maturity in about 4 years.

An elaborate courtship of head and/or forelimb vibrations occurs.

The adult males of all are smaller than the adult females—some significantly so.

228

Graptemys barbouri

Abundance Locally common, the Barbour's map turtle is restricted in distribution to the panhandle's Apalachicola River drainage.

Habitat The Barbour's map turtles is a riverine species that is not known to migrate over land. In Florida this species occurs in the Apalachicola and Chipola rivers. It also ascends some of the feeder creeks of these rivers.

Size This species is tremendously dimorphic. Females routinely attain and exceed 9 in. in carapace length. Some may attain a foot in length. Males are rarely larger than 4.5 in.

Reproduction Barbour's map turtles breed in the spring of the year and females lay the first of 2 or more clutches 2–3 weeks later. Each clutch usually contains a dozen or fewer eggs, but a large, healthy female may nest 4 or more times annually. Sandbars and other sandy riveredge situations are the preferred nesting sites. Incubation seems lengthy, taking 70 or more days.

Coloration/pattern The carapacial ground color is gray to olive-brown. A prominent, black, vertebral keel is present in Barbour's map turtles of all ages, but is particularly prominent and saw-like on juveniles and males. Old females may lack any highlights. Juveniles and males have numerous yellow map-like lines in each carapacial scute including the marginals. The plastron is cream to yellow-olive with each scute outlined with dark pigment. The skin of the head and limbs has a ground color of olive or olive-gray. A very broad yellow-green blotch occurs posterior to each eye. This may curve up onto the snout between the eyes or break behind the eyes leaving the interorbital marking a discrete blotch. A broad curving bar on the chin parallels the lower jawline. A series of thin dark and light lines outline the posterior edge of the postocular blotches. The neck and limbs bear many thin greenish-yellow lines. Adult females have a very enlarged head and massive, crushing jaws. Take care not to be bitten by one. Males have a normally-sized head. Despite its comparative subtlety of color, most observers find this a very pretty turtle.

TURTLES AND TORTOISES

Similar species Range, coupled with the saw-like vertebral keel, should identify this turtle in the field. See also the Escambia map turtle [146].

Behavior This very wary turtle is both difficult to approach in the field and a very powerful swimmer. It occurs in riverine situations with a rather strong current. Barbour's map turtle basks extensively, usually on exposed snags, but occasionally on riveredge sandbars.

Comments Florida considers this turtle a species of special concern. It may not be collected for commercial purposes.

146 ESCAMBIA MAP TURTLE

Graptemys ernsti

Abundance In Florida the range of this newly described species is bordered by the Escambia River drainage on the west and the Yellow River drainage on the east. Suitable stretches of river can hold considerable populations of this turtle. Yet, due to its limited distribution, it should be considered a vulnerable species.

Habitat This riverine species occurs in swiftly flowing waters of fairly large rivers and creeks. It prefers areas with many exposed snags and logs upon which it can bask.

Size Females with 11-in. carapaces have been found. Males are adult at about 4.5 in.

Reproduction Several clutches of as many as 10 eggs each are laid annually. The nesting site is usually on a sand bar or more rarely a sandy shore. Incubation duration is about 75 days. Hatchlings have a carapace length of about 1.5 in.

Coloration/pattern Carapace color is olive-gray, gray, or olive-brown. A map-like pattern of dark-edged, light lines is present on all carapacial scutes, including marginals. The pattern is best defined on juveniles and males and may be all but obscured on old adult females. A black vertebral keel is present. This is most prominent on juvenile and male examples. The plastron is yellow but dark pigment is present along the seams of the scutes. The yellow-olive postocular and interorbital blotches are discrete. There are light lines on the neck and limbs. There is a light chin blotch at each outermost edge of the lower mandible.

Similar species Barbour's map turtle has a broad, curved bar on the chin paralleling the lower jawline. Barbour's map turtle does not occur in the Escambia-Yellow River drainages.

Behavior Like all map turtles, *G. ernsti* is wary and very difficult to approach. It suns extensively on protruding snags and branches, and seldom comes fully ashore except for the purpose of egg-laying.

Comments Until rather recently this turtle was considered conspecific with the Alabama map turtle, *G. pulchra*. It, and a more westerly species were recognized as distinct in 1992.

Commercialization of the Escambia map turtle is prohibited in Florida. Possession is limited to 2 per person.

DIAMONDBACKED TERRAPINS
Genus Malaclemys

As currently understood, there are 5 subspecies of diamondback found in Florida. The possibility exists that the diamondbacks of the Upper Keys are of a yet undescribed race. All have gray(ish) to nearly black carapaces and (usually) spots or streaks of black on a gray skin. The carapace usually shows prominent growth annuli. Dark pigmentation may follow the ridges of these annuli. Only one, the ornate diamondback, could even come close to being called brightly colored. This Florida west coast race has an orange center in each carapacial scute.

Because of their variable color and patterns, the several subspecies are difficult to identify. Knowing the origin of a specimen and checking the relative shape of the carapace from above may help.

The diamondbacks of the northern keys (from Key Colony Beach northward) are badly in need of research. They do not comfortably fit all criteria for any of the currently described subspecies.

These are turtles of brackish and saltwater habitats. Diamond-backed terrapins continue to exist, typically in diminished numbers, in suitable remaining patches of mainland habitat. Offshore island populations of some races seemingly remain more robust. In bygone years, these turtles often entered and succumbed in underwater crab traps. All races are now difficult to find, and one, the mangrove ter-rapin of the Lower Florida Keys, seems particularly so.

TURTLES AND TORTOISES

147 ORNATE DIAMONDBACKED TERRAPIN

Malaclemys terrapin macrospilota

Abundance Although the various diamondbacked terrapins still occur all along the Florida shoreline and on many of the keys and islands, all are greatly reduced in number. The ornate diamondback is a west coast resident that occurs roughly from the panhandle's Choctawatchee Bay to Key Largo.

Habitat The diamondbacked terrapins are residents of brackish and saltwater marshes, estuarine areas, coastlines, and similar habitats.

Size Females of the ornate diamondbacked terrapin attain a carapace length of 6–7.5 in. Males are smaller, often being only 4.5–5.5 in.

Reproduction As might be expected, larger female diamondbacks lay larger clutches than smaller ones. But with that said, clutches of Florida diamondbacks are not large to begin with. Between 4 and 8 eggs are normally laid in each clutch, but females often nest several times annually. Incubation duration is variable according, apparently, to both soil temperature and nest depth. Incubation may vary from 60–85 days. Hatchlings are 1–1.5 in. long.

Coloration/pattern The ornate diamondback has a gray(ish) carapace with orange scute centers and a gray skin that is profusely or sparsely dotted with black. A dark vertebral line (actually a very low keel) is present. The keel of some specimens is more prominent than that of others and may have a bulbous protuberance at the rear of each central scute. Females usually have a proportionately larger head than males. The plastron is dark and may be smudged with dark pigment. The center keel of some hatchlings may be so bulbous that the babies look deformed.

Similar species The various diamondbacks are the only turtles in Florida that are gray(ish) in color, that have normal feet (not flippers), that have a grayish skin speckled or marked with black, and that inhabit salt or brackish water. For additional subspecies accounts see "Comments." Any of the other emydine turtles that enter saltwater will have yellow-striped heads and necks.

Behavior These are wary turtles and difficult to observe. They may be seen (with binoculars) basking on, or walking between oyster beds and mudflats. Diamondbacks may be active year-round in Florida.

Comments Only 40 years ago diamondbacked terrapins were relatively common in Florida. Even 15 years ago, chats with crabbers disclosed that many diamondbacks of various subspecies still were being caught (and often drowned) in crab traps. By 10 years ago, many fewer diamondbacks were seen, and it now takes a concerted search, or more than a modicum of luck, to find one.

Besides the ornate diamondback, there are 4 additional described races, and, seemingly, one that is, as yet, undescribed, found at various points along the Florida coastline. Where the ranges of any two abut, difficult to identify intergrades occur. Older examples are usually darker than young ones, and barnacles may attach to the shell and obscure some characteristics. We suggest that you rely primarily on distribution when attempting identification of diamondbacked terrapins.

148 CAROLINA DIAMONDBACKED TERRAPIN

Malaclemys t. centrata

Occurring as far south on the east coast of Florida as southern Flagler County, this is a variable and pretty turtle, which has a fairly light to very dark, (usually) almost unicolored, carapace and prominent growth annuli. The head and limbs are light-gray, spotted or weakly streaked with black. The sides of the carapace are nearly parallel when viewed from above. When of the darkest color, this race does not have prominent darker middorsal markings but, if the carapace is light in color, the low, vertebral tubercles are usually darker than the surrounding shell.

149 Mississippi Diamondbacked Terrapin

M. t. pileata

At the far side of Florida, from the panhandle area of Choctawatchee Bay westward to (and beyond) the state line, we may encounter the very dark colored Mississippi diamondbacked terrapin. The carapace is grayish-black to charcoal. The vertebral tubercles are often at least slightly darker than the surrounding shell color. Except for the black cranial area, the skin of the head, neck, and limbs is light to dark gray and may be spotted, weakly streaked, or almost unicolored. The upper mandible is dark, giving the appearance that the turtle is wearing a mustache.

150, 151 Mangrove Diamondbacked Terrapin

M. t. rhizophorarum

South of Marathon, on Florida's Lower Keys, we enter the realm of the very pretty, rather poorly known, and seldom seen mangrove diamondbacked terrapin. It is a rather dark race; the carapace is blackish and there is a vertebral keel. The plastral seams are variably (but often broadly) edged with black pigment. The top of the head is black. The sides of the face and the neck are usually light gray. The head and neck markings may be nearly absent, may be prominent discrete spots, or may be coalesced into heavy, irregular black stripes. The upper mandible is usually dark. The overall appearance is very pleasing.

Despite often being referred to the race *M. t. rhizophorarum*, the diamondbacked terrapin found at the southernmost tip of the Florida mainland and the Upper Keys [151], is, most likely, an undescribed race. It is particularly variable in coloration and pattern. Its status is currently being researched.

M. t. tequesta

This race of diamondback usually has a grayish carapace, which may lack the dark rings that outline the (usually) prominent annuli. The center of each carapacial scute *may* be lighter than the rest of the shell. A weak vertebral keel is present. The raised vertebral tubercles *may* be darker than the surrounding shell. The sides of the head, neck, and limbs are light gray and the spots of the face are big (but are *usually* not stripes) and boldly black. The center of the head is dark and a variably dark mustache is usually present.

152

COOTERS, RED-BELLIED TURTLES, AND SLIDERS
Genera Pseudemys and Trachemys

These are the big pond turtles of Florida, which, in one species or another may be found over the entire state. The sliders of the genus *Trachemys* were long considered a *Pseudemys*. The accounts for *Trachemys* may be found on pages 162–163.

The sliders and cooters are persistent baskers, but slide into the water at the first sign of disturbance. The females are often larger than the males. The males of some have elongated front claws that are used during their aquatic courtship rituals.

Babies are brightly colored (usually green with darker markings dorsally), adults are usually less so. Old adult males of some species become suffused with pattern obliterating melanin and may look virtually black or olive-black. The heads and necks of most are strongly striped.

Location of the highest point on the carapace may be as important in reaching a positive identification as are shell and head pattern.

Compare the pattern and marking color on the second costal scute.

Because of the release of unwanted specimens, the popular pet turtle, the red-eared slider, *Trachemys scripta elegans,* has become the most widely distributed turtle in the world. Besides the Mississippi drainage (to which it was native), it occurs virtually throughout the

TURTLES AND TORTOISES

235

United States (including Florida, of course), in France, Japan, Australia, and other countries as well.

Hatchlings and young specimens are largely insectivorous, but larger specimens of many species are primarily herbivorous.

All may be difficult to identify, especially if dry. Wet shells show age-obscured patterns best. The field marks mentioned will usually allow you to make a positive identification, but these marks can vary on some specimens.

Taxonomy of many of these big turtles is in disarray. We have opted for conservative taxonomy here.

The races of *Pseudemys concinna* are considered river cooters. The races of *Pseudemys floridana* are usually pond and ditch cooters. The races of *Trachemys scripta* are called sliders.

153 MOBILE COOTER

Pseudemys concinna mobilensis

Abundance Mobile Cooters remain common throughout their range. They are restricted in distribution to the panhandle of Florida, from Wakulla and Leon counties, westward.

Habitat This is a species of springs, spring runs, rivers, and large creeks. Mobile cooters may also be encountered in brackish and salty estuaries.

Size This is a large species of freshwater turtle. Females regularly attain 11 in. in length and occasionally reach a foot in carapace length. Males are usually somewhat smaller.

Reproduction River cooters typically construct 3 nests, a principal center nest into which most of the clutch is laid, and a satellite nest on each side which usually contain only a few eggs each. Following the deposition, the central nest is usually covered carefully and largely obliterated, but less care is shown in covering the subordinate nests. Predators, such as raccoons, often find and pillage the subordinate nests but are less apt to locate the main nest. As with most turtles, clutch (and, perhaps, egg) size varies with the size of the female; the largest females produce the most and largest eggs, and nest most often during each season. From 8–24+ eggs are laid in each clutch, and healthy females have been found to nest up to 6 times in a season. Females may need to wander far from the water to find a suitably exposed nesting spot. Incubation takes 2½–3 months. Hatchlings are about 1.5 in. long.

Coloration/pattern Hatchlings are a pretty, busily patterned green. Adults are equally busily patterned, and dark brown to nearly black. The carapacial markings of old adults are difficult to discern. The second costal scute contains a stylized C in the upper rear corner. The arms of this C can continue on and close in the next scute, forming an O. Consider *only* the part of the marking in the second scute. The plastron is yellow with dark pigment following the scute seams. Ocelli occur on the underside of each marginal. Each ocellus involves the rear of one marginal scute and the anterior of the next.

The head and legs are very dark with well defined orangish markings. There is a rather broad orangish interorbital stripe, which usually is not tipped on the snout by a >; in other words, this marking *usually* does not form an arrow. Males have greatly elongated foreclaws.

Similar species Chicken turtles have a single broad stripe on the forelimb, a narrow head, a very long neck, and an unmarked plastron. Florida cooters have an unmarked plastron and no C on the second costal scute. Yellow-bellied sliders have prominently yellow cheeks. Red-eared sliders have red post-orbital bars. Florida red-bellied turtles have an arrow between the eyes and a single broad (usually orange) vertical bar in the second costal scute.

Behavior This is a very wary turtle that usually does not allow approach. Binoculars will help with long-distance identification. Eliminate as many similar species as possible, taking the range into account, and go from there.

Comments Although some authorities consider *P. c. mobilensis* an invalid subspecies, there remains much controversy on this. We have chosen to follow the tentative conclusions of Dundee and Rossman, and the more definite conclusions of Ernst, Lovich, and Barbour, and recognize this race. If it is found that the subspecies *P. c. mobilensis* is invalid, the river cooters of the Florida panhandle would be of intergrade status.

154 SUWANNEE COOTER

Pseudemys concinna
suwanniensis

The taxonomic status and range of the
Suwannee cooter are also in question. Some
authorities consider it allopatric, and interpret the
range as being on Florida's western peninsula from
Hillsborough to Dixie counties. Such interpretation is in
error. The impression of allopatrism is the result of
inconclusive sampling rather than reality. Actually, Wakulla
County in the eastern panhandle, is the dividing line
for the two contiguous races.

The Suwannee cooter is very similar to the Mobile cooter in most
respects. However, it is larger, with females regularly attaining a 16-
in.+ carapace length, and the head stripes are paler. Striping is often
white, pale yellow, or greenish-yellow. The ground color is very
dark. Positive identification can be problematic.

155 FLORIDA COOTER

Pseudemys floridana floridana

Abundance This is a common turtle that is distributed widely in northern peninsular Florida and
throughout the panhandle.

Habitat This turtle is pretty much a generalist in its
choice of aquatic habitats. It is found in sloughs, marshes,
slow areas of rivers, ponds, lakes, and most other water
bodies.

Size Although the largest females can exceed 15 in., most
are smaller, with 8–12 in. the usual size for both sexes.

Reproduction Like the Mobile and Suwannee cooters, the Florida
cooter digs a main nest and (usually 2) subordinate nests. The main
complement of eggs is placed in the main chamber with a few in each
of the subordinates. The main nest is carefully concealed when deposition is completed. Often less care is shown in obliterating the tell-
tale signs of the satellite nests. Clutch size varies from 8–20+, and
large, healthy females routinely nest several times annually. Depending on soil temperature and nest depth, hatching occurs in 60–90
days. Hatchlings are 1–1.25 in. long.

Coloration/pattern This big dark (often olive-brown), cooter has a busy carapacial pattern of light (often pale green) markings, but lacks the C that identifies the river cooters. There is often a broad light vertical bar on the second costal. This may be forked at its extremities. The marginals bear oval ocelli. The yellow to pale orange plastron is unmarked. Hatchlings are a much brighter green than the adults.

Similar species Chicken turtles have a narrow head, long neck, and single broad stripe on the forelimbs. Mobile and Suwannee cooters have a light letter C on the second costal, the yellow-bellied slider has a large yellow cheek patch and the red-eared slider has a broad, reddish, postorbital stripe. The Florida red-bellied turtle has a yellow arrow extending to the snout from between the eyes.

Behavior This turtle basks extensively on exposed snags or non-vegetated areas of the shoreline throughout most of the year. Florida cooters often bask with other sympatric species. It may be inactive during the coldest days of winter.

Comments Florida cooters are known to hybridize with river cooters, producing difficult to identify specimens. Sometimes the best an observer can do is say that a questionable specimen most closely resembles one or the other species.

156 PENINSULA COOTER

Pseudemys floridana
peninsularis

Because of a distinctive head pattern, the southern representative of the species is more easily identified. The peninsula cooter occurs throughout peninsular Florida to Levy, Alachua, and Duval counties.

It, too, is big (to 14 in.+), dark, and has the highest point of the shell anterior to midpoint. The head is patterned with numerous stripes, but there is a hairpin on each side of the head behind the eyes. The open ends of this continue well onto the neck.

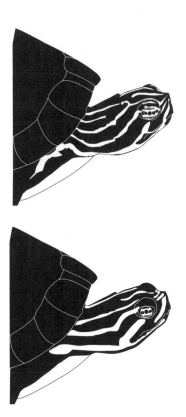

The peninsula cooter (top) has a light "hairpin-shaped" marking behind the eye. The Florida red-bellied turtle (bottom) has a light line between the eye and a light forward-directed **V** on the nose. Together these form a spear-shaped marking.

157 FLORIDA RED-BELLIED TURTLE

Pseudemys nelsoni

Abundance This beautifully colored turtle is common over the entire peninsula and occurs in an apparently disjunct population in the Apalachicola region of the peninsula.

Habitat The Florida red-bellied turtle occurs in nearly any permanent body of freshwater—ponds, lakes, ditches, canals, rivers, and streams.

Size This is a big, thick-shelled turtle that occasionally exceeds a foot in length. Females are the larger sex.

Reproduction From 8 to 25+ eggs are laid in each clutch. Females may nest several times annually. Female *P. nelsoni* may dig their nest either into the soil or into an alligator nest. Incubation takes 50–80 days. Hatchlings are about 1.25 in. long.

Coloration/pattern Hatchlings are green with a busy dark carapacial pattern. The plastron is often a bright orange to red orange with large but discrete dark spots along the seams of some scutes. Adults are olive-brown to nearly black with vertical orange bars in each costal. The plastral pattern and color fades. The plastron is often an unrelieved orange-yellow or yellow. Submarginal markings are entirely dark rather than ocelli. Males are often more brightly colored than females. A suffusion of melanin sometimes largely obscures the colors of old red-bellies of both sexes. There are few yellow lines on the dark head. The most constant identifying mark is the arrow. The shaft is between the eyes and the point contours the snout. The jaw style is also diagnostic for this species in Florida. A medial notch in the upper jaw is edged on each side by a downward projecting cusp. Males have long foreclaws.

Similar species When this turtle is in hand or within suitable binocular distance the arrow between the eyes is a good diagnostic tool. The orange (juvenile specimens) to yellow (larger specimens) plastron and vertical orange costal bars should further assist in a positive identification.

Behavior Although wary, the Florida red-bellied slider may allow closer approach than congenerics. These are among Florida's most beautiful turtles.

Comments Although a wary turtle that is usually best observed with binoculars, it has become acclimated to the presence of people in state and federal parks, etc. where it has long been protected.

Box Turtles
Terrapene carolina ssp.

These are the most divergent of Florida's emydine turtles. All are primarily terrestrial in habits, with only one, the Gulf Coast box turtle, readily entering deep water. In fact, most box turtles are distressed if in the water and bob on the surface like corks as they clumsily paddle to land.

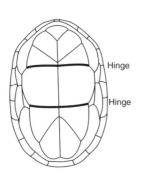
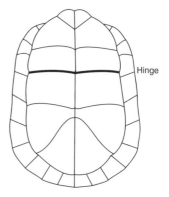

The plastron (bottom shell) of the mud turtles (left) has two hinges while that of the box turtles (right) has a single hinge.

The forefeet are stubby and short, the rear feet are rather typical but unwebbed. These turtles all have comparatively highly domed carapaces, although on the Gulf Coast box turtle this is often centrally flattened.

The plastron of adult box turtles is prominently hinged crossways and is attached at the bridge by tough cartilage. The hinge is nonfunctional at hatching but fully so by the time the box turtle is half grown.

There is some indication that populations of box turtles are being adversely affected (in some areas of the country, seriously so) by predation by the introduced tropical fire ant.

158 FLORIDA BOX TURTLE

Terrapene carolina bauri

Abundance Once common to abundant, populations of the Florida box turtle are now reduced in number. However, the species is still present, often in considerable numbers, wherever suitable habitat remains. This race ranges from Key West northward to the Georgia state line. It is replaced in the panhandle by other races (see "Comments").

Habitat The Florida box turtle may be found in open mixed woodland, damp pasture edges, marshes, periodically flooded pine flatwoods, and other such areas. These are primarily terrestrial turtles that may enter shallow water but are uncomfortable in water of a depth where they must swim.

Size Males, the larger sex, attain a carapacial length of a little more than 6.25 in. Females are adult at 4–5 in.

Reproduction Breeding occurs in the late winter and early spring in the southern part of the state and in the spring in the north. The usual clutch consists of from 2–5 (rarely to 7) eggs, which are laid in a freshly dug hole that at times barely contains them. The incubation duration is 55–68 days. Hatchlings are about 1.25 in. long.

Coloration/pattern The Florida box turtle has a narrow, highly domed carapace with the highest point *posterior* to midpoint. Its color is deep brownish-black to black with radiating yellow lines and a yellow vertebral keel. There are two yellow stripes on the sides of the face, which is rather light in color. The skin of the leg apices and neck is also light. The plastron is yellow with variable dark markings.

Hatchlings are colored like the adults, but the yellow carapacial radiations are broken into irregular spots. The vertebral keel is yellow, and dual yellow cheek lines are present. The eyes of both sexes are dark.

Box turtles derive their common name from the muscular hinged plastron that allows them to close tightly (like a box). The hinge is undeveloped in hatchlings, only poorly developed in juveniles, but well developed by the time the turtles are half grown. Most Florida box turtles have only 3 toes on each hind foot. Adult males have a prominent concavity in the rear lobe of their plastron. This helps them remain positioned for the breeding sequence.

Similar species Box turtles are the only highly domed terrestrial turtles found in Florida that have a *single* plastral hinge (see other subspecies accounts in [159–161]). The aquatic mud turtles are less colorful, smaller, lower domed, and have two plastral hinges.

Behavior Box turtles are primarily terrestrial but will readily enter the shallow water of a sloped ditch or rain puddle to drink and soak. Of the 4 races supposedly found in Florida, only the Gulf Coast box turtle readily enters deep water.

TURTLES AND TORTOISES

159 Eastern Box Turtle

Terrapene carolina carolina

If it occurs in Florida at all, the eastern box turtle does so only in the extreme northeastern section of the state along the Georgia state line. Most specimens show characteristics intermediate between the eastern and Gulf Coast races. Only from northeastern Baker County are found box turtles showing typical eastern characteristics.

The eastern box turtle is less highly domed than the Florida. It is also slightly more oval, slightly larger, and very differently colored.

Although these turtles are of variable color, the carapace, head, neck, and limbs of the eastern box turtle are usually brown or brownish with irregular olive, orange, or yellow markings. The plastron may be similarly or somewhat differently colored. Either the dark or the light color may predominate. Males often have bright red irides; those of females are buff or brown. Males, which are the larger sex and which have a variable degree of flaring to the rear marginals, have a prominent concavity in the rear lobe of the plastron. This race tends to have 4 toes on the hind feet.

160 Gulf Coast Box Turtle

Terrapene carolina major

With adult males attaining a carapace length of 7.5 in. (rarely to 8.5 in.), the Gulf Coast box turtle is the largest of Florida's box turtles. It is also the most aquatic and occasionally may be seen walking or foraging on the bottoms of ponds, puddles, or canals. It also forages terrestrially. *Terrapene c. major* is found in its pure form only in the woodlands, stream- and canal-edges, pinewoods, and marshes of the southern Florida panhandle. Areas of possible racial-intergradation exist where the ranges of the various subspecies abut.

The Gulf Coast race is a dark box turtle. The ground color (which usually predominates) is brown or black, and the variable carapacial markings are yellowish or olive. Males often have red irides; those of the females are dark. Rather than being highly domed, the carapace of this race is depressed centrally. The plastron is usually darkest anteriorly and males have a prominent concavity in the rear lobe. Males are the larger sex. Most unintergraded Gulf Coast box turtles have 4 toes on each hind foot. Where intergradation with either the Florida or three-toed box turtles occurs, the rear toes may number either three or four. Old adult Gulf Coast Box Turtles have a prominent flaring to the posterior marginals. Old males often have a variable amount of white on their faces. This may be restricted to the anterior chin and mandibles or so extensive that it involves the whole head.

161 THREE-TOED BOX TURTLE

Terrapene c. triunguis

In its pure form, the three-toed box turtle does not enter Florida. However, because its influence may be seen in the Gulf Coast box turtles found in the Florida Panhandle along the Alabama and Georgia borders, we mention it here.

In its non-intergraded form the three-toed box turtles are usually quite dull in coloration. The carapacial ground color is horn, olive, tan or buff with or without lighter radiations or teardrop-shaped markings. Eye color does not differ significantly by sex. The plastron is yellowish or olive and devoid of markings. Males often lack the rear-lobe plastral concavity that is so prominent in other races. Variable red and/or white markings may be present on the dark cheeks. This is a small race. It is often fully adult at 4–5 in. This race usually has 3 toes on each hind foot.

162 YELLOW-BELLIED SLIDER

Trachemys scripta scripta

Abundance This is a common pond slider throughout the northern one third of the state, including the panhandle.

Habitat The yellow-bellied slider is common to abundant in the (usually) heavily vegetated ponds, lakes, canals, ditches, and other such bodies of water throughout its range.

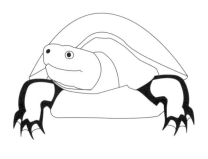

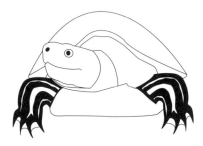

Comparative foreleg striping of the chicken turtles (top) and the yellow-bellied slider (bottom).

Size Typically these pretty turtles attain an adult length of 5–8 in. Some exceed 10 in. Adult males are usually somewhat smaller than the females.

Reproduction Mating occurs in the spring and egg-laying follows shortly thereafter. Females can lay from two to several nests of 8-17 eggs at roughly monthly intervals. They may wander well away from the water in search of their nesting site. Depending on temperature and ground moisture levels, incubation lasts 55–90+ days.

Coloration/pattern The coloration of this slider varies with age. Hatchlings have a greenish carapace with many darker and lighter markings. The head is greenish with extensive areas of yellow on the sides of the face and diagonal yellow lines from the snout to the chin. The limbs are also greenish and bear *several* stripes (fore limbs) or spots (rear limbs) of yellow. The skin to each side of the tail is vertically striped with green and yellow.

With growth the green in the ground color is lost and the carapace, limbs, and head darken to an olive drab or olive-black. The yellow markings of the carapace broaden but dull to an olive-yellow or a pale olive-green. The yellow of the cheeks and snout are the last of the markings to dull (if they ever do).

Old specimens may be almost uniformly black (with the oldest males being the darkest), but at least vestiges of the yellow cheeks usually remain visible.

Juveniles, sub-adults, and young adults have prominent, dark, rounded, markings on the lower surface of the marginals and on the anterior plastron. Most sexually mature males have elongated front claws.

Similar species This is the only turtle of Florida with prominent yellow cheeks (see the red-eared slider [163]). If identification is in doubt, compare also the accounts for the various river and Florida cooters [153–156] and the Florida red-bellied turtle [157]. The chicken turtle has an extraordinarily long neck and only a single yellow stripe on the front of its forelimbs.

Behavior Yellow-bellied turtles bask extensively on exposed snags and banks or on mats of surface vegetation, but are wary and difficult to approach. They are best observed from a vehicle with binoculars. Babies may often be found foraging atop floating mats of *Hydrilla* or other such vegetation. (Also see pages 235–236.)

163 RED-EARED SLIDER

Trachemys scripta elegans

Native to the Mississippi River drainages, now occurs in Florida's waters. As a matter of fact, because of releases of unwanted pet red-ears, this non-native turtle may now be found from the freshwater retention ponds of the southernmost Keys northward throughout the state. Intergrades between this and the native yellow-bellied slider are seen with increasing frequency *throughout* the range of the latter.

For six (or more) decades, the red-eared slider has been prominent in the pet trade of the world. It is the little "green" or "painted" turtle that was once seen in the pet departments of nearly every five- and ten-cent store and pet shop in the USA. Federal health regulations have now curtailed its availability somewhat, but it is still readily commercially available to those who want it.

Hatchlings of the red-eared slider have carapaces of green patterned with numerous *narrow* lighter and darker lines. The submarginal and plastral scutes are patterned with irregular dark ocelli. The face and limbs are green with numerous yellow stripes. The very broad red temporal stripe, from which this turtle takes its name, is usually prominently evident.

Colors and pattern dull with age. Males are often duller than females of a similar age. Old males can be entirely devoid of pattern and nearly a uniform dark-olive to olive-black in color. This species attains a carapace length of 7–12 in. Sexually mature males have elongate front claws.

The presence of the red-eared slider in Florida's waters (indeed, throughout much of the world) presents an unequaled and unwanted story of success. It seems that wherever the turtle is released it takes hold and thrives. Unwanted pet specimens should be placed in caring foster homes, never released into the wild. (Also see pages 235–236.)

MUD AND MUSK TURTLES
Family Kinosternidae

Collectively, the Florida representatives of this family are small turtles with rather highly domed carapaces, that are basically aquatic in habits. They often occur in shallow water situations and some wander far afield in search of new habitats.

Our musk turtles have plastrons so reduced in size that they offer little protection to the turtle's soft parts, and pointed conical noses. The plastron of the mud turtles are larger (but still small) and the noses are not as pointed.

The plastron of the mud turtle has 2 hinges, but the abdominal scutes are rather rigidly affixed to the bridge. Thus, the front lobe

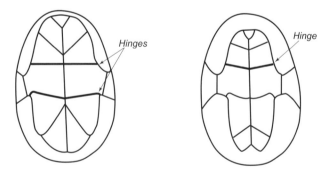

Mud turtles (left) have a comparatively large plastron with two hinges; musk turtles (right) have a reduced plastron with one hinge.

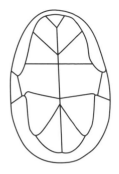
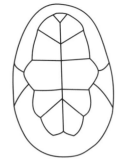

Kinosternon subrubrum subrubrum   *Kinosternon subrubrum steindachneri*

The rear lobe of the plastron of the eastern mud turtle (left) is wide and the bridge (the connector between the carapace and the plastron) is wide. The rear lobe of the plastron of the Florida mud turtle is smaller and the bridge is narrow.

(consisting of the gular, humeral and pectoral scutes) and the rear lobe (consisting of the femoral and the anal scutes) are movable to a degree. Musk turtles have a movable front plastral lobe.

Adult male musk and mud turtles have a heavy, enlarged tail that is usually tipped with a curved spur.

These turtles all have strong jaws and will bite if restrained or prodded and given the opportunity.

The carapacial patterns (of those species which have them) may be obscured by age and nearly impossible to see when the shell is dry. Immersing the turtle in water may heighten color and pattern.

A musky exudate is produced in glands that are situated where the skin meets the bridge of the shell.

164 STRIPED MUD TURTLE

Kinosternon baurii

Abundance This is an abundant turtle that occurs in most freshwater and some brackish water situations throughout peninsular Florida and the Keys.

Habitat Ponds, lakes, swamps, marshes, canals, ditches, estuaries and most other weakly-brackish situations are all used by this small turtle. At times it may be found far from water, hunkered down under boards, leafmats or other terrestrial debris.

Size Most striped mud turtles are adult at 3.5–4.25 in. Rarely are they a full 5 in. long.

Reproduction Adult females lay several clutches of 1–4 eggs. The nesting site may be in wateredge soil or in decaying aquatic vegetation, either at water's edge or in thick floating mats. Incubation takes 3–4 months. Hatchlings have a carapace length of 1 in.

Coloration/pattern Striped mud turtles have a black, brown, or duskily translucent carapace color. There are usually three longitudinal yellowish lines on the carapace (carapacial stripes are typically lacking in Gulf Hammock and Okefenokee populations). The plastron is olive-yellow to orange with dark pigment outlining each scute. The head is basically dark but there are 2 variably prominent stripes on each side of the mottled face and a yellowish chin stripe.

Similar species The common musk turtle also has face stripes but lacks carapacial stripes and has a reduced plastron (see diagram page **248**).

Behavior The striped mud turtle may be active by day, but actively forages in water edge situations after nightfall. It may bury deeply into the mud when its water source dries, or it may strike out across country in search of another. Populations often concentrate in the puddles that form as their home waters dry.

Comments Many of the striped mud turtles from the lower Keys have a particularly translucent carapace. They also seem to have a proportionately shorter snout. These were long designated as the nominate subspecies and provided the name of *K. baurii baurii*. The upper Keys and mainland populations were then called *K. baurii palmarum*. It is now felt that the populations are not sufficiently distinct to be designated as subspecies. Despite this, the Lower Key populations are considered endangered and are protected.

165 FLORIDA MUD TURTLE

Kinosternon subrubrum
steindachneri

Abundance Common, but not often seen in the concentrations associated with the striped mud turtle. The Florida mud turtle occurs throughout the southern three quarters of the peninsula.

Habitat Although the Florida mud turtle is often found sympatrically with the striped mud turtle, it is never as common as the latter. Ponds, cypress heads, flooded flatwood situations, river edges, and estuarine situations are among its habitats.

Size This is a small mud turtle with a big head. Its adult size is usually 4 in. or less.

Reproduction Adult females produce several clutches of 3–5 eggs during the spring and summer months. The nests may be dug in sand, soil, or decaying vegetation. The hatchlings, which emerge after a 3+-month incubation, are about an inch in length.

Coloration/pattern The carapace and head of this turtle are a warm to dark olive-brown. The posterior edge of each carapacial scute, including the marginals, may be outlined by dark pigment. There may be yellowish spots on the cheeks, and the jaws of many specimens are lighter than the head. Many males develop a very enlarged head. The plastron is orangish. The rear lobe of the plastron of this subspecies is of reduced size. Hatchlings have a roughened carapace and pinkish plastron.

Similar species The striped mud turtle is darker and usually has carapacial stripes. Where the arranges of the eastern and the Florida mud turtles abut, distinguishing the two will be a problem. See [166].

Behavior This is a highly aquatic turtle that is less prone to long overland journeys than the striped mud. However, the Florida mud turtle does wander and may be found in terrestrial situations. It secludes itself by day but comes into the shallows to forage at night.

TURTLES AND TORTOISES

166 MISSISSIPPI MUD TURTLE

K. s. hippocrepis

At least some of the eastern mud
turtles of the extreme western panhandle show
some characteristics of the more westerly Mississippi
mud turtle. West of Florida, this race is typified by having two well defined but irregular stripes on each side of
its head. Mud turtles of the westernmost peninsula often
show at least indications of the lower cheek stripe, but seldom, if ever, have any indications of the upper (canthal)
stripe. Although the head patterns of the two are very similar, the Mississippi mud turtle lacks the 3 carapacial stripes
that distinguish most populations of the striped mud turtle.

167 EASTERN MUD TURTLE

Kinosternon subrubrum
subrubrum

This is found in Florida in a narrow band
from the Georgia border southward to Taylor,
Columbia and Duval counties and westward
throughout the panhandle.

The Eastern mud turtle is very similar to the Florida
but has a proportionately larger rear carapacial lobe as
well as a proportionately broader bridge.

Male eastern mud turtles do not seem to develop the
enlarged head often seen on males of the Florida race.

Eastern mud turtles often wander far from water and may be
found beneath terrestrial debris.

Sternotherus minor minor

Abundance The loggerhead musk turtle is a
common turtle of the clear springs and spring-fed rivers
of the northern one half of the Florida peninsula and
the eastern panhandle.

Habitat It is invariably associated with flowing,
freshwater habitats and their associated overflows and
drainages.

Size An adult size of 5 in. is attained by this species.

Reproduction Adult females usually lay several clutches of 2–5 eggs
early each summer. Little effort is made at concealing the nests,
which may be situated against a tree, stump, rock, or other promi-
nence, or merely be scratched into the ground litter. Incubation takes
about 3 months. Hatchlings average 1 in. in carapace length.

Coloration/pattern The high, 3-keeled carapace may vary through
several shades of brown and has downward radiating dark lines that
are most prominent on the costal scutes. The head is grayish and is
liberally peppered with black dots. The small plastron is yellowish.
Old males are very dark in overall color, develop an enormous head,
and may have light mandibles. Hatchlings have a light tan carapace
and a bright pink plastron.

Similar species Mud turtles have proportionately larger plastrons
(see diagram page **248**).

Behavior Although loggerhead musks are highly aquatic, they do
occasionally move about on land. They occasionally bask by ascending protruding snags or cypress knees or exposed, sloping tree
trunks. They are active both by day and night, but are more apt to
enter shallow water situations after dark.

TURTLES AND TORTOISES

169 STRIPED-NECKED MUSK TURTLE

Sternotherus minor peltifer

From Walton County westward in
the panhandle, the loggerhead musk turtles
begin to show the influence of the more westerly race.

The carapace is proportionately flatter and the two
dorsolateral keels are less prominent. The overall color
may be darker and the head and neck spots coalesce into
stripes. This race still prefers creeks and streams but also
inhabits nearby lakes, reservoirs, and can be particularly
common in impoundments.

170 COMMON MUSK TURTLE

Sternotherus odoratus

Abundance This species is abundant throughout the state.

Habitat The common musk turtle may be found in virtually any still or slowly flowing water source.

Size The carapace length of adults of this common turtle
ranges from 3–4.5 in.

Reproduction In Florida, female common musk turtles
begin nesting early in the spring. Each female may nest 2 or more
times and the usual clutch size is 1–5 eggs. The 1-in.-long hatchlings
emerge after about 2½ months of incubation.

Coloration/pattern Old adults have an olive-black (rarely olive),
black-stippled, to solid black, smooth, rather highly-domed carapace.
The small plastron is horn color. Males have considerable expanses
of skin showing between the plastral scutes; females have almost
none. The skin of the head and limbs is dark, and there are 2 variably prominent yellow lines on the side of the head. The carapace of
the hatchlings is usually black in color and rough, with a strong
medial keel and a weak dorsolateral keel on each side.

Similar species Striped mud turtles have striped faces but also usually
have carapacial stripes, which the common musk turtle lacks.

Behavior Despite its aquatic propensities, the common musk turtle
often wanders extensively on land. Common musks occasionally

enter shallow water in great numbers at dusk during the spring breeding season.

Comments This is one of the most abundant turtles in Florida. At night they walk, rather than swim, along the bottom of their pond or lake in search of worms or insects. These turtles can and will bite hard if carelessly restrained.

Primitive Side-Necked Turtles
Family Pelomedusidae

This family of turtles is restricted in distribution to South America, Africa, the Seychelles Islands, and the island continent of Madagascar.

In bygone years, many species were commonplace in the American pet trade, but many are now classed as endangered species and are seldom seen.

Several species of African mud turtle continue to be imported for the pet marketplace, and of these, *P. subniger,* the East African black mud turtle, is the most often seen. It is a powerful but secretive species and has, reportedly, been established in Dade County for considerably over a decade.

The fact that it folds its neck and head sideways under the anterior lip of the carapace, rather than withdrawing them in a vertical S, will help in identifying this turtle.

Although very aquatic, turtles of this genus are known to wander widely and to be able to survive droughts by digging deeply into the mud as their ponds dry.

171 East African Black Mud Turtle

Pelusios subniger subniger

Abundance The status of this predacious East and South African turtle in Florida is not known with certainty. It is so secretive and aquatic that it may be easily overlooked. It is thought to be only tenuously established and present only in Dade County.

Habitat Although it may wander extensively on land, this is a primarily aquatic turtle associated in Florida with man-made ponds and canals.

Size This turtle is known to attain a shell length of about 8 in., but Florida specimens seldom exceed 6 in.

Coloration/pattern The rather smoothly domed carapace is an unpatterned dark brown to black and the hinged plastron is usually yellowish. The plastral scutes may have dark seams or a variable amount of dark pigment may extend onto the scutes themselves. Concentric growth rings are usually at least weakly visible. Dorsally, the broad head is often the same color as the carapace but may be prominently mottled or reticulated with lighter pigment. The head color fades on the cheeks and shades to yellow(ish) on the jaws and chin. The snout is short. The hidden soft parts and the rear of the legs are olive-gray to gray. Two short barbels are present on the chin. Sexually mature males have variably concave plastrons and elongate, thickened tails.

Reproduction Little is known about the reproductive habits of this species in Florida. Egg clutches seem normally to number 5–12, and a 2-month incubation period seems normal. Hatchlings have comparatively flattened carapaces and measure slightly more than an inch in length. The plastral hinge is undeveloped. It is not known whether this species has multiple clutches.

Similar species Although American mud turtles have domed carapaces and hinged plastra, none are as large as an adult *P. subniger*. Additionally, the kinosternids are, collectively, more elongate and have a longer, sharper nose. Finally, American mud turtles are either of lighter shell color or, if a dark species, usually have prominent yellow facial stripes.

Behavior Although rather bold when under water, if removed from that element, black mud turtles are shy, withdrawing into their shell and remaining there for quite considerable durations. The head is folded sideways under the anterior overhang of the carapace, and the plastron can be rather tightly closed. In captivity these turtles are omnivorous. It is suspected that this is also so in the wild.

Comments The stronghold of this species in Florida seems to be a single, meandering, man-made lake where they were released by an animal dealer. Despite having connections to permanently flooded nearby canals, black mud turtles have not been reported in these related drainage systems.

TORTOISES
Family Testudinidae

This family is represented by only this single species in all of eastern North America. Two conspecifics occur in the western U.S. and northern Mexico and there is one other in north central Mexico. The genus contains only these 4 species.

Typically, tortoises are restricted to upland areas with sharp drainage. The gopher tortoise is no exception. It occurs virtually throughout the state, but is absent from wetlands, swamps, and marshes. It can be common on high, dry, offshore islands, but in general has been seriously reduced in number in the last half decade. The elevated, rapidly drained habitats required by the gopher tortoise are also coveted by humans. There can be no question about which of the two is winning the contest.

These terrestrial vegetarians dig extensive home (and occasionally satellite) burrows.

An upper respiratory ailment is afflicting many tortoises in most populations. The ultimate outcome of this potentially serious health problem remains unknown.

172 GOPHER TORTOISE

Gopherus polyphemus

Abundance The gopher tortoise is still widely distributed in Florida, but is now of spotty distribution. It seems that some populations have been largely (or entirely) extirpated and that remaining populations are in decline.

Habitat Sandy, open scrub habitats; turkey oak-longleaf pine associations; sandy, vegetated coastal dunes; and other well-drained habitats with ample, low herbaceous growth are used by the gopher tortoise.

Size This is a large tortoise that is made to look even larger by its highly domed, but flat-topped carapace. Although 10–13 in. is the normal size, 15 in. is the current confirmed record.

Reproduction Gopher tortoises are slow to reproduce and have a high hatchling mortality. The nest is dug into the apron of sand at the mouth of the burrow, or nearby in another suitable area in the late spring or early summer. Although up to 12 eggs may be laid by old, healthy females, most clutches number between 5–9 eggs. The hatchlings can vary in size, but average about 1.5 in. in carapace length. Incubation takes about 3 months.

Coloration/pattern Adult gopher tortoises are merely big, tan or brown (sometimes almost black) turtles that, when young, show prominent growth annuli. The plastron is somewhat lighter than the carapace in color. The head is rounded, the neck is fairly short, the digging forefeet are broad, flattened and spadelike with stout claws, and the rear feet are club-like. Hatchlings are quite brightly colored. They have a yellowish head and limbs, and their carapace has peach or yellowish colored centers to the dark-edged carapacial scutes.

Similar species None. Box turtles, the only other terrestrial turtles with highly domed carapaces, have a hinged plastron.

Behavior These tortoises dwell in (sometimes extensive) colonies and dig burrows that may exceed 15 ft in length, 6 ft in depth and are sufficiently wide to allow the turtle to reverse face at any given point. Hatchlings may construct a burrow of their own or temporarily bunk with an adult. Numerous other reptiles and amphibian species also use gopher tortoise burrows for refuge. Breeding male gopher tortoises produce a clucking sound.

Comments Because of habitat degradation, including fragmentation, the continued presence of the gopher tortoise over much of its range on the southern peninsula and in other areas with burgeoning human populations is far from assured. This is one of the most thoroughly studied reptiles in Florida, and we know what is necessary to assure the continued success of the species. The question now is, Are we willing to provide the basic necessities?

SOFTSHELLED TURTLES
Family Trionychidae

Three species of softshelled turtles occur in Florida. Only one, however, ranges widely. With a record weight of 71 lbs, the Florida softshell is also the largest soft-shell species in North America.

Softshelled turtles are almost fully aquatic. They are powerful and agile swimmers that have fully webbed feet. Two of the three species often bask while in the water (the Florida softshell often

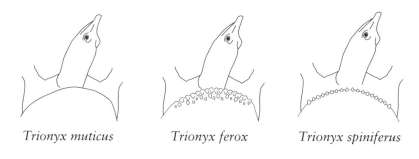

Trionyx muticus   *Trionyx ferox*   *Trionyx spiniferus*

Trionyx muticus   *Trionyx ferox*
                     Trionyx spiniferus

The spiny softshelled turtle (top right) has spines on the leading edge of its rounded carapace. The Florida softshelled turtle (center left) has flattened, hemispherical, bumps on the front of its carapace. The anterior of the carapace of the smooth softshelled turtle (top left) lacks spines and bumps.
Both the Florida and spiny softshelled turtles have a lateral ridge on their septum (bottom right); the smooth softshelled turtle lacks the septal ridge (bottom left).

comes ashore to bask), choosing shallows that the sun's warmth can easily penetrate. Collectively, softshells have a long neck and a Pinocchio nose.

The Florida softshell also diverges from the norm by selecting ponds, lakes, swamps, canals and other quiet, rather than flowing, waters, as its preferred habitat.

Softshells have the rounded or oval (when viewed from above) carapace covered with a thick, leathery skin rather than keratinized scutes. Although the center of the shell is comparatively rigid, the edges of the carapace are flexible. There are only 3 claws on each of the fully webbed feet. Males have a greatly enlarged tail that extends well beyond the edge of the carapace.

The valid generic name for the members of this genus is currently in question. Until more universal agreement is reached by taxonomists, we continue to follow the suggestion of Webb (1990) and use *Trionyx* as the generic name for all.

173 FLORIDA SOFTSHELLED TURTLE

Trionyx ferox

Abundance Common in quiet waters throughout the state.

Habitat Of the 3 softshelled turtles in Florida, this
species is the only one to preferentially choose non-
flowing waters for its home. The Florida softshelled turtle
is common to abundant in ponds, lakes, canals, ditches,
swamps, marshes, cypress heads, and other such habitats.

Size There is a tremendous disparity in the adult size of
the two sexes of this species. Females regularly exceed a foot in carapace length and the largest female specimen confirmed to date measured 24.75 in. Males most often measure 6–10 in. long at maturity,
but Moler (1997) has mentioned many that were substantially larger
and one that measured 18 in. over the curve of the carapace.

Reproduction An average-large female Florida softshelled turtle lays
10–25 eggs per clutch. As far as is currently known, the record clutch
contained 38 eggs. Several clutches are laid each summer. The nest is
constructed in a sandy location but may be obscured from the water.
The nest may sometimes be only a few feet from the water line, but is
often much more distant. Incubation takes somewhat more than 2
months. The hatchlings measure about 1.5 in. long.

Coloration/pattern Because of the many, large, dark, spots on the
carapace, at first glance, hatchling Florida softshells seem to be a
solid olive-green to olive-black. In fact there is a narrow, light olive-
tan reticulum separating the carapacial spots. A yellow to olive-yellow band edges the carapace. The plastron is dark olive-gray and the
dark head is busily spotted and striped with yellow.

With growth, both sexes fade to an olive-tan to olive-brown, but
males are more apt than females to retain some of the juvenile pattern. Head markings darken and obscure with age.

When viewed from above, the carapace of this species is oval. The
anterior edge of the carapace is studded with somewhat flattened
(low hemispherical) tubercles. There is a horizontally oriented ridge
on the nasal septum.

Similar species The other species of softshells are more rounded
when viewed from above, have a light carapace with dark spots, and
well defined light lines on the sides of the face.

Behavior Sedate while in the water, when on shore a fair-sized Florida softshelled turtle becomes a formidable adversary. The long neck and strong jaws are to be carefully reckoned with. Besides the jaws, the raking claws of a carelessly handled specimen can leave deep scratches.

This species basks far more extensively than either of the other softshells of Florida. Banks, exposed snags, mats of floating vegetation, and tangles of sub-surface sticks are used for basking sites. Florida softshells occasionally wander far afield and are frequently seen crossing roadways.

Comments There is considerable human pressure on these softshells. A thriving fishery catches and prepares them for human consumption, and the babies are frequently seen in the pet trade.

174 GULF COAST SMOOTH SOFTSHELLED TURTLE

Trionyx muticus calvatus

Abundance Although having a wide range in the southeastern United States, this species is known to occur in Florida only in the northern reaches of the Escambia River, Escambia County. It is possible that it occurs elsewhere on the northwestern panhandle. The Gulf Coast softshell is common in the state within its very restricted range.

Habitat This turtle is most common where extensive, open, sandbars occur.

Size Females of this softshelled turtle reach 10.5 in. (rarely a little more); the smaller males vary 4–6-in. in carapace length.

Reproduction In Florida, as elsewhere, this turtles nests on open sandbars. It seems that this species always nests where the water is always visible from the nests. Nests have contained 6–31 eggs, but normally range from 8–20. Florida females lay fewer and larger eggs than specimens from farther north. Following an incubation period of somewhat more than 2 months, the 1.5-in. hatchlings emerge. A female lays several clutches a summer.

Coloration/pattern The carapace of this softshell has a ground color of olive-tan to light-olive-brown with numerous, well-separated, large, dark spots. A single black line follows the carapace near the rim. The plastron is lighter in color than the brownish underside of the carapace. There is a dark-edged yellow line on each side of the head. The forelegs are not strongly patterned, there are no bumps of any description on the anterior edge of the carapace and there is no horizontal ridge on the nasal septum. Males tend to retain the carapacial spots of babyhood. The carapacial spots become obscured on large female specimens.

Similar species The Florida softshell is big, dark, and strongly oval when viewed from above. The Gulf Coast spiny softshell has small ocelli—not large dark spots—marking the carapace and 2 or more dark lines delineating the rear of the carapace. Both of these species have either tubercles or spines on the anterior edge of the carapace.

Behavior This is a wary and difficult-to-approach species. If carelessly grasped they will scratch with vigor, and are perfectly capable of delivering strong bites. Following hatching and prior to dispersal, hatchlings may be found in the shallow waters at the edge of sandbars. This species is adept at burying itself in the sand in water shallow enough to allow its snout to break the surface when the turtle's long neck is extended.

A full study of life history and exact range of this species in Florida is badly needed.

Comments This is the most uncommon, and smallest, of Florida's 3 softshell species. It is hoped increased awareness will disclose that its Florida range may be somewhat greater than currently thought.

175 GULF COAST SPINY SOFTSHELLED TURTLE

Trionyx spiniferus asperus

Abundance This species is common in the panhandle rivers from Gadsden County westward and in the St. Mary's River in Baker and Nassau counties.

Habitat This is a riverine species, but it may also occur in lakes and large ponds.

Size Like other softshells, the Gulf Coast spiny is dimorphic. Females commonly attain a carapace length of 7–12 in. and occasionally grow to 16 in. Adult males are about half that size.

Reproduction This softshell lays several clutches that average about 16 eggs in number. Occasionally 25 (or more) eggs are laid by large females. The incubation takes about 2½ months. Hatchlings are 1.25 in. long.

Coloration/pattern The carapacial color of the Gulf Coast spiny softshell is tan to olive-brown. There are dark ocelli in the central area of the carapace and dark spots closer to the edge. The plastron is about the same color as the underside of the carapace. There are at least 2 dark lines bordering the edge of the carapace. There are 2 dark-edged yellow lines on each side of the face. These converge and meet on the neck. The feet are heavily spotted and streaked. A horizontal ridge is present on the nasal septum. The anterior of the carapace bears conical spines.

Similar species The shell of this species is round when viewed from above. The Florida softshell is oval when viewed from above and darker. The carapace of the Gulf Coast smooth softshell is marked with solid dark spots—not ocelli. This latter species lacks anterior spinous processes on the carapace and horizontal extensions on the septum.

Behavior This is an active, agile, turtle that is entirely at home in the water. It easily negotiates considerable current. It is wary and difficult to approach.

Comments Like all softshells, this species is an agile swimmer, and is fully capable of chasing down and consuming small fish. At least as often, however, the turtle secludes itself in river-bottom silt and sand ambushes fish that stray within reach of the long neck and strong jaws.

PERIPHERAL TURTLES

Anecdotal reports exist of two subspecies of painted turtles having been seen or taken in Florida. While there is a chance that the southern painted turtle may occur naturally in isolated ponds of the western panhandle, there seems little likelihood that this is the case with the eastern painted turtle, which has been seen in heavily populated Duval County. The painted turtles are contained in the family Emydidae.

PAINTED TURTLES
Family Emydidae

176 SOUTHERN PAINTED TURTLE

Chrysemys picta dorsalis

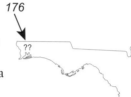

176

Abundance This turtle is abundant to the north and west of Florida, and is known to occur in the lower Alabama River.

Habitat The southern painted turtle inhabits ponds, marshes, lakes, and slowly flowing rivers.

Size While specimens 4–5 in. are commonly seen, occasional adults of this turtle attain a 6-in. carapace length.

Reproduction Clutches of 4–9 (sometimes more) eggs are known. Most females lay 2–4 clutches annually. The 1-in. hatchlings emerge following a 2½-month incubation.

Coloration/pattern This turtle has a smooth black to brown carapace with a well defined orange vertebral line. The plastron is usually an unrelieved yellow. Yellow lines are apparent on the brown head. Both sexes and all sizes are colored similarly.

Similar species No other turtle species or subspecies has an orange vertebral line.

Behavior Southern painted turtles bask persistently, climbing out of the water onto snags and exposed banks to do so.

Comments There are periodic anecdotal reports of southern painted turtles being seen in Florida's westernmost counties. No sightings have been verified.

177 Eastern Painted Turtle

Chrysemys picta picta

There are also reports of the
eastern painted turtle, having once
occurred in ditches and ponds of Duval County in
Florida's northeasternmost corner. If so, these were
assuredly "releasees," escapees, and/or their progeny.
Recent sightings are lacking and this turtle may now
be extirpated in the state.

The eastern painted turtle has a carapace of black,
lacks a vertebral stripe, and has red markings on both
the upper and lower surfaces of the marginal scutes. The
plastron is (usually) an unmarked yellow. The black head has yellow
markings, the legs have red and yellow markings.

←177

GLOSSARY

Aestivation—A period of warm weather inactivity; often triggered by excessive heat or drought.

Alveolar ridge (or plate)—A broad crushing plate posterior to the mandibles.

Ambient temperature—The temperature of the surrounding environment.

Anterior—Toward the front.

Anulli—The growth rings on the carapace of some turtle species.

Anus—The external opening of the cloaca; the vent.

Arboreal—Tree dwelling.

Bridge—The "bridge of shell" between fore and rear limbs that connects a turtle's carapace and the plastron.

Brille—The clear spectacle that protects the eyes of lidless-eyed geckos.

Carapace—The upper shell of a chelonian.

Caudal—Pertaining to the tail.

Chelonian—A turtle or tortoise.

Cirri—Downward projecting appendages associated with the nostrils of some male plethodontid salamanders.

Cloaca—The common chamber into which digestive, urinary, and reproductive systems empty and which itself opens exteriorly through the vent or anus.

Congeneric—Grouped in the same genus.

Cranial crests—The raised ridges on the top of the head of toads.

Crepuscular—Active at dusk and/or dawn.

Deposition—As used here, the laying of the eggs or birthing of young.

Deposition site—The nesting site.

Dichromatic—Exhibiting two-color phases; often sex-linked.

Dimorphic—A difference in form, build, or coloration involving the same species; often sex-linked.

Direct development—As used with amphibia, complete development within the egg capsule; no free-swimming larval stage.

Diurnal—Active in the daytime.

Dorsal—Pertaining to the back; upper surface.

Dorsolateral—Pertaining to the upper side.

Dorsolateral ridge—A glandular longitudinal ridge on the upper sides of some frogs.

Dorsum—The upper surface.

Ecological niche—The precise habitat of a species.

Ectothermic—"Cold-blooded."

Endemic—Confined to a specific region.

Endothermic—"Warm-blooded."

Femoral pores—Openings in the scales on the underside of the hind legs of some lizards.

Femur—The part of the leg between the hip and the knee.

Form—An identifiable species or subspecies.

Fracture plane—A naturally weakened area in the tail vertebrae of some lizards; a natural breaking point.

Genus—A taxonomic classification of a group of species having similar characteristics. The genus falls between the next higher designation of "family" and the next lower designation of "species." Genera is the singular of genus. It is always capitalized when written.

Gravid—The reptilian equivalent of mammalian pregnancy.

Gular—Pertaining to the throat.

Heliothermic—Pertaining to a species that basks in the sun to thermoregulate.

Herpetologist—One who indulges in herpetology.

Herpetology—The study (often scientifically oriented) of reptiles and amphibians.

Hybrid—Offspring resulting from the breeding of two species.

Intergrade—Offspring resulting from the breeding of two adjacent subspecies.

Interstitial—Between the scales.

Juvenile—A young or immature specimen.

Keel—A carapacial or plastral ridge (or ridges) or a longitudinal ridge on the scales of some lizards.

Lamellae—The transverse divisions that extend across the bottom surfaces of the toes of anoles and geckos.

Larvae/larval—Pertaining to the aquatic immature stage of some salamanders.

Lateral—Pertaining to the side.

Lateral fold—A longitudinal expandible fold that is found on the lower sides of anguid lizards.

Lateral ridge—A longitudinal ridge of skin that runs along the sides of some curly-tailed lizards.

Mandibles—Jaws.

Mandibular—Pertaining to the jaws.

Melanism—A profusion of black pigment.

Mental—An often large secreting gland on the chins of some salamanders.

Metamorph—A baby amphibian that is newly transformed to the adult stage.

Metamorphosis—The transformation from one stage of an amphibian's life to another.

Middorsal—Pertaining to the middle of the back.

Midventral—Pertaining to the center of the belly.

Monotypic—Containing but one type.

Naso-labial groove—A groove between the nostril and upper lip of plethodontid salamanders.

Nocturnal—Active at night.

Nominate—The first named form.

Ocelli—Dark or light-edged circular spots.

Ontogenetic—Age related (color) changes.

Oviparous—Reproducing by means of eggs that hatch after laying.

Papillae—Small fleshy, nipplelike protuberances.

Paratoid glands—The toxin-producing shoulder glands of toads.

Parthenogenesis—Reproduction without fertilization.

Phalanges—The bones of the toes.

Photoperiod—The daily/seasonally variable length of the hours of daylight.

Plastron—The bottom shell.

Poikilothermic (also **ectothermic**)—A species with no internal body temperature regulation. The old term was "cold-blooded."

Pollywog—A tadpole.

Postocular—To the rear of the eye.

Race—A subspecies.

Rugose—Wrinkled, warty, or rough.

Scute—Scale; especially the large scales on a turtle's shell.

Setae—The hairlike bristles in the lamellae on the toes of anoles and geckos.

Sibling species—Two or more similar appearing species supposedly derived from the same parental stock. Sibling species are often unidentifiable in the field.

Species—A group of similar creatures that produce viable young when breeding. The taxonomic designation that falls beneath genus and above subspecies. Abbreviation, "sp."

Subcaudal—Beneath the tail.

Subdigital—Beneath the toes.

Subocular—Below the eye.

Subspecies—The subdivision of a species. A race that may differ slightly in color, size, scalation, or other criteria. Abbreviation, "ssp."

Subsurface—Beneath the surface.

Supraocular—Above the eye.

Supratympanal—Above the tympanum.

Sympatric—Occurring together.

Taxonomy—The science of classification of plants and animals.

Terrestrial—Land-dwelling.

Thermoregulate—To regulate (body) temperature by choosing a warmer or cooler environment.

Trogloditic—Dwelling in caves.

Vent—The external opening of the cloaca; the anus.

Venter—The underside of a creature; the belly.

Ventral—Pertaining to the undersurface or belly.

Ventrolateral—Pertaining to the sides of the belly.

Vocal sac—The distendable, resonating pouch of skin on the throats of male anurans.

BIBLIOGRAPHY

The following listing is only a few of the publications that pertain to Florida herpetology. They are, however, among the more important contributions.

Altig, Ronald, 1970. "A Key to the Tadpoles of the Continental United States and Canada." *Herpetologica* 26 (2): 180–207.

Ashton, R. E., Jr., S. R. Edwards, and G. R. Pisani, 1976. "Endangered and Threatened Amphibians and Reptiles of the United States." Lawrence, Kansas: Soc. for the Study of Amphib. and Rep., Herp. Circ. no. 5.

Ashton, R. E., Jr., and P. S. Ashton, 1985. *Handbook of Reptiles and Amphibians of Florida. Part II, Lizards, Turtles and Crocodilians.* Miami: Windward Publishing.

_____, 1988. *Handbook of Reptiles and Amphibians of Florida. Part III, The Amphibians.* Miami: Windward Publishing.

Bart, Henry L., Jr., Mark A. Bailey, Ray E. Ashton, Jr., and Paul E. Moler, 1997. "Taxonomic and Nomenclatural Status of the Upper Black Warrior River Waterdog." *Journ. of Herp.* 31(2): 192–201.

Bartlett, R. D., 1988. *In Search of Reptiles and Amphibians.* New York: E. J. Brill.

_____ and P. P. Bartlett, 1995. *Iguanas—A Complete Pet Owner's Manual.* Hauppauge, New York: Barron's Educ. Series.

_____, 1996. *Frogs, Toads, and Treefrogs, A Complete Pet Owner's Manual.* Hauppauge, New York: Barron's Educ. Series.

_____, 1997. *Anoles, Basilisks, and Water Dragons, A Complete Pet Owner's Manual.* Hauppauge, New York: Barron's Educ. Series.

Behler, John L. and F. Wayne King, 1979. *The Audubon Society Field Guide to North American Reptiles and Amphibians.* New York: Alfred Knopf.

Carr, Archie. 1952. *Handbook of Turtles.* Ithaca, New York: Cornell Univ. Press.

Conant, Roger and Joseph T. Collins, 1991. *A Field Guide to the Reptiles and Amphibians of Eastern and Central North America,* 3rd ed. Boston, Massachusetts: Houghton Mifflin.

Collins, Joseph T., 1997. *Standard Common and Current Scientific Names for North American Amphibians and Reptiles.* Lawrence, Kansas: Soc. for the Study of Amphib. and Rep., Herp. Circ. no. 25.

Duellman, William E. and Albert Schwartz, 1958. *Amphibians and Reptiles of Southern Florida.* Gainesville, Florida: Bull. of the Florida. State Mus. No. 3.

Elliott, Lang, 1992. *The Calls of Frogs and Toads* (audio tape), Eastern and Central North America. Ithaca, New York: Lang Elliott Nature Sound Studio.

Ernst, Carl H. Jeffrey E. Lovich, and Roger W. Barbour, 1994. *Turtles of the United States and Canada.* Washington: Smithsonian.

Godley, J. Steve, 1983. "Observations on the Courtship, Nests and Young of *Siren intermedia* in Southern Florida." *The Amer. Midland Naturalist:* 215–219.

Halliday, Tim and Kraig Adler (eds.), 1986. *The Encyclopedia of Reptiles and Amphibians.* New York: Facts on File.

Iverson, J. B. and P. E. Moler, 1997. "The Female Reproductive Cycle of the Florida Softshell Turtle (*Apalone ferox*)." *Jour. of Herp.* 31(3): 399–409.

Moler, Paul E., 1990. "A Checklist of Florida's Amphibians and Reptiles" (Revised). Tallahassee: Florida Game and Fresh Water Fish Comm.

Moler, Paul E., (ed.), 1992. *Rare and Endangered Biota of Florida, Volume III. Amphibians and Reptiles.* Gainesville: University Press of Florida.

Neill, Wilfred T., 1951. "A New Subspecies of Salamander, Genus *Pseudobranchus,* From the Gulf Hammock Region of Florida." Silver Springs, Florida. Ross Allen's Reptile Inst.

_____, 1971. *The Last of the Ruling Reptiles.* New York: Columbia Univ. Press.

Reno, Harley W., Frederick R. Gehlbach, and R. A. Turner, 1972. "Skin and Aestivational Cocoon of the Aquatic Amphibian," *Siren intermedia. Copeia* (4):625–631.

Schwartz, Albert and Robert W. Henderson, 1991. *Amphibian and Reptiles of the West Indies.* Gainesville, Florida: Univ. Press of Florida.

Smith, Hobart M., 1946. *Handbook of Lizards.* Ithaca, New York: Comstock.

Tennant, Alan, 1997. *A Field Guide to Snakes of Florida.* Houston, Texas: Gulf Pub.

Webb, Robert G., 1962. "North American Recent Soft Shelled Turtles (Family Trionychidae)." Univ. of Kansas Publ. Mus. Nat. Hist. 13(10):429–611.

_____, 1990. "Trionyx." *Catalogue of American Amphibians and Reptiles:* 487.1-487-7.

Wilson, Larry David and Louis Porras, 1983. *The Ecological Impact of Man on the South Florida Herpetofauna.* Lawrence, Kansas: Univ. of Kansas.

Wright, A. H. and A. A. Wright, 1949. *Handbook of the Frogs and Toads,* 3rd ed. Ithaca, New York: Comstock.

INDEX

DICK AND PATRICIA BARTLETT

A veteran herpetologist/herpetoculturist, **R. D. (Dick) Bartlett** has 40 years' experience in studying, photographing, and educating people about reptiles and amphibians. Mr. Bartlett is the founder of the Reptilian Breeding and Research Institute, a private facility dedicated to herpetofauna study and support. The author of 3 books and more than 425 related articles, he has co-authored 10 additional books with his wife, **Patricia,** who is a museum director in Gainesville, Florida.